AMIGA FORMAT presents...

Get the most out of your Amiga 1993

Mark Smiddy ▪ Gary Whiteley ▪ Maff Evans ▪ Phil Gladwyn
▪ Lawrence Hickmott ▪ Dave Winder ▪ Stuart Campbell ▪
Jonathan Davies ▪ Toby Simpson ▪ Ian Wrigley
EDITOR Rod Lawton

Get the most out of your Amiga 1993

Get the Most out of your Amiga 1993
Copyright © 1993 Future Publishing
All rights reserved. No part of this book may be duplicated, stored in a retrieval system or used as part of any other book, database, program or other commercial application without the publisher's express written permission.

Book design and production Rod Lawton

Cover design Mark Nottley

Cover photography Rob Scott

Authors Mark Smiddy, Gary Whiteley, Maff Evans, Phil Gladwyn, Lawrence Hickmott, Dave Winder, Stuart Campbell, Jonathan Davies, Toby Simpson and Ian Wrigley

First published in 1993 by Future Publishing, Beauford Court, 30 Monmouth Street, Bath, Avon BA1 2BW. Tel: 0225 442244

ISBN: 1 898275 00 9

Printed in the UK by Beshara Press

Acknowledgement of copyright and trademarks
This book contains copyright or trademark product names owned by the companies which produce them. Description of these products without mention of their legal status does not consitute a challenge to this status. The authors and Future publishing fully acknowledge such copyright names or trademarks.

Why are we here?

Get the Most out of your Amiga 1993 is the third in a series which began in 1990. Since then, however, the Amiga market has developed drastically, and this 1993 edition has been completely rewritten to cope with this Amiga boom.

But what's it all about? Well, as any Amiga owner knows, the Amiga is the best 'home' computer you can buy. However, it's lumbered with a reputation as a 'games machine'.

Now it just so happens that the Amiga is the best games machine – it still boasts more, better, and generally cheaper,games titles than the all-conquering dedicated games consoles.

But the Amiga can do a lot more besides. If it wasn't so good at playing games, people might look at its other abilities a bit more closely. The fact is that the Amiga is a formidable word processing tool, it's capable of professional-quality design and publishing, it can handle 3D modelling and computer-aided design, and its abilities in the fields of animation, video titling and multimedia are legendary.

The point is that the Amiga doesn't just do these things *quite* well. It does them *extremely* well. Job-for-job it will regularly outperform high-end PCs, for example, and for a fraction of the cost.

And that's what this book is about – getting the most out of your Amiga. We aim to show you what it can do, what the jargon means, which products are best and what to do next.

Is space finite?

Well, we're not too sure about the universe, but unfortunately the space within this book certainly *is* finite. And there are things we would have loved to have squeezed in but couldn't. Like all the cheating devices now available for games players. And the increasingly important role the Amiga is playing in education, both in the classroom and at home. And how ARrexx, the programming language now bundled free with Amigas, opens up whole new areas and potential... but these will have to wait for another time.

We set out to write a book about the Amiga and found out that *ten* books wouldn't do it...

Preface
By Marcus Dyon, Editor of Amiga Format magazine

Owning an Amiga is a great adventure – you have in your possession one of the world's most powerful personal computers. But at times, things can get a bit confusing, especially if you're a new or recent owner. That's when you should reach for your copy of **Get the Most out of Your Amiga** 1993.

This book gives you a handy guide to the whole spectrum of Amiga usage, whether it be getting started with the machine or areas of use like graphics, music and comms. And whether you feel like relaxing with a great game or expanding your system with some new hardware, **Get The Most** has the info you'll need to get the job done. And as if all that weren't enough we've included two program-packed disks to show you some of the Amiga's true potential. Enjoy!

About Amiga Format
If you find the information in this book useful – and believe me, you will – you might like to take a look at Amiga Format magazine (unless you read it already, of course!). Every month we bring you the latest news on products and software under development from all around the Amiga world. Once they are finished (and only *when* they are finished), we review them to help you decide if they're the type of thing you want to own. We also bring you features on new and exciting ways to use your Amiga, and if you're stuck, we help you out. All this, plus a program-packed coverdisk for the bargain price of £3.25 a month.

How to use this book

Get the most out of your Amiga 1993 reflects the whole spectrum of Amiga use, from games-playing, to programming, to business to desktop publishing and more. The book, therefore, is broken down into sections dealing with each of these specific fields. And each section is written by a known expert in that field.

The idea is firstly to explain what's involved in each of these areas, what the terms mean and what equipment and knowledge you need, and secondly to point you towards the best products currently on the market.

The idea is that you should get a picture of the tremendous range of the Amiga's abilities, be able to find out a whole load more about any area that interests you and then find out what you should do or which software or hardware you need to look at next in order to take it a stage further.

We're assuming that you're all Amiga nuts, but not that you're complete 'wireheads'. We don't believe in jumping in at the deep end and just spouting loads of jargon for the sake of it. Who needs it? But then, computing jargon is here to stay, so we've used lots of margin notes throughout the book to explain what some of the more outrageous gibberish means.

Books, of course, can do more than just tell you things – they can save you time and money! Our experts have collected loads of handy little tips, and you'll find those spread liberally throughout the book too.

Finally, we've picked out the best products in each are, and given a brief summary of the each – together with info on where to get them. But that's enough waffle. Let's get on with the book!

WHAT DOES IT MEAN?
You'll find nearly 200 of these margin notes throughout the book, explaining away those ghastly techie terms.

HANDY ADVICE
Our experts know all the tips and wrinkles for getting the best out of the Amiga and its software/hardware.

PRODUCTS WE RATE
These are recommended products in any one field. Call the number printed to check the latest prices and availability.

WHERE TO GET GAMES
In our top 25 Amiga games section, look out for this icon – it tells you where to get the games.

The authors

Mark Smiddy
Mark Smiddy has written four books on the Amiga, is regarded as a foremost expert in AmigaDOS and has been a consultant editor on Amiga Shopper magazine since its inception. Mark considers computers dumb and thinks intellectual bores should be lined up against a wall and shot. Not necessarily in that order.

Gary Whiteley
Gary Whiteley is an ex-oilfield geologist with ten years of professional video experience, seven of those using Amigas. He has worked on a wide range of projects, including community videos, pop promos, broadcast commercials and feature films. He also has a wide knowledge of many Amiga-related subjects, including 3D animation and graphics.

Maff Evans
Maff Evans first started out in the world of computers by coding art packages for the BBC micro (Model B – the forefront of technology). He's been writing reviews for the computer press in 1988 and is now the reviews editor of Future Music, Britain's best-selling music technology magazine. In his spare time heplays with electro-band Maschine Manitou.

Philip Gladwin
Philip Gladwin has worked for years in various branches of computing. Many abortive attempts to make lots of easy money have led him and his Amiga to put together more business plans than he cares to remember – leaving him poor, but well-qualified to write the business chapter!

Lawrence Hickmott
In 1978 Lawrence Hickmott started out in newspaper publishing. Ten years on, new technology, made available by the Amiga, helped him take a new turn in publishing. Since then, in a daily grind of publishing and reviewing, he has taken to promoting the Amiga as a superb desktop publishing instrument.

The authors

Dave Winder
Dave Winder is a comms expert extraordinaire. He knows all there is to know about protocols, modems, archivers, terminal software, bulletin boards… and he actually explains it in English, too!

Stuart Campbell
Stuart Campbell is reviews editor on Amiga Power, the magazine with 'attitude'. The man has a mind like a diamond, a tongue like a knife and a pen like a long yellow thing with an inky bit at the end. If this man doesn't like a game, the whole world gets to hear about it. If he *does* like it… well then, the whole world gets to hear about it…

Jonathan Davies
Jonathan Davies has been reviewing Amiga games for far longer than most people would consider healthy. He also compiles, somewhat reluctantly, The Last Resort for Amiga Power each month, attempting to assist people who're stuck in games. He's 22, always looks forward to Christmas, and was really cross when Sky TV bought Beverly Hills 90210.

Toby Simpson
Toby Simpson is lead programmer for Millennium Interactive Ltd. He designs and writes computer games. He is not strange in anyway, has never met aliens, drinks an abnormally large amount of single malt scotch whisky and has yet to successfully grow any plant whatsoever. In his spare time, other than being particularly odd, he goes caving… for some reason.

Ian Wrigley
Ian Wrigley is a journalist and computer consultant. He specialises in what he calls "the two coolest computers" – the Amiga and the Apple Mac – and is a Consultant Editor of Amiga Shopper, where he writes the regular PD World column. He also specialises in drinking Guinness and Boddington's Bitter.

Get the most out of your Amiga 1993

Contents...

1: The history of the Amiga　　1
The Amiga's only been going since 1985, but already it's had an eventful and colourful history. Find out how the machine has evolved, the major landmarks in its development and how your machine fits into the Amiga family tree.

2: Setting up your Amiga　　13
You've signed the cheque, you've brought it home, you've got the lid off the box – now comes the worrying bit, getting your brand new Amiga up and running. It's easy when you know how – and we show you how.

3: Workbench basics　　19
So how do you change your preferences, then, and what do all the menu items do? And what do these icons mean, and what's a window? And… and… oh look, just go and read it for yourselves, why don't you?

4: Painting, modelling, multimedia and DTV!　　43
Just about every Amiga owner will already have a copy of the wonderful Deluxe Paint, but your Amiga can do so much more. Did you know you can title your own videos, for example? Or make your own animations? Maybe so. But how about 'morphing'? That's the digital technique that can turn Volvos into horses (seen the TV ad?) and human beings into monsters. The Amiga can do that too. And then there's the buzz-word of the '90s – multimedia – the mixing of real-world images, sounds and text. And how about virtual reality? The Amiga is right up there at the cutting edge.

5: Making music　　75
An Amiga will help you compose, edit and even play your own music. It's cheaper, easier to get on with and a darned sight better-looking than your average indie band hopeful. (Ever tried putting an ad in the paper?) What your Amiga can't do, of course, is provide the talent. But then you must be pretty smart to have bought an Amiga in the first place…

Contents...

6: Getting down to business   85
What, the Amiga? A business machine? Yup. There's a whole heap of dedicated Amiga business software out there, from databases, to spreadsheets to accounts packages. You don't have to spend £1,000 on a bland three-box PC clone to run your own business – and then find you've got to spend another £500+ on software. Not when you've got an Amiga...

7: From word processing to DTP...   101
From composing a nasty letter to British Rail to publishing your own national magazine (in colour!) – the Amiga can do it. Don't believe us? Well you're just going to have to take a look, aren't you? We'll show you the difference between word processing, word publishing and desktop publishing, and unlock the secrets of PostScript printing – the system that lets your Amiga produce printed pages indistinguishable (yes, we do know what we're saying) from those in *any* book, magazine or brochure.

8: Going on-line   123
If computers are such powerful, logical beasts, how come it's such a nightmare getting them to talk to each other? We unravel the mysteries of Communications, a strange, arcane art handed down through generations of computer users, all sworn to secrecy. Until today. We show you how to link up your Amiga to the big, wide world and its big, wide communications networks.

9: The top 25 Amiga games   131
Mega Drive? What's that? SNES? Never heard of it. Imagine an Amiga without a keyboard. That's how useful a games console is. The fact is the Amiga is still the best games-playing machine the word has ever seen – and it also boasts some of the best *games* the world has ever seen. What? You want to know what they are? Very well. We reveal the 25 best Amiga games of all time.

Get the most out of your Amiga 1993

Contents...

10: Essential game tips   163
Stuck in your favourite game? Well maybe – just maybe – we can help you out. We've got tips, passwords and/or cheats for all of the following: Another World, Batman – the Movie, Carrier Command, Defender of the Crown, Dyna Blaster, E-Motion, Epic, F-29 Retaliator, Falcon, Fantasy World Dizzy, Fire and Ice, Flood, Gem'X, Future Wars, Gobliiins, Hook, Humans, Hunter, Interceptor, James Pond, Kick Off 2, Kid Gloves, Last Ninja 3, Lemmings, Lotus Esprit Turbo Challenge I, II and III!, Midnight Resistance, New Zealand Story, Oh no! More Lemmings!, Pinball Fantasies, Populous I and II, Premiere, Rainbow Islands, Robocod, Robocop 3, The Secret of Monkey Island, Shadow of the Beast II... look, this is stupid. If printed the whole list we'd have to stick an extra fold-down bit of paper on the bottom of this page. You must have got the idea by now.

11: Programming   197
It's all very well going out and buying software for your Amiga, but there are three reasons for learning to write programs yourself: (a) because you think you might like to earn a living at it, (b) because you can't afford to buy commercial software, (c) because no-one's *written* the program you need, (d) because, well, you simply like tinkering around with programs. Sorry, that's four reasons. We explain what it all means and how to get started.

12: Public Domain and Shareware   207
"There's no such thing as a free lunch". That's what they say, anyway. The thing is that as far as public domain software goes, no-one's found the catch yet! This is genuinely free software that will only cost you a small handling charge to get hold of. And while it might be free, that doesn't mean it's 'cheap'. It just goes to show you *can* have your cake and eat it.

13: Upgrading your Amiga   225
The Amiga can do lots of extremely powerful and amazing stuff, but the machine you bought may not have sufficient hardware built in as standard. We show you how you can fit more RAM, speed up your processing, and increase your Amiga's storage space.

Contents...

14: Choosing and using a hard disk 233
Floppy disks are cheap these days, and pretty reliable. But they can only store so much and – be honest – how often do you update the labels on your disks? (You have got labels on your disks, haven't you?) There are two reasons for investing in a hard disk (if your machine hasn't already got one): (a) more space to store files and applications, (b) less chance of having your data corrupted, (c) you know where to find things, (d) you can store files too large to fit on a floppy. Sorry, that's *four* reasons (oh no, not this again).

15: Choosing a printer 239
Gone are the days when a printer was a rattly thing that sat in a corner churning out dotty text at the rate of about five lines per week. These days you can choose from 9-pins, 24-pins, bubble-jets, inkjets and laser printers. But which one do *you* need? How do you choose a printer and, more importantly, how do you get it working with your Amiga?

16: The disks 247
Amazing, isn't it? We've just produced the biggest, fattest, most comprehensive Amiga guide yet published and it's not enough! Not on its own, anyway. Just because we like to show you as well as tell you, we're including two disks packed with Amiga programs for you to try. Programs specially selected to give you a glimpse of the Amiga's true potential.

17: AmigaDOS reference 257
On your Workbench disk is an icon labelled Shell. It's not the remains of a prawn vindaloo, but an extremely sophisticated and powerful interface between you and the guts of your Amiga. It's kind of like Workbench without the friendliness but with a whole lot more power. So much power, it would take an entire book to explain it. Which is why we've settled on an exhaustive command list, including command name, syntax and a brief description of its use. If you've never used AmigaDOS before, take care! If you have, but you're missing a concise, up-to-date, well laid-out alphabetical list of all AmigaDOS commands... well, you're not any more.

The history of the Amiga

Just how did the world's greatest home computer come about? Mark Smiddy dusts down the history books and tells the story...

The Amiga Family Tree

The better-specified models are to the right of the tree and the later models are towards the bottom. (ECS) and (AGA) mark the introduction of bigger and better chip sets

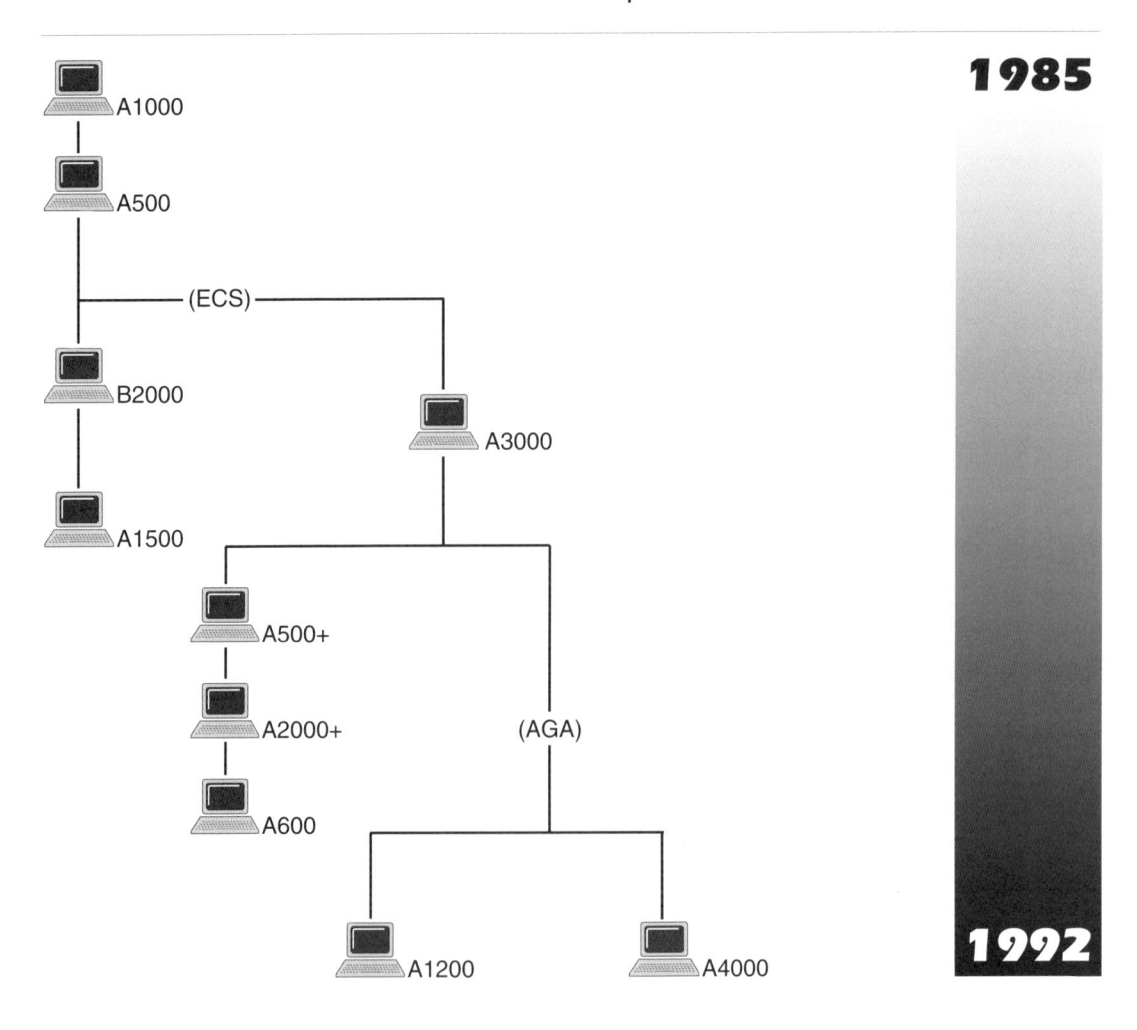

1985

- A1000
- A500
- (ECS)
- B2000
- A3000
- A1500
- A500+
- A2000+
- (AGA)
- A600
- A1200
- A4000

1992

The history of the Amiga

ECS, AGA

Part of the Amiga's formidable power comes from its dedicated chips (chipsets). The introduction of the new ECS and later the AGA chipsets represent upgrades to the Amiga hardware.

It seems strange to reflect it all started less than ten years ago – when a group of talented designers left a Atari to form their own business. Working on a budget tighter than Hulk Hogan's trunks and the disguise of a joystick manufacturer, Hi-Torro created a machine which has (millions of dollars and man-hours later) become a legend it its own time. The first machine to offer a multi-tasking operating system to home users as standard, yet one which is also capable of impressive feats in sound and graphics. The machine was code-named – "Loraine"; a less than awe-inspiring title later changed to "Amiga" when the company came out of the Silicon Valley woodwork. This was a more catchy nickname (Latin-American for girlfriend) which placed them before Apple in the telephone directory.

Better than a PC?

Technologically (and metaphorically) speaking, the Amiga blew the IBM PC systems clean out of the water: nothing could hold a candle to it. Nevertheless it is a matter of ancient computer history that the Amiga failed with a bone-crushing thump: even though, on the merits of specifications alone, it should have laid the PC to rest. The PC could (and still only can) directly access 640K of base memory.

Let's set the record straight: the latest PCs may be fast but even the most powerful 80486 based PC-machines have to use special software to access extra memory. Adding to the confusion, there are two completely incompatible standards. A memory-page based system (EMS) which works on most processors giving multiple 384K RAM pages located above the 640K base memory and a direct system (XMS) requiring a 386 or better.

Although clever software can emulate both these in real-time, many games are not compatible with the drivers. This is fine if you like fiddling with your machine's configuration – but a real nuisance the vast majority of the time. Go ahead, buy a PC – you'll regret it later.

The Amiga failed in the first instance because IBM already had a foothold. But the fact the machine is not a world standard does not detract from it in any way. Many other machines have tried to compete with the PC, some from huge manufacturers. Many have faded into the leagues of the irrelevant, some have died altogether.

Much of the PC's success has been attributed to the quality (and quantity) of software. IBM (and its much copied machine) continues to keep its lead not because it has the best machine – but because industry is unwilling to accept change. The industry made its own bed – and we all know the cliché... But we do not all have to lie in it. Read on and discover why.

The A1000 is born

The A1000 was the first commercially available Amiga – a machine greeted with universal adoration and acclaim in all quarters. Never before had so many colours been available on a home micro. The A1000 was fashioned along the lines of the increasingly popular three-box design pioneered by IBM for their burgeoning Personal Computer.

However, in the days when the massive IBM corporation were still building comparatively slow 8/16-bit machines, Amiga standardised on Motorola's more recent 16/32-bit processor (also found in Apple's ground-breaking Lisa and Macintosh series). This gave the machine full 16-bit architecture and the advantages that offered, plus versatile colour and sound capabilities. Other standard software included computer-synthesised text-to-speech and a full window-based operating system.

8-BIT/ 16-BIT/ 32-BIT

A computer's power is usually judged according to the power of its main processor. An 8-bit processor can handle 8 bits of data simultaneously, a 16-bit can handle 16 bits and so on. Every doubling of 'bit-handling' capacity multiplies the machine's power enormously (far more than 'twice'), and involves far more complex hardware.

The history of the Amiga

> **OPERATING SYSTEM**
> Computers are not intelligent things. Not only do you have to tell them what to do (using a program), you also have to tell them simply how to think (using an 'operating system'). Operating systems vary according to the computer's manufacturer, and differences here are the principal reason why a program written for one machine won't work on another.

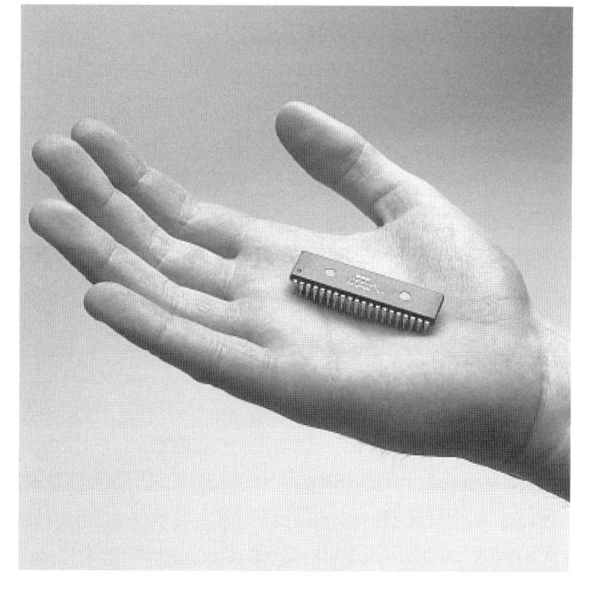

This was what started it all – Motorola's ground-breaking 68000 processor.

The A1000 is an attractive machine, but here is a cautionary note for anyone thinking of buying one now: don't! The A1000 ceased production years ago and very little of today's hardware is directly compatible with it. Also, the operating system is soft-kicked from floppy disk.

Amigas become affordable

Commodore has been called a few names for its handling of Amiga (the company, not the machine) – but it must not be forgotten it developed the machine into what it is today. Without Commodore, the Amiga would have curled up and died like so many machines since. Commodore took the machine and ploughed millions into the development of the first truly affordable machine, the A500.

> **A1000**
> Don't buy one! It's a good machine, but incompatible with much modern hardware and software.

When released in the UK the A500 came with an integral, full size keyboard; version 1.2 of the Kickstart operating system on ROM

The history of the Amiga

At around £500, the A500 was the first 'affordable' Amiga.

and complementary disk-based Workbench. Plus, at £500, it cost half what the old model did. 512K standard memory was easily expandable to 1Mb with a real-time clock, and extra memory soon became available through the external expansion slot. Later additions such as an optional external hard drive took the machine into a league of its own.

Many saw the A500 as a games machine. Indeed, it was marketed as such. Although some did find their way into serious use, such as DTV (DeskTop Video) and music, the vast majority remained with games users. Later A500 machines were fitted with a 1.3 Kickstart to support the new auto-booting hard disks and were greeted with jeers from games players. Still later models came with improved custom chips allowing for better graphics, although the big change did not come until the release of the A500+. This machine had newer custom chips the Kickstart from the A3000 machine.

Inevitably, the new system brought its problems, but the improvements were spectacular – the whole WIMP interface had been overhauled, having been given a much more professional look. And it's now much faster to boot.

> **AUTO-BOOTING**
> The Amiga usually has to be started up with a Workbench floppy disk, but now it's possible for machines with hard drives to load the necessary 'booting' software from these – automatically – when you switch on.

> **WIMP INTERFACE**
> Stands for 'Windows, Icons, Menus and Pointers'. A much friendlier computer interface than the traditional 'command line'. Now all you have to do is point to what you want, rather than having to know exactly what to type.

Get the most out of your Amiga 1993

The history of the Amiga

EXPANSION PORT
A connector, fitted either internally or externally, that allows you to plug in extra memory, a disk drive or a whole range of 'peripherals'.

With the introduction of the Zorro bus, the Amiga became as 'expandable' as the all-conquering IBM-compatibles.

The expandable Amiga

The A1000 had poor expansion capability – apart from the (non-standard) ports for printer and serial; plus video and disk drive. RAM and other expansion capabilities were limited to a sideways expansion similar to that found on the A500. IBM had had devised a better system, making their machine more versatile. The CPU, BIOS and control hardware was housed on a motherboard and everything else fitted into expansion slots, including the expansion ports, disk controllers, video cards and so on.

The Amiga already had all this on the motherboard so the Commodore expansion system was free to accept any manner of things. More powerful than the IBM system, the Amiga's "Zorro 2" bus can accept Amiga cards and a large number of IBM-PC cards too. In addition to the standard Amiga expansion bus, the B2000 has separate processor and video slots. Also, the 16-bit wide architecture as standard is much faster than the standard 8-bit bus slots in PC clones. (IBM also has developed other bus standards but only the 16-bit, "AT" version has made any real impact and many cards are still just 8-bit.)

Get the most out of your Amiga 1993

Other than expansion, separate keyboard and 1Mb standard memory, there is little to separate the A500 and B2000 machines. Although the slot expansion system allowed hardware developers to implement some very jazzy gadgets, the machine's speed was still largely inhibited by a base 7.14MHz processor. Even though external developers had already demonstrated high-speed 68030 processors, the machine would be judged by outsiders in its most basic form, and while the B2000 was having its day, a sub-8MHz processor was nothing special.

Commodore attempted to bridge the gap between the A500 and B2000 by re-specifying the machine with a standard hard disk and releasing a twin-drive version called the A1500. The A1500 proved to be a dead duck because the press and public viewed it as a cop-out; and neither machine ever really sold in large numbers – out-gunned by the versatile base machines.

The A500 is Dead!

There will always be rumours – and before the wraps were off the A500+, rumours started to circulate that a new machine was just around the corner. Sure enough, the A300 as it was then known became a reality – but to the surprise (and horror) of many – journalists and developers included, the new A600 replaced the A500 machine.

This bitter shock saw the demise of the infamous sideways expansion to be replaced by the newly developed PCMCIA and the death of the numeric keypad. Some pundits thought Commodore management had gone soft and regarded the machine with outrage. "It'll never sell! Why did they kill a winning formula?" they wanted to know. Reliability was high and not long after A600 machines started selling in numbers, the price dropped by a remarkable 25 per cent to just £300. Exactly what informed

MHZ

Stands for MegaHertz. It's the way a processor's speed is measured, and the higher the number, the better. The chip type is still a more important measure of its power, though.

The history of the Amiga

COLOUR DISPLAYS
Why all the big deal about 16-colour and 256-colour displays? Well, the larger the number of colours that can be displayed simultaneously, the more realistic and attractive the screen displays. The greater the number of colours, though, the more processing power needed to handle them.

The A500 was finally phased out in favour of the new A600 – a radical departure from previous machines.

sources had been predicting – although a nasty shock for those brave enough to buy an early machine.

On specification, the A600 is broadly similar to the A500+ it replaced, although the inclusion of an internal modulator makes the machine far more convenient for those using the machine on a standard television system.

A1200: "Beyond the rainbow"

In the days when IBM had comparatively poor 4 and 16-colour displays, the Amiga had a vast lead. But by the time the A3000 was coming on stream, things had changed dramatically. Years had passed and little had changed in the way of standard hardware. IBM and its developers had come up with vastly improved displays capable of 256 simultaneous colours on flicker-free, very high resolution displays.

Amiga's HAM mode, although amazing in its day, looked poor in comparison and had proved too slow to be usable in everyday games environments – still a major selling point. Besides which,

The A1200 boasts breathtaking graphics capabilities, thanks to a brand new set of custom chips.

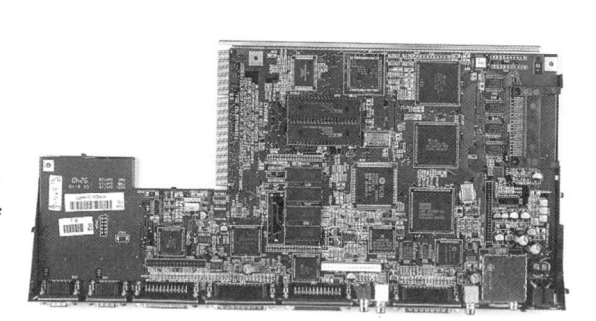

32-BIT DATA BUS
It's one thing having a processor than can handle 32-bit information, but it's a bit of a waste of time if the data bus – the wiring carrying data to and from the processor – is 16-bit. A 32-bit processor is easy to build... a 32-bit data bus is not. However, the A1200 has a 32-bit data bus, hence the description 'true 32-bit architecture'.

the base machine's processor was still the 16/32 bit Motorola engine running at sub-8MHz.

Late in 1992 the bubble burst and the long expected change came – the A500 slot was filled by a new machine, the A1200. This has a totally revamped set of custom chips known as the AGA set and is capable of 256,000 colours! The new machine is also based on a much faster Motorola 68020 processor – similar in performance to Intel 80286/386 used in modern PC systems. Sound is still a weakness on the latest machines (being 8-bit), but Commodore apparently has plans to fix this soon.

Like the A600 before it, the A1200 affords RAM expansion via the PCMCIA slot and while this is more expensive than earlier systems it is standard and the price will come down. More importantly, the machine has internal slots for a hard drive and processor expansion – and such cards are already available with floating point maths units too.

Although not as obvious to the untrained eye, though, the A1200 has full 32-bit architecture throughout: including the graphics

The history of the Amiga

ZORRO BUS

The latest internal expansion system for the Amiga. The new Zorro 3 bus can be configured to 32-bit operation, meaning very fast data handling.

chips. This means the screen displays are much faster and slicker than ever before because less processor time is required to get graphics on the screen.

Compare this to the majority of current IBM clones with 16-bit graphics boards and many (286, 386SX and 486SX) which are still based around 16-bit architecture. The sort of specifications PC fans are slow to admit.

Faster and better...

When it was introduced, the A3000 heralded the first major change for the Amiga in years. The ugly, though functional, steel case on the B2000 was replaced by a more attractive and slimmer version in a cream finish. The machine was first offered in two versions: 16 and 25MHz, although the slower one was soon dropped through low demand.

Other specifications are similar to the A500+ although the major architecture is full 32-bit rather than 16-bit of the smaller model. Internal expansion is similar to that of the A2000, although the new Zorro 3 bus, while backwardly compatible with Zorro 2, can be configured to 32-bit, giving a massive increase in speed.

All Amiga 3000 machines come with hard disks (minimum 52Mb) and a floating point unit for maths intensive software. The operating system is Kickstart/Workbench 2.04 soft kicked (like the A1000) and easily upgradable.

A major innovation found in the A3000 is a screen de-interlacer, which can provided high-frequency, very high-resolution displays without any of the annoying flicker which makes them unusable on the lower machines. This gadget does, however, require the use of a special monitor, which adds to the price.

Current flagship of the Amiga range is the A4000. Based around a 68040 processor, it's the most powerful Amiga yet.

A4000: "Leading the field"

The A4000 is the cream of the current models. It is to the A1200 what the A3000 is to the A500Plus. Essentially the two machines are based on the same sort of hardware, but the bigger version has a better, faster processor; a maths co-processor, more RAM expansion and of course, the Zorro 3 bus connectors.

Setting up your Amiga

The Amiga is the most powerful complete home computer system in existence. No other machine offers the same facilities in terms of ease of use, colour potential and sheer versatility. This section will help you connect the machine and get the most from it in a comfortable workplace where it will enjoy a long and fruitful life…

The Amiga is a mass of complex electronics, so does not require food, drink or household solvents. All it needs is an uninterrupted supply of electricity and a clean area in which to live. Your machine should be located where it will not be exposed to bright sunlight or extremes of heat, cold, dust... or prying fingers.

Your work area should be well-lit to avoid eye strain and the machine should be placed at a height where you can easily reach the keyboard while sitting in a relaxed position. Placing the machine on a thick-pile Axminster carpeted floor should be avoided. Such surfaces do not afford sufficient ventilation and there is a distinct possibility of someone standing on it! Choice of a suitable chair is largely personal preference – but a backrest should be considered essential and one with lumbar support is handy.

If you must work on an existing household table, ensure the mouse is placed on a custom-made mouse mat – a magazine will not do! (Even if it *is* Amiga Format) This keeps the mouse rollers clean and avoids the inevitable surface wear through the constant motion of the mouse's pads – even the non-stick PTFE variety. (Victorian inlaid tables look better without six inches square of mouse scratches.)

If the machine is to be placed under a custom-built workstation, such as those from MFI, ensure it has enough room to "breathe". Good circulation above and below single unit models (A500, 600, 1200 etc.) is essential to keep the electronics cool and ensure long-life. The power supply block for smaller machines should be placed on a level surface above floor level – somewhere it cannot get kicked and accidentally switched off. Larger machines have an internal fan and this too must have at least four inches of clear air

MOUSE

A small, hand-held device used to move a pointer or other cursor around the screen. Mice are found in all modern computer systems since they are easy to relate to. A trackball is nothing more than an inverted mouse with a large ball.

Get the most out of your Amiga 1993

Setting up your Amiga

PTFE

Polytetrafluoroethylene: Commonly called Teflon. This is the most slippery substance known to man and is used as the "feet" of many modern mice. While the PTFE feet will not scratch a wooden tabletop, the little bits of dirt and grit they invariably attract, will.

space to provide adequate ventilation for the power supply and other components.

Connecting up your Amiga

All wiring should be laid out as neatly as possible behind the machine and out of direct pathways – to avoid family members (and pets) getting caught in the network. Cats and tame birds should be kept well away: members of the parrot family especially are quite capable of biting clean through a mouse's tail and rendering the machine useless. Similarly, dogs love to chew and the on-site maintenance contract does not cover a half-digested keyboard.

Important: never, ever connect or disconnect **any** external equipment while the machine is switched on. Most of the expansion sockets are fitted with a pair of tapped nuts – to accept small screws fitted to the plug. They are there for a good reason and should be used. And screw them down firmly with a small terminal screwdriver – not a knife.

Plugging into a TV?

If the machine is being connected to a domestic television, ensure the modulator cable is well clear of the power supply. Electromagnetic radiation, while not directly harmful to humans in such small doses, will cause fluttering and wavy lines on the display.

The external modulator used with some Amigas has to be connected to the left and right audio outputs via the supplied Y-connector. If the audio/video quality is poor, you may need to alter the position of the tiny slider switch on the modulator. The modulator is prone to falling out of its socket and thus damaging internal hardware: this should be borne in mind if the machine is to be pulled from under a workstation.

Getting better sound

Many modern televisions, including portables, come with a SCART/Peritel connector. Although this is intended for direct connection to a VCR or satellite receiver, it can easily be used with an Amiga – the correct cable is available from most large suppliers. Such leads can also carry stereo sound to the TV, but a better option is to connect the machine to the auxiliary equipment socket on a domestic hi-fi or "ghetto blaster".

A far better solution is to invest in a pair of amplified speakers. Those typically sold for the purpose are cheap – around £30 – but not particularly good quality. A better option, if budget allows, are those intended for CD walkmans and are available from most high-street "brown goods" specialists including Dixons, Tandy and Currys. You'll need the type with fitted phono (RCA) connectors – the 3.5" mini plug employed on the low-cost models will not do. The £60+ such speakers cost will seem expensive until you hear these amazing units in action – a must for music freaks and dedicated gamers.

Plug-in extras

If you intend using your machine for more serious purposes a hard disk, printer and possibly even a modem will be the order of the day. Some late-model Amigas can accept an IDE hard disk internally, whereas other machines require an external box. The exact choice depends on the machine in question – however, always buy the largest capacity budget allows: and never anything less than 40Mb – you'll regret it later. External hard disks offer the choice of IDE or SCSI interfaces, and while the IDE option is often cheaper, the SCSI type are more versatile. As before connect these devices to the machine while it is switched OFF: turn them on before you switch on the Amiga and off after the machine is powered down.

MODEM

Stands for Modulator-Demodulator – a gadget used to convert a serial bitstream (computer data) into sound waves suitable for transmission/reception over an audio link. Typically used on telephone lines, but sometimes found on amateur (HAM) radio.

IDE

Stands for Integrated Drive Electronics. A type of hard-disk interface mainly used on the PC – and occasionally found on low-cost Amiga drives. IDE is a low-cost interface to implement but less versatile than SCSI.

Get the most out of your Amiga 1993

Setting up your Amiga

SCSI

Stands for Small Computer Systems Interface. An accepted standard used to connect hard disks and other specialised hardware to micros. Pronounced "Skuzzy" – you'll see this term a lot.

Buying a second-hand Amiga?

If you have bought this book then we can assume you have already bought your Amiga. However, if you are thinking of changing the machine or just buying a spare, the second-hand market is a good place to start. Here are some rough guidelines on what to look out for and what to avoid.

A1000: Unofficially, Commodore refuse to support the machine, so backup is limited – except through user-groups. An interesting footnote to this is that Commodore Germany once marketed a revised A1000, called the A2000, and although the two machines look different, they are essentially the same and some suppliers tend to be economical with the truth. Caveat emptor.

A500: Examples range from £150-£300, depending on what extras have been fitted and the age of the machine. Potential buyers would be wise to look for an A500+ model – the more modern machines are less fraught with problems than many suggest and have a more usable operating system. An unofficial Kickstart 1.3 system is now circulating which should offer some degree of compatibility with very old software.

A600: Tend to hold their value and a good example with extras can cost more than the shop price. Although not the best Amiga buy, they are a good step for those on a budget.

A1200: At the time of writing, reliability is in some doubt due to a minor design bug. Second-hand machines sell for £350 upwards so a new model is a better bet until the machines are at least a year old and the prices have stabilised.

A1500/B2000: £700 should secure a basic A1500 and expect to pay about £800 for a basic A2000 with hard disk: both with a

CBM 1084S monitor. Many machines will have much more hardware and possibly better monitors – be prepared to haggle.

A3000: Good second-hand examples can be had for around £1200, making them an excellent choice if you want power without the latest graphics potential. When buying one of these machines remember they originally cost a lot more – so the seller is likely to want more than it's really worth.

A4000: Too new and exclusive for there to be a good second-hand market in these – save up and buy one new.

Workbench basics

Workbench is the Amiga's advanced graphical interface and allows even the most tenderfoot user to gain access to the machine's basic functions. Workbench provides enough functions to start applications and look after all types of disk housekeeping: creating new drawers, moving files around and deleting defunct data.

Workbench is a safe environment when compared to AmigaDOS and can even give basic access to the machine's multi-tasking capability. The function reference provided here covers Workbench 2 and 3 only. Although the terminology is the same for earlier versions, many of the facilities are not available.

Boot Options

Workbench is a disk-based operating system – that means all the major software is executed from disk. In order to do this you must boot the machine with a special disk in the internal drive. Some Amigas have hard disks and the Workbench is started automatically when they are switched on. However, there is more to booting than meets the eye. Holding both mouse buttons down immediately after reset brings up the Amiga Early Startup screen – the one shown here is from Kickstart 3 – the one featured in Kickstart 2 is similar.

These options give extra control over the machine's initial configuration: the sort of things that are not possible after Workbench has been activated. Some of the options are designed

AMIGADOS
Amiga Device Operating System. A set of low-level commands used to control everything from the keyboard and screen to the printer and disk drives. AmigaDOS is not for the faint hearted.

MULTI-TASKING
Multi-tasking: the ability to run more than one program at once – each thinking it has complete control of the machine.

The Amiga Early Startup screen (from Kickstart 3)

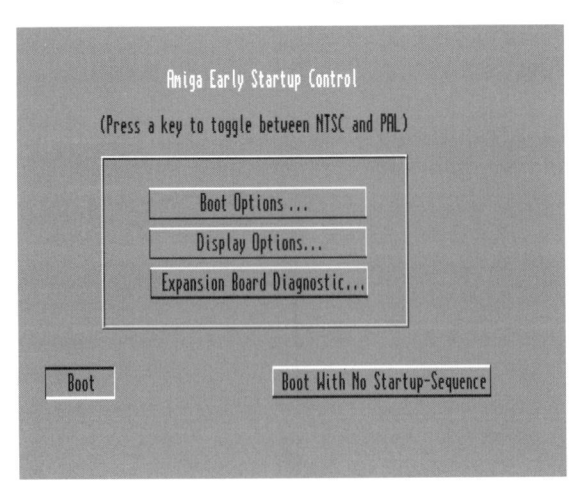

Workbench basics

BOOT
To reset the machine by cycling the power or pressing CRTL–A–A.

to provide compatibility with older software, although in practice this is rarely the case – software either works or it doesn't.

Early Startup

The Early Startup allows you to boot the machine normally or without a Startup-sequence. Booting without a startup-sequence is reserved for folk with an intimate knowledge of AmigaDOS since it drops you directly into a Shell without any initial configuration. Clicking one of the other buttons takes you to the Boot or Display options screens: the expansion board diagnostic is of little use so it will not be discussed here.

KICKSTART
The machine's operating system. Software held on chip inside the machine rather than on a floppy disk. Although faster than disks, such ROM storage is less easy to alter.

The boot options control the boot device and allow you to switch off other bootable devices without actually having to disable or physically remove them. Note that at least one device must be active at any time – any device's status can be toggled by clicking on its name.

Once a device has been disabled it can only be enabled by resetting the machine. The boot device allows you to select which hard or floppy disk to boot from. This is rarely necessary because

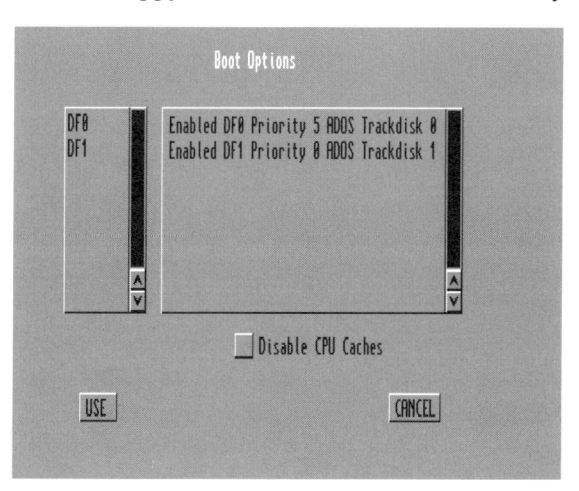

Workbench boot options let you select devices to boot from.

Get the most out of your Amiga 1993

the Amiga always attempts to boot from the internal floppy disk first, other drives are searched according to their priority later.

The disable CPU caches check box should be selected to provide compatibility with badly written programs that modify themselves or their data areas directly. This technique was widely used on 8-bit processors and proved effective with the smaller 68000 series engines. Later CPUs have internal caches which increase speed but cause self-modifying code to crash.

BOOT SCREEN
A primary boot screen may be accessed by holding down the left mouse button only while the machine is starting.

Display Options

The selection available on this screen depends entirely on which Amiga model is in use. The PAL/NTSC option can be used on most monitors and some televisions to increase the display update from 50 to 60 cycles per second which is easier on the eye and has a side effect of speeding up some games. The Chip selection only affects the mode types available from Workbench and Workbench launched programs such as Deluxe Paint AGA. Applications that address the hardware directly such as games will not be affected by any of these.

CACHE
A small amount of RAM (Random Access Memory) on the CPU used to store instructions or data. Caches create a noticeable increase in speed because the processor does not have to waste time "fetching" the information from main memory.

Choose your display type with the display options screen.

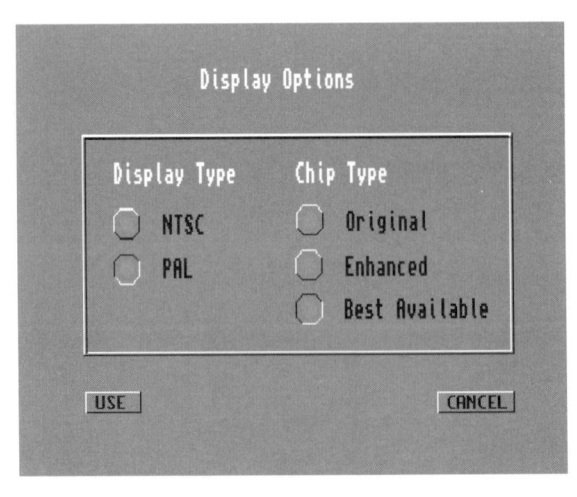

Get the most out of your Amiga 1993

Workbench basics

Using Workbench

Workbench is very easy to use – more so since it received a major re-vamp for version 2 (covered here). When you insert a disk it will appear on the Workbench as an icon. The disk's contents can be examined by double-clicking it or selecting it and choosing Open from the "Icons" menu.

A typical window and its gadgets is shown below – note the title bar for a disk window shows information about the disk and available space – provided the disk is inserted. When a disk is removed from the machine its icon will remain on the display until all windows belonging to it (and programs using it) are removed or closed. The icons you are like to see most are shown on the next page.

The system is entirely object-based. You may select a single icon by clicking on it or several icons by holding down the Shift key

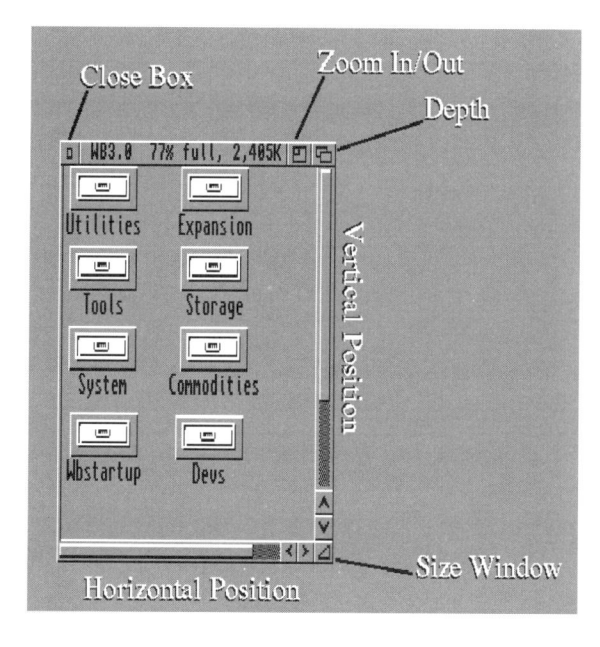

A typical Workbench window complete with 'gadgets'.l

Typical Workbench icons

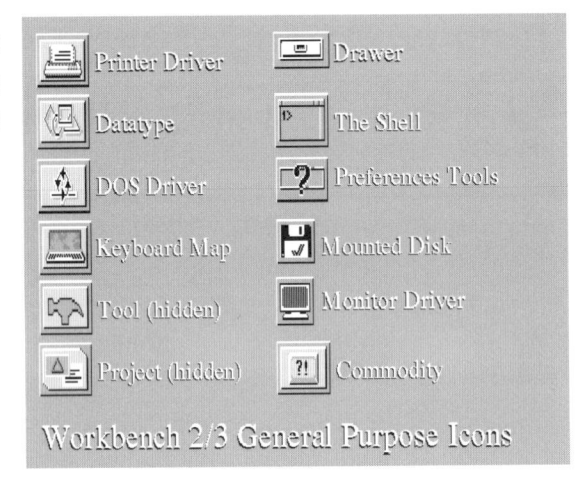

Printer Driver	Drawer
Datatype	The Shell
DOS Driver	Preferences Tools
Keyboard Map	Mounted Disk
Tool (hidden)	Monitor Driver
Project (hidden)	Commodity

Workbench 2/3 General Purpose Icons

DRAGGING
Holding the left mouse button while moving the mouse.

while selecting them. A quick extended selection is available by dragging a box around them. A combination of both methods may be used to select many icons – but the Shift key must be held down to keep the selection valid. Also, once an icon is selected it cannot be unselected without clearing the whole lot and starting again.

Workbench basics

TOOL

An Amiga application that creates or modifies something. The analogy comes from the idea a workman uses tools to do a job and a job in progress is a Project.

The Preferences Editors

Workbench has fully configurable user-environment – everything you see and hear and react to can be changed, from the screen colours to the icons themselves.

There are literally dozens of settings, all controlled from 15 different tools. Options can be set temporarily by selecting the Use gadget or made permanent by selecting Save.

The next few pages in this section explain what they do...

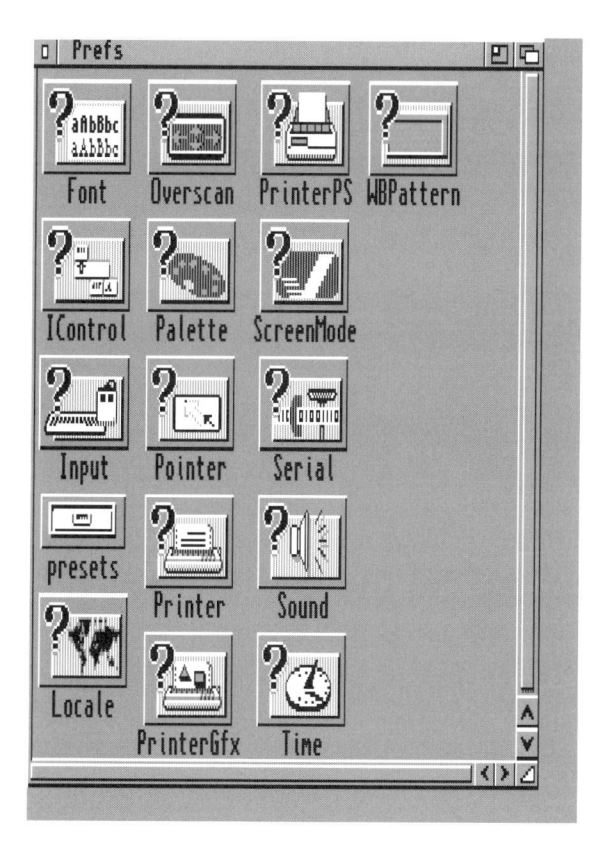

Workbench can be highly customised! All these icons reperesent tools for altering user preferences.

Get the most out of your Amiga 1993

Font — Controls the system fonts. Up to three fonts can be used at the same time, although large and/or proportional fonts should be avoided.

IControl — Controls the Intuition functions for moving screens and icons. Screen drag is the most useful function – holding the left mouse button plus a qualifier allows the entire screen to be moved.

Input — Define the mouse and keyboard speeds. Mouse acceleration is a useful option to leave on when you get used to the device.

Locale — Determines the generalised country settings such as language. The map also shows world time with respect to GMT.

Overscan — Sets the physical screen size. The Amiga's screen can be expanded into the normal screen borders giving more effective room for Workbench.

Palette — Sets the screen colours. The number of available colours is determined by the screen mode in use.

> **INTUITION**
> A set of 'libraries' for creating typical Amiga menus in your own programs.

> **QUALIFIER**
> A special key on the keyboard. Usually one of the Amiga keys located either side of the spacebar or the CTRL/ALT keys.

Workbench basics

BORDER

An area of the screen which frames the working area – the mouse, for instance, is bound by the screen borders.

Pointer — Defines both the normal arrow pointer and the clock "busy" pointer shown by Workbench. The main pointer is also shared by other non-Workbench applications.

Printer — Allows you to select a printer driver from those available in the DEVS/Printers drawer. This option does not work correctly on single floppy disk machines with Workbench 3.

PrinterGfx — Sets the default printer graphic preferences. Note: do not select high-density printing on a colour printer. Colour adjustment makes the colours on the printer more accurate to those displayed on screen.

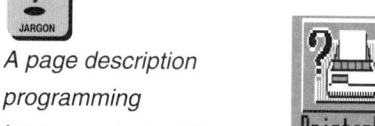

POSTSCRIPT

A page description programming language devised by Adobe for high-quality printout using low-cost devices. Usually only written by applications and rarely touched by human hands.

PrinterPS — Determines the options used by a Postscript printer – such as an expensive Laser printer. Consult your printer's manual for more information.

ScreenMode — Allows you to pick a new screen display from those available. (The actual list depends on which monitor drivers have been placed in the DEVS/Monitors drawer.) This works in conjunction with the Overscan too. Do NOT attempt to select a multiscan or other esoteric monitor if you are using a domestic television display.

Serial — Determines the current settings for the serial (RS232) port. These options must be set correctly for a serial printer or if you are using the AUX: device from AmigaDOS – otherwise they can be ignored since all good "comms" software will configure the port itself.

Get the most out of your Amiga 1993

Sound — Sets the effect when the Intuition attempts to flash the screen. On most systems, the screen flash is actually a beep through the speaker but the Amiga has no internal sound capability. Since most Amiga monitors (including TVs) support sound you can use this tool to set a more useful beep or even a sample – such as a scream or piece of music.

Time — This is used to set the date and time using a simple calendar-like interface. The save gadget also sets the machine's internal battery-backed up clock if one is fitted.

WBPattern — Sets the backdrop pattern for the Workbench window and drawer windows. Generally speaking, these should be left alone since although dots might look nice they make the display hard to read.

Workbench basics

The Workbench menus
Ever wondered what they all do? Well here's a complete menu breakdown, listed from the left, detailing each menu item in turn:

1. Workbench
These menu commands control the look of the Workbench screen.

WINDOW
A framed area of the screen where a program can display something such as text or a picture.

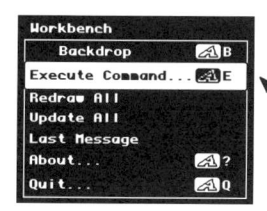

Toggles the Workbench window on and off. When the window is off, Workbench behaves like an empty screen, when the window is active, it can be sized and depth arranged with other windows.

Gives access to any normal AmigaDOS command without the hassle of opening a Shell window. When the command is executed, Workbench opens a temporary window which is closed automatically when the command terminates. The contents of the requester are buffered so the command may be executed or edited in many different ways. (This function relies on the AmigaDOS LoadWB and Path functions to work correctly.)

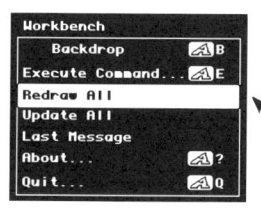

Does an instant re-draw of all the Workbench icons. It does not re-read any current settings or changed disks and is only required when badly written software has "damaged" the display in some way.

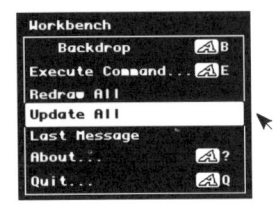

Re-reads all mounted disks and open drawers and re-draws the entire display. This function is only useful when something has been deleted or created via an AmigaDOS command OR you have changed file protection flags from the **Icons... Information** screen.

Repeats the last message communicated by Workbench. The message appears across the title bar.

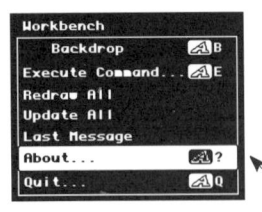

Produces copyright and version information about the Workbench and Kickstart fitted. Note the keypress is Left Amiga-Shift-/.

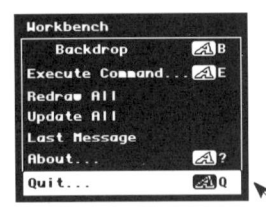

Exits the Workbench program. This function only works if all the applications started by Workbench have been completed.

2. Window

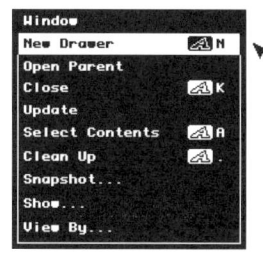

This function creates a new drawer and is only available when a suitable (disk or drawer) window is open and active. The new drawer is automatically given the name "Unnamed1" and the **Icons... Rename** function is called. See that function for more information. If a drawer is created by accident it must be deleted or dragged to the trashcan.

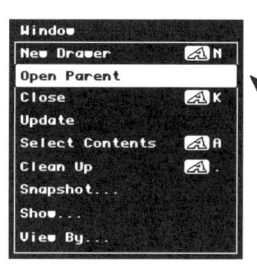

The **Parent** operation is only available when a drawer or disk window is active. It activates the "parent" window of the active window and brings it to the front. If the drawer has been closed it is opened. The facility has no affect on disk windows whose natural parent is a disk icon.

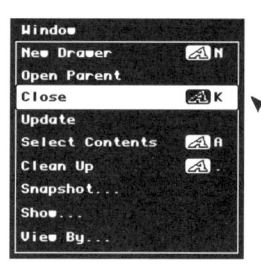

This function closes the currently active window. It is only available when a disk or drawer window is open and active.

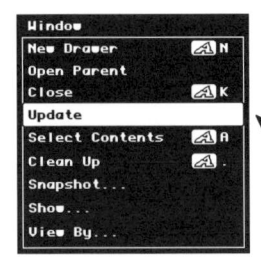

Similar to the Workbench menu's "Update All" this re-reads the contents of the currently active drawer and re-draws all the icons. Only available when a disk or drawer window is active.

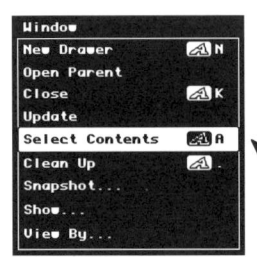

In icon view, this selects ALL icons in the current window – even if they are not currently visible. This function may be used after **Window... Clean Up** and before **Icons... Snapshot** (or **Icons... UnSnapshot**) to work on the entire contents of a drawer. The facility may also be used on the Workbench window.

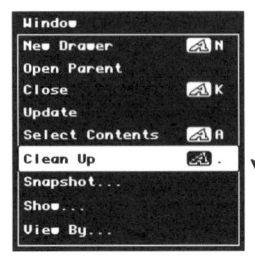

This function is available when the currently active disk or drawer window is in icon view (see **Window... View By**). It forces Workbench to sort all the icons by size so they all fit neatly in the window – even if not currently in view. Although fast, this method is not usually as neat as performing it manually yourself. The function is available from the Workbench window when active although it does not arrange the positions of the windows.

Workbench basics

This generic function is found both here and on the icons menu. **Snapshot** is used to remember the position, size and settings of any object: it's a little like setting and saving the preferences.

Snapshot... Window holds the size and position of the current window. The window can be move and re-sized, but when it is closed and re-opened it will return to the last Snapshot size and position. The positions of the horizontal and vertical sliders are also memorised, as are the current settings of **Window... Show** and **Window... View By**. If the Workbench window is selected, the position of the **Backdrop** function is remembered. Note: the individual icons in the window are not affected by this function.

Snapshot... All works exactly like **Snapshot... Window** but operates on all currently open windows, active or not, including the Workbench window.

Show... Only Icons sets the default position for all new drawers and disks. It tells the Workbench to display icons for all files which have an associated "dot-info" file at AmigaDOS level. Beginners should leave this setting as it is.

Show... All Files – when this function is selected the window is updated and pseudo-icons are created for all files and drawers in the current window. This function is also tied to the **Window... View By** facility.

Get the most out of your Amiga 1993

This menu option determines how the window will be displayed. If **Show... All Files** is active, files without "dot-info" icons will be shown too.

View By... Icon – files are shown by icon – this is the default setting and is best left alone until you get used to the Workbench.

View By... Name – the contents of the window are shown as a text listing – sorted by filename. This function is similar to the AmigaDOS command, List and generates a lot of information. Files can be selected by clicking their names and drawers may be opened by double-clicking. Other functions such as "Window... Select All" can be used in the same way. Note that "dot-info" files are not shown in the listing although they will be copied automatically if required.

View By... Date – files are sorted according to their creation date.

View By... Size – files are sorted according to their size in bytes. Drawers (which have no size attached) appear first.

Workbench basics

3. Icons

The features listed on this menu work on specific icons or groups of icons. The functions are only available when a suitable icon is selected.

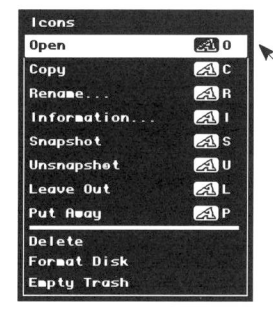

DOUBLE-CLICKING
To press the right-hand mouse button twice in quick succession.

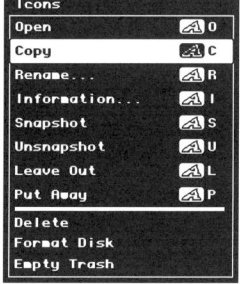

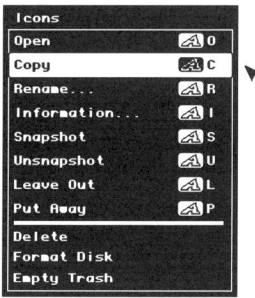

If a drawer or disk is selected it is opened, if a tool is selected Workbench attempts to execute it. This is exactly the same as double-clicking an icon. This function also works in text views. You may open an application's "deposit" pseudo icon if one is available – this will usually activate the application and may open a new window. Individual applications differ on this point.

CLOSING WINDOWS
You may close a window by clicking its close box even while Workbench is still reading the disk it belongs to.

This creates an exact copy of the selected icon(s). If a Drawer, Project, Disk or Tool is selected it is copied in the same directory. If a drawer is selected, the entire drawer and its contents are copied: this can take some time and may fill all available disk space. If a Disk is selected, Workbench calls the DiskCopy utility automatically. It is important to note: if a "Left out" icon is copied, the duplicate is created in the original parent directory.

Get the most out of your Amiga 1993

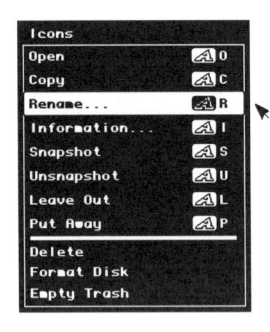

A text requester appears with the name of the selected icon and allows you to enter a new name. While the gadget is active the A-X keypress clears all the text. You may select multiple icons for this function – they will be renamed one by one. You may Rename an application's "deposit" although this will only work for the current invocation.

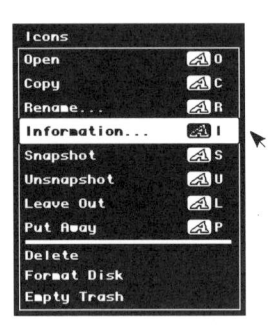

Calls the information screen for the selected icon(s). See 'Inside Information' later in this chapter.

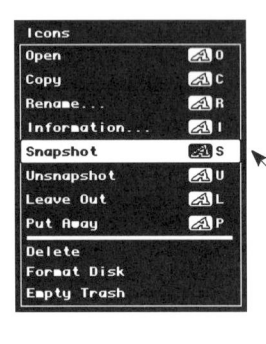

Freezes the icon(s) in its current position relative to the top left corner of the current window. This option can be used more efficiently if **Select... All** is called first.

SPACES IN NAMES

Spaces are allowed in names, but should be avoided as a rule.

Get the most out of your Amiga 1993

Workbench basics

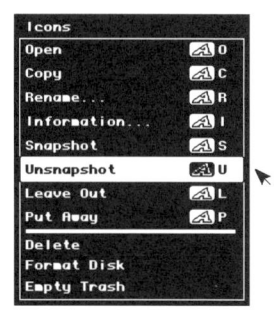

Unfreezes the icon's position and allows Workbench to place it anywhere it wants. The affect of this facility may be viewed instantly by selecting **Window... Update**.

"LEFT OUT" ICONS
If a "Left out" icon is copied, the copy is placed in the original drawer – not on the desktop.

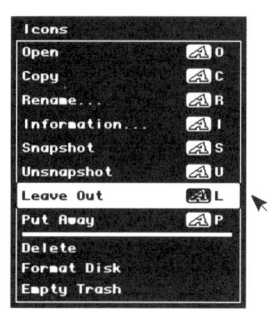

The selected icon(s) is placed on the desktop for easy access and **Snapshot** may be used to fix the icon in position. The Trashcan cannot be left out.

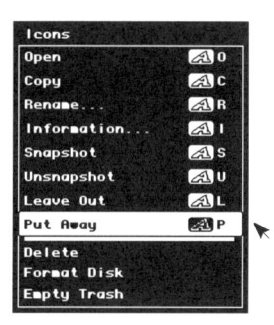

The selected icons(s) is replaced back in its original drawer. You cannot put disk icons away.

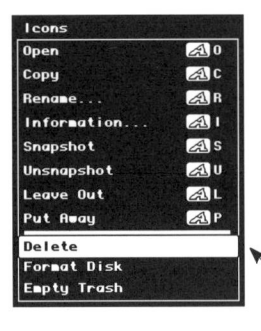

The selected icon(s) is removed permanently from the disk. If a drawer is selected the entire drawer and its contents (including any other drawers) are removed. Icons cannot be deleted if their "Deletable" has been switched OFF in the information screen, nevertheless this facility should be used with extreme caution.

The selected disk is formatted. If the disk is already formatted it can be quick formatted, although this option should not be used if the disk has developed any hard errors.

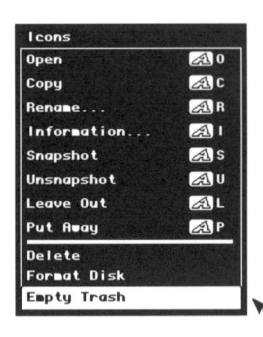

The selected Trashcan is emptied. This option is only available when a Trashcan icon is active. Note: every disk has its own trashcan – so the trashcan cannot be "Left Out"!

4. Tools

The functions listed here depend mainly on running applications. **ResetWB** is the only default option.

Restarts the Workbench application, redraws the screen and re-reads any mounted disks – a last resort so use sparingly.

Getting inside information

The Information window is used to obtain specific details about any displayed icon. This screen can also be called when an object is being displayed in a text view to edit particular options or preferences.

There are five different icon types including two pseudo-icons available when **Icons » Show... All Files**:

Trashcan: This is the simplest icon type and is actually just a drawer, although it has a special meaning to Workbench. The only usable information for this icon is the Last Changed date. This shows the date and time something was last placed in the trash or removed from it. An icon in the trash can be used as if it were on the Workbench, but it can be removed if you change your mind. Once the trash is emptied the icons cannot be retrieved. You must only move something to the trash on its own disk – if the disk does not have a Trashcan, the icon must be deleted to remove it.

Drawers are the Workbench extension of AmigaDOS directories. If the **Icons » Show... All Files** option is active, private AmigaDOS directories will appear. You may attach a comment to any drawer but the Tooltypes array has no effect. Hidden drawers are displayed without a Tooltypes array.

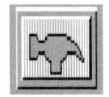

A **tool** is an application, software, a program – call it what you will: something we use to create or work with. An art program is a tool to create images whereas a word processor is a tool used to create text. The files saved by such programs are called projects: things created by tools. The application's size is displayed in disk blocks used and bytes. The number of blocks used is determined by the type of disk in use – but addition to the standard display, two user-editable options are available for tools:

Stack: The amount of stack allocated to the task when the program is launched by Workbench. If that sounds complicated – it's because it is: leave this option alone; the stack size is determined by the programmer and that's all you need to know at this stage. This option is not available for pseudo icons.

Tooltypes: This list allows users to set initial configuration options for certain tools and these will usually be detailed in the documentation. Not all tools provide for Tooltypes and this selection is never available for pseudo icons. Generally speaking, the Tooltypes mirror the options directly selectable from AmigaDOS. It is important to note, however, the tooltypes list (strictly called an array) is case-sensitive, so options must be entered as detailed: usually in capital letters followed by "=". Some Workbench tools (Workbench 3's MultiView is a good example) come with example settings bracketed out.

Project: These icons are only created by tools and also have a tooltypes array. Large applications may use the individual tooltypes to save different settings with each project. Such settings may be edited with care. The Tooltypes saved with a project will override those set for the main tool. Another option available here is the "Default Tool". This is the

Workbench basics

name and AmigaDOS path for the tool to launch when the project is opened or double-clicked.

Disks are also known as volumes. The information is limited and quite technical. All disks have a Default Tool of "SYS:System/DiskCopy" which seems logical enough. The date and time shown for a disk shows when the disk was last formatted – disks more than two years old should be copied and re-formatted since after this time the data may become unreliable: especially if they are accessed a lot.

42

Painting, modelling, multimedia and DeskTop Video!

If you've got an Amiga then you might already have a pretty good idea of its graphics abilities. But to give you the full story on the machine's now legendary power, here's Gary Whiteley

If you thought that Amigas were just games machines then you couldn't be more wrong! They can be used for all kinds of "serious" applications too – graphics, animation, video production, 3D modelling, digitising real-world images and a whole lot more, as you'll find out in other chapters of this book.

With a suitably-equipped Amiga, and the right extras, anything is possible – right up to broadcast-quality television work. But since this is still pie-in-the-sky for many of you perhaps we should begin with a few more down-to-earth explanations and possibilities.

So let's first take stock of the graphics potential which lies behind so many of the Amiga's great talents.

> **HAM**
> *(Hold And Modify) – A ground-breaking Amiga graphics mode capable of providing 4096 colours on-screen at any time in screen sizes up to 384 x 580.*

HAM, HiRes and AA chips

Although a new generation of Amigas with vastly improved graphics capabilities is now beginning to make its mark, the majority of Amigas around the world still use "old" technology for their pixel wizardry. The basis of all this dates back to the Amiga's pre-Commodore design days in the mid-1980's when innovatory ideas such as HAM were being developed.

The "normal" Amiga graphics modes cover quite a range – anything from 4096 colours on a 320 x 256 pixel lo-res screen to 16 colours on a full overscan, 768 x 580 Hi-res interlace screen. Note that all of these screen modes (or Resolutions) can be displayed on any suitable monitor – for instance Commodore's own 1084 or Philip's 8833 models, or even on standard TV sets if necessary.

The trouble is that resolution is a thorny concept to explain because, at least as far as graphics are concerned, the Amiga is an extremely flexible beast. With the new "AA" chip set included in

> **SCREEN RESOLUTION**
> *Refers both to the dimensions of the Amiga's graphic output (in pixels) and to the number of colours it contains (in bitplanes). For instance, Interlace could be up to 384 x 580 and up to 5 bitplanes (32 colours).*

Painting, modelling, multimedia and DeskTop Video!

PIXEL

The smallest graphics unit (or Picture Element) which is used in the making of an electronic image. Pixel size varies according to resolution – higher resolutions have smaller pixels.

the new Amiga 1200 and 4000 models it is now possible to have screen displays in up to 262,000 colours on screen in even PAL hires-interlace overscan sizes whereas previous models could only manage 16 colours tops at such sizes.

Typical Amiga PAL screen sizes (pixels)

Lo-Res	320 x 256
Lo-res Overscan	352 x 290
Lo-Res Interlace	320 x 512
Lo-Res Interlace Overscan	352 x 580
Hi-Res	640 x 256
Hi-Res Overscan	704 x 290
Hi-Res Interlace	640 x 512
Hi-Res Interlace Overscan	704 x 580

PAL

The UK television standard which defines how our TV systems work and the specifications of the signals that they receive.

Resolution also depends to some extent on the amount of memory that the Amiga is fitted with, since computer images need memory to actually be displayed (quite a lot, usually). In some situations there may not be enough memory to display Hi-res pictures, for instance.

Now that we've skimmed through the basics of screen resolution let's briefly turn our attention to 24-bit – or "TrueColour" mode. Since one bit (short for bitplane, in this case) can contain 2 colours it follows that 24 bitplanes can contain a total of 16,777,216 colours. If you don't believe me multiply 2 by itself 24 times!

24-bit represents the peak of computer graphic quality and can be used to display breathtakingly life-like images. But the Amiga itself is not yet capable of displaying such images from its own hardware so an additional card needs to be added. There are, however, many programs capable of generating 24-bit files, and in many cases, these form the basis of professional graphics on the Amiga.

Note that although it would require an almost impossible screen resolution of 5150 x 3250 to actually display ALL the possible 24-bit colours, the advantage comes from having such a wide colour palette that colour graduations appear smooth and natural-looking.

RAM, disks and other hard stuff

Now whilst I appreciate that many of you will be too skint to buy much else after shelling out for a new Amiga (and hopefully a good RGB monitor too), I'm going to have to give you some tough news.

Most basic Amigas – and I'm talking about all except the 4000 here – will require a fair number of extras if you want to get even remotely serious with them:

❶ Firstly, graphics need memory, and animated graphics need plenty of it – particularly when working with lots of colours and large scale images. So the first recommended purchase is memory – as much as you can afford. An extra 2Mb makes a good starting point.

❷ Secondly, many programs will load quite happily from the Amiga's internal disk drive but you'll soon find that the constant disk-swapping becomes irksome. So the next treat has to be an extra floppy drive.

❸ Thirdly, once you start getting really serious you'll notice that your bedroom/study/lounge soon becomes infested with floppy disks, a sure indicator that it's time to consider buying a new hard drive (or upgrading to a larger one).

> **HARD DRIVES**
> Buy the largest hard drive you can afford. Anything less than 40Mb capacity is almost certainly a false economy.

Painting, modelling, multimedia and DeskTop Video!

ACCELERATORS

A1200/3000/4000 computers are already fitted with fast processors so don't need an accelerator.

There are two more things which those contemplating serious Amiga graphics should consider. The first is an accelerator. This will not only speed up many of the Amiga's normal processes but also improve the playback speed of animations and the creation of 3D rendered images. The second is a 24-bit card, because good as the new AA graphics modes are, they still don't have the pristine quality which 24-bit can provide.

Then of course you will need some software – recommendations on best buys are to be found as you go through this section. But first let's explore some of the ways the Amiga can be used for graphics.

What do you use yours for?

Because graphics applications come in many flavours it's not always easy to neatly pigeonhole them. And because of the Amiga's IFF file format work from one program can be easily incorporated into many others. For instance, an animation made with Deluxe Paint can be played back as part of a DTV presentation with a program such as Scala or used as an animated surface texture for a 3D object in a 3D modelling program like Imagine 2. So the following categories are used for convenience and are not cast in stone.

IFF

Interchange File Format. A standard Amiga file format which is used by many programs to allow the easy exchange of images and animations from one application to another.

Two-dimensional painting

Where 2D graphics are concerned the first words that spring to mind are "Deluxe Paint", one of the original programs for the Amiga, and still going from strength to strength.

Why? Because electronic painting is fascinating – and much cleaner than its messy real-world counterparts. 2D programs such as Deluxe Paint IV paint directly onto the Amiga's monitor screen with light and can even be used for making animations – anything

Get the most out of your Amiga 1993

from cartoons to business presentations, flying logos and psychedelic rave art.

But, for all this, 2D programs are still somewhat limited because (in theory) they can only operate within the flat plane offered by a TV screen – i.e. the horizontal and vertical planes only.

Although several innovative paint programs have vied for the crown over the relatively short history of the Amiga, none has approached the success of Deluxe Paint amongst graphics users – from games designers and professional animators to kids and grandparents.

Deluxe Paint IV £89.99

From: Electronic Arts. Tel. 0753 549442
Minimum Requirements: 1Mb RAM (3Mb recommended)

With far more features than there is space to list here, everyone from the beginner to the professional Amiga artist should have Deluxe Paint IV in their software collection. In fact, many of the

Deluxe Paint IV still sets the standard for Amiga point packages.

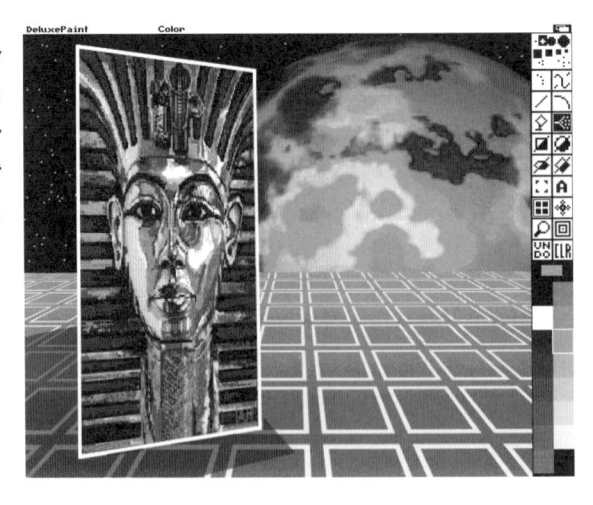

Painting, modelling, multimedia and DeskTop Video! 49

BRUSH
A chunk of graphic 'clipped' from an image which can be moved and pasted in another position.

Amiga's most enduring images and games have Deluxe Paint to thank for their existence.

Some of its abilities include support for HAM (and soon AA modes) and all "normal" IFF resolutions, full video overscan, animation, animated brushes, a wide range of painting and brush manipulation tools, text support, perspective, stencil functions – and plenty more.

I can't recommend Deluxe Paint IV too highly. OK, it doesn't do everything an Amiga artist will ever need, but if you only ever buy one paint program for your machine, this should be it. It comes complete with an excellent manual and a range of tutorial examples to set you off on the right track. Then it's up to your imagination.

Still the best all-round paint and animation software, Deluxe Paint IV offers an excellent introduction to electronic graphics.

✔ Personal Paint £59.99
From: Micro-PACE UK Ltd. Tel: 0753 551888
Minimum Requirements: 1Mb RAM (more recommended)

Although resembling Deluxe Paint in many ways, Personal Paint is actually much more an image processor than a paint program. With no HAM support the actual painting side is rather limited (unless you have an AA-equipped Amiga) in comparison to Deluxe Paint and there are no animation facilities, though there are one or two innovative features in this program that Deluxe Paint doesn't have.

Where Personal Paint scores most highly is in the range of image formats it can load and convert (though, oddly, not JPEG). Once

Get the most out of your Amiga 1993

More of an image processor than paint program, Personal Paint is no match for DPaint – but is still good value.

loaded, these images can have a whole range of image processing functions applied to them to produce effects such as embossing and texturing.

Whilst Personal Paint is no substitute for Deluxe Paint IV it is well worth considering as a relatively cheap image processor with paint functions included.

Three-dimensional modelling

Although the display area of a monitor is only two-dimensional, it is possible to make 3D worlds within the Amiga and display the results on screen. By also representing the third dimension (depth) the basis of what is now referred to as Virtual Reality can be produced.

Within a 3D program whole families of objects can be built, coloured, textured, given movement and turned into complex – and often very lifelike – still images or animations. The laws of physics can be blatantly flouted or simulations of real-world objects can be made to visualise new designs before committing

JPEG

A special compression technique to dramatically reduce the size of an image file whilst causing minimal quality loss on decompression.

Painting, modelling, multimedia and DeskTop Video!   51

VIRTUAL REALITY
A catch-all to describe the creation of interactive 3D computer environments.

actual resources to them. And worlds of fantasy can be made flesh – within the confines of the computer, of course. With a program of the power of VistaPro even entire landscapes can be realistically modelled.

While there are quite a few 3D programs around, the most popular two are undoubtedly Imagine 2 and Real 3D. User loyalty is generally very strong to either one product or the other but both programs can be (and are) used by professional animators and artists.

Other programs which deserve a mention are Caligari, which is available in various forms and the oldie but goldie Sculpt 3D.

Finally, perhaps the best 3D software for the Amiga is NewTek's Lightwave 3D but only owners of a Video Toaster (which is limited to US standard video output only, making it pretty useless for the majority of UK Amiga users) can use it.

✔ Imagine 2   £269
From: Digital Multimedia Services. Tel: 0702 206165
Minimum Requirements: 3Mb RAM, 40Mb hard drive (accelerator recommended)

Whilst Imagine 2 isn't perfect (what is?) it offers a very wide range of features – not least the ability to produce some stunning 24-bit images.

Imagine contains all the tools necessary to model 3D objects, give them a wide range of surface properties, arrange them in a 3D world and light them as required. Then they can be brought to life by animating them and playing back the resulting file or saving each frame singly to video for brilliant quality animation.

Get the most out of your Amiga 1993

Imagine 2 is a professional-quality 3D modelling package.

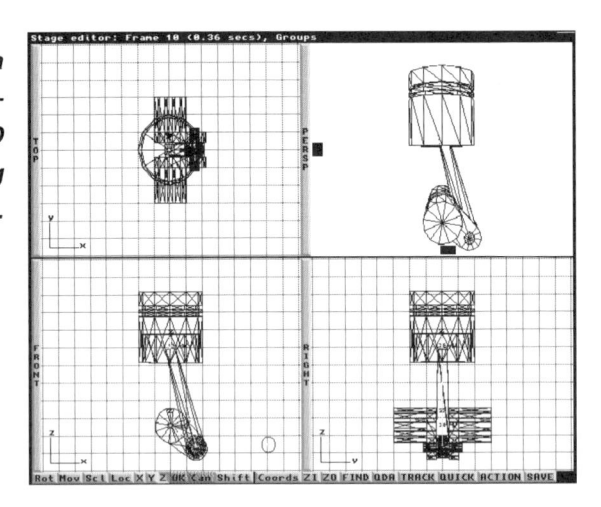

A 3D image (below) rendered by Imagine 2.

Imagine 2 isn't a program for the faint-hearted and it requires a great amount of user-application because it is so wide-ranging.

If you are an impatient soul then DON'T buy Imagine 2 (or any other 3D program for that matter) since you'll only ever be frustrated by it. But treated with respect Imagine is capable of

Painting, modelling, multimedia and DeskTop Video!

IMAGINE 2 BOOKS
Look out for tutorial books on Imagine 2. They really can help.

producing marvels. Mind you, the manual could do with some improvement! Imagine 2 is a piece of flexible, full-featured 3D modelling and animation software capable of professional quality results.

Real 3D Classic £TBA (£100?)

From: Alternative Image. Tel. 0533 440041
Minimum Requirements: 1Mb chip + 2Mb fast RAM

Now that Real 3D 2 is available, Real 3D Classic (the original Real 3D) has been substantially reduced in price.

Like chalk to Imagine's cheese, Real 3D Classic is also capable of producing professional-quality 3D modelling and animation, though it is a little out on a limb in that its object format is poorly supported by other programs. However, its simpler approach to modelling and animation has won a Real 3D lot of friends amongst Amiga graphics users – though I have to admit I'm still an Imagine fan myself.

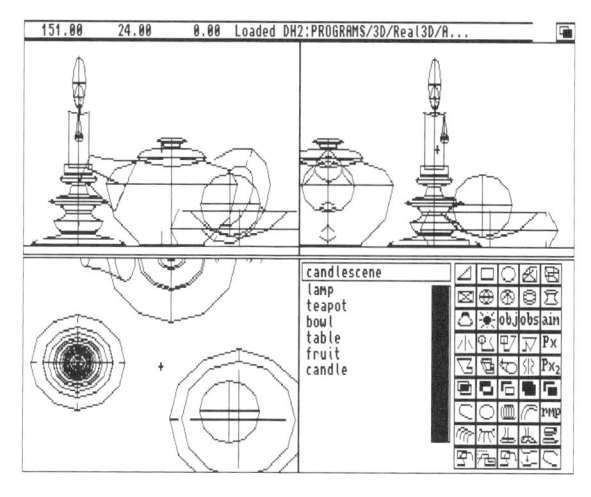

Real 3D Classic is in some ways simpler to use than Imagine 2, yet whether it will dislodge that program from top spot remains to be seen.

Get the most out of your Amiga 1993

An image reddered by Real 3D Classic.

Some features, such as surface mapping, are much more straightforward with Real 3D and others, like modelling, are more basic. Its animation and object layout might also be considered simpler than Imagine's, but in my eyes you simply choose one program or t'other.

Real 3D is a viable alternative to Imagine 2. Simpler to use, not quite as comprehensive, but nonetheless one of the best introductions to 3D work.

SURFACE MAPPING
A technique for clothing a 3D object with a bitmap graphic for greater realism and simpler modelling.

Pixel 3D 2 £99.95

From: Digital Marketing International. Tel. 0753 686000
Minimum Requirements: 1.5Mb RAM (accelerator recommended)

Unlike Amiga graphics formats, 3D objects aren't readily interchangeable between different programs. This is where a program like Pixel 3D comes in – allowing conversion between a range of object formats (but not Real 3D...).

Get the most out of your Amiga 1993

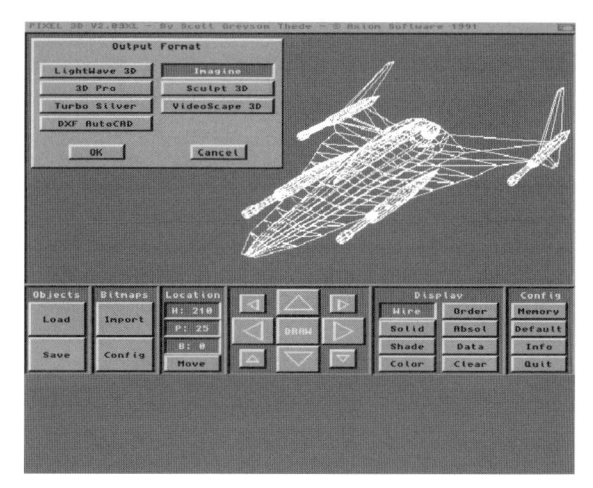

Painting, modelling, multimedia and DeskTop Video!

Pixel 3D 2 can convert objects from a range of 3D modelling programs into counterparts' formats (but not Real 3D).

It can also change a 2D image into a 3D object – perfect for extruding company logos for 3D animations and do a number of other clever tricks to help with 3D modelling. A very useful 3D utility program.

Become a video producer!

Perhaps DeskTop Video is best described as a catch-all for anything to do with computers and video production. This means that video titling, morphing, genlocking, single-frame animation recording and even digitising could be included in DTV.

MORPHING
Changing one image or form into another via a sequence of intermediate formS.

Basically, if it involves video input and/or output then it is probably DTV – unless it is Multimedia, of course. (Oh dear – ed.)

The most talked-about aspect of DTV at the moment is probably morphing – the process of changing one digital image into another over time. Once a hideously expensive process only indulged in by Hollywood producers, morphing is now within the grasp of many Amiga users.

Painting, modelling, multimedia and DeskTop Video!

With such a wide range of applications and products, DTV software could cover several pages alone. Probably the most common DTV activity is video titling, so we'll look at that, take in genlocks and mention morphing too.

Scroller 2 £80

From: Alternative Image. Tel. 0533 440041
Minimum Requirements: 1Mb chip RAM (2Mb chip RAM recommended).

Scroller 2 is a non-multitasking video titling package which does far more than its name suggests. It comes with a range of typefaces, something which is rather important when video titling. It has a wide range of text effects and can easily be programmed to mix and match these together. Scrolling is very smooth and can be instantly set to any of nine speeds.

For most general domestic work Scroller 2 is ideal – though there's no reason why it can't be used for more upmarket productions either. Its biggest drawback is that it can only run from the original disks – not from hard drive or backups. A strong

TYPEFACE
A collection of letters, numerals etc which share a common style and design.

Scroller 2 is an excellent low-end video titling package – if only it could run from hard disk.

Get the most out of your Amiga 1993

showing and available to all Amiga users. Pity it doesn't run from a hard drive, though.

✓ Broadcast Titler 2 £229.99
From: Micro-Pace UK Ltd. Tel. 0753 551888
Minimum Requirements: 1Mb chip + 1Mb fast RAM (hard drive recommended).

SUPERHIRES
An extended graphics mode which can double the screen resolution of a non-AA standard Amiga. Requires Super Denise chip.

A truly dedicated video titler, Broadcast Titler 2 is a program for the Amiga DTV professional. With a very wide range of functions, text effects, wipes, ability to use backgrounds and brushes, triggering, adjustable speeds and much more, Broadcast Titler 2 is almost certainly the best Amiga video titler – but with a price to match.

By using anti-aliased (i.e. jaggy-free) fonts high quality can be obtained – even better if you have the SuperHires version which can take advantage of the Amiga's Super Denise chip (if fitted) to provide very high resolution. A versatile, high quality dedicated titling software, but you pay for that power.

BROADCAST TITLER 2
* FONT FEATURES *
- Accepts 256 Character International Fonts
- Uses All Accents/Symbols
- Sharper Anti-aliasing
- New Character Borders
- Automatic IFF BrushText Fill
- Accepts Amiga/Color Fonts

INNOVISION TECHNOLOGY

Broadcast Titler 2 is a program for the DeskTop Video professional.

Morph Plus £199.95

✓ GOOD BUY

From: DMI plc. Tel. 0753 686000

Minimum Requirements: AmigaDOS2.X (or greater), 1Mb chip RAM, 4Mb fast RAM (more fast RAM and a hard drive recommended)

Morph Plus, as one of three currently available morphing packages, probably offers the best overall results at the moment – though it is run very close by Image Master (see Image Processing below).

Morphing takes some learning to get the techniques worked out, but once you've found your way around Morph Plus's interface and manual you shouldn't have too much trouble.

Morph Plus can handle still morphs, moving morphs, still warps and moving warps as well as an impressive range of image manipulation and distortion functions – sort of like a miniature Art Department Professional. For quality work I'd certainly recommend Morph Plus over the cheaper (but less accommodating) CineMorph from GVP.

MOVING MORPH
The results of morphing between two sets of moving images to provide realistic transitions in motion.

Morph Plus is a professional morphing tool – but it costs accordingly.

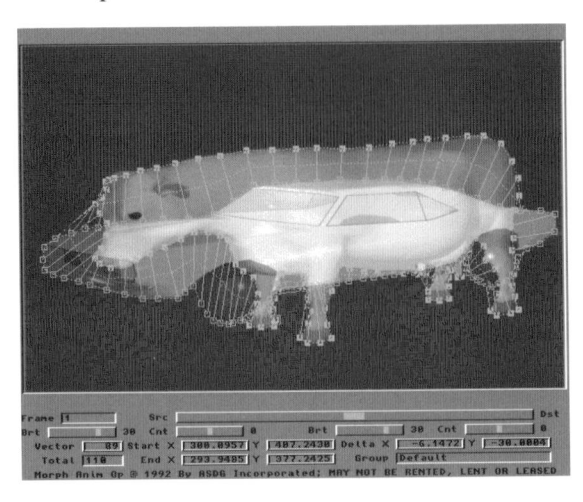

Get the most out of your Amiga 1993

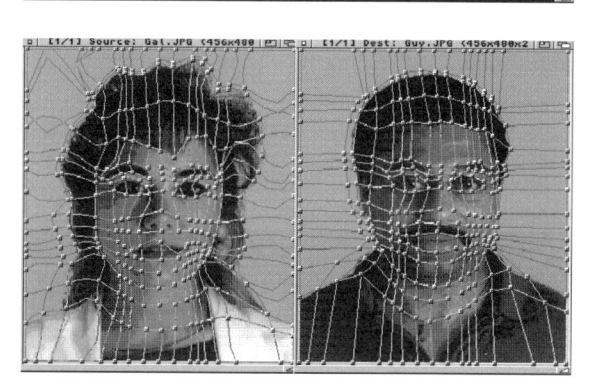

Cinemorph is not as well-featured as Morph Plus, but the price is much more accessible.

✓ Cinemorph   £99.95

From: Silica Systems. Tel. 081 3091111

Minimum Requirements: AmigaDOS 1.3 (or greater), 512K chip RAM, 2Mb fast RAM.

WARP

The process by which one image is dragged into the shape of another. Coupled with a cross-fade this is the basis of morphing.

A dedicated morphing program, and currently the cheapest way to experience morphing, CineMorph offers a wide range of morphing features and its relatively low cost will make this an attractive prospect for many.

But be warned – it can be quite awkward to use because of its method of defining morphing points. Otherwise it produces very acceptable results and also makes Amiga-compatible animations directly – which the others don't.

Cinemorph is a capable morpher which is well-priced, though not as flexible as other programs.

The Rendale 8802 FMC Genlock is a good genlock at a good price.

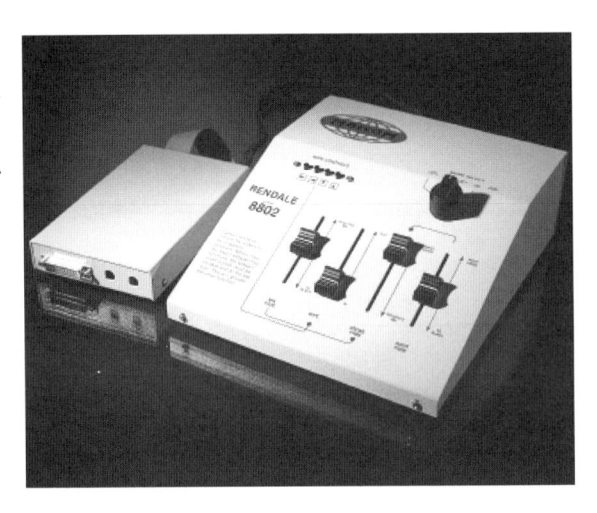

✔ Rendale 8802 FMC Genlock £178
From: Marcam Ltd. Tel. 0604 790466.
Minimum Requirements: An Amiga and a video deck or camera.

One of the longest-established Amiga genlocks and still one of the most reliable, providing good quality signals and locking onto most composite video signals with ease. The 8802 has to be connected to the Amiga's RGB port but has a pass-through to let you still use a standard RGB monitor (unlike some other low-cost genlocks).

This version also allows cross-fading between Amiga and video images, has a fade to black feature and has a choice of genlocking modes. A clean, reliable and good-value genlock.

The multimedia revolution

The new buzzword amongst media people, Multimedia covers a range of applications which involve more than one data source (e.g. CD audio, video tape, Laserdisk, MIDI music devices and

RGB PORT
The best quality Amiga video output, which is used when high-quality is required.

GENLOCK
A device for overlaying computer graphics onto video images.

Painting, modelling, multimedia and DeskTop Video!

Amiga graphics) all choreographed by one master program to produce a complete presentation.

The individual parts will usually be produced using other software and data gathering techniques such as sound sampling and video filming, but always with the final result in mind.

A multimedia production is rather like making a TV program, except that the results are "broadcast" by the computer itself, along with the relevant playback devices. The current Amiga multimedia champ is SCALA's Scala MM200, though there are several others in the field.

Oddly, Multimedia has long been the dark horse of Amiga applications, but with programs like Amiga Vision and, especially, Scala, the situation is happily changing for the better. Indeed, one family of products really does deserve your attention – and that's Scala.

✓ Scala £99, £149, £399

GOOD BUY **From:** SCALA UK: Tel. 0920 444294

Minimum Requirements: These will vary according to software version.

The range of Scala products complements both the range of Amiga products and the needs of every user level and all versions can produce straight-forward DTV presentations which include graphics, wipes, and text.

Scala HT (Home Titler) is for the A500, A600 or CDTV enthusiast and gives easy entry into the multimedia arena, with a range of typefaces, brushes and wipes and up to 8 colours in Hi-res

The Amiga is a top multimedia tool, thanks to packages like Scala MM (MultiMedia).

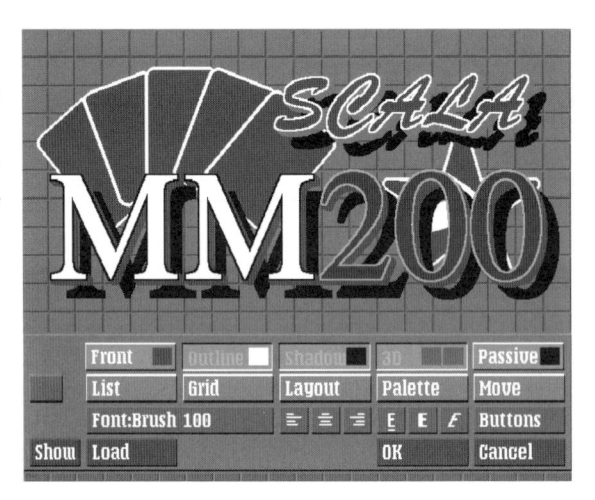

overscan. A program especially tailored for the domestic videographer. Requires 1Mb RAM minimum.

Scala VS (Video Studio) includes a range of high-quality backgrounds and additional wipes and is more suited to semi-pro and advanced home use. Also has basic sound handling. As a halfway house between HT and MM the entry requirements may be a little high for many users. Requires 1Mb chip + 2Mb fast RAM and hard drive minimum.

Scala MM (Multimedia) is a top-end multimedia product – able to control an ever-expanding range of external hardware, including MIDI music equipment, Laserdisks, CDTV audio, video decks (and lots more) and integrate their output into a fully-fledged multimedia presentation. It can also utilise sampled sound and play back animations. For serious users Scala MM has already established itself as a multimedia leader – on any computer platform! This really is the Amiga multimedia king, though the need for the (anti-pirate) dongle can be troublesome at times.

Painting, modelling, multimedia and DeskTop Video!

BACK-GROUNDS
Design your own background for Scala with a paint program like Deluxe Paint IV.

Requires 1Mb chip + 3Mb fast RAM and hard drive minimum. (2Mb chip RAM recommended)

Using real-world pictures

How do you accurately copy a logo if you aren't an artist? And how do you turn a section of video into an animation clip? The answer is simple – use a digitiser.

The great thing about digitising is that almost anything from the real world can be captured from a video signal and used as a template for further work. Again, extra equipment is required – a video camera or other video source (such as a video deck with rock-solid pause) and, naturally, a digitiser.

ROTO-SCOPING
A technique for tracing over live action (traditionally film but now also video and digitised images) to capture subtle movements into new graphic characters.

The principle is simple: a video image is fed into the digitiser, where it is separated into its three basic components – Red, Green and Blue (RGB). Some digitisers require an external electronic colour splitter for this but nowadays most have one built in. An exception occurs when a black and white video camera is used, and coloured filters have to be used in front of the camera lens instead – again one for each of the RGB splits.

Once grabbed, an image (or sequence of images) can be stored in a suitable format for further use, e.g. HAM, 24-bit etc and then be used as a basis for rotoscoping, company logos, animations, DTV backgrounds, diagrams, database files and so on.

Like other Amiga products, there are a wide range of video digitisers are available, all of which have their own merits. There are two main types – Slow Scan and Fast Scan – which depend on whether the digitiser has on-board memory into which to grab a video image or not. The advantage of fast scan digitisers is that they can grab a frame in the time it takes to display it – i.e. 1/25th of a second and hold it as long as required in memory whereas to digitise an image with a slow scan digitiser the source needs to be perfectly still – whether from video tape or in front of a camera – as scanning can take several seconds or more.

✓ Vidi-Amiga 12 £99.95
GOOD BUY **From:** Rombo Limited. Tel. 0506 414631
Minimum Requirements: 1Mb RAM (more recommended)

Rombo's Vidi-Amiga 12 is a small black box which has to be attached to your Amiga's parallel and disk drive ports. It can accept either composite or S-VHS video inputs and is controlled by its own software.

As a slow scan digitiser it does require a perfectly still image for colour work. But because it is very fast it can grab in black and white in almost real-time – which makes it ideal for grabbing sections of video for subsequent reprocessing into colour animations.

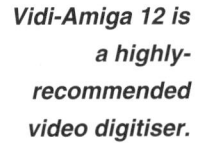

Vidi-Amiga 12 is a highly-recommended video digitiser.

Get the most out of your Amiga 1993

Painting, modelling, multimedia and DeskTop Video! 65

S-VHS VIDEO

A video format where the colour and brightness information are processed separately for better quality images.

Vidi-Amiga 12 can produce output in all the regular Amiga resolutions plus the new AA modes and can grab multiple frames into memory and play them back as an animation. So the more memory the Amiga has, the bigger the animation can be.

Picture quality is excellent and the range of tools for manipulating the images – both stills and animations – is outstanding for a unit of this price. Highly recommended.

VLab Par, VLab £382, £341

From: Amiga Centre Scotland. Tel. 0896 87583
Minimum Requirements: 1Mb RAM, AmigaDOS 2.x or greater (hard drive highly recommended)

VLab Par is one of two models, both identical in all but price and fitting. VLab Par is an external version which (naturally) connects to the parallel port of any suitable Amiga whilst the other version is an internal card for Amiga 1500/2000/3000/4000 models only.

Both are fast scan digitisers capable of grabbing a frame from composite video in next to no time in sizes up to full PAL

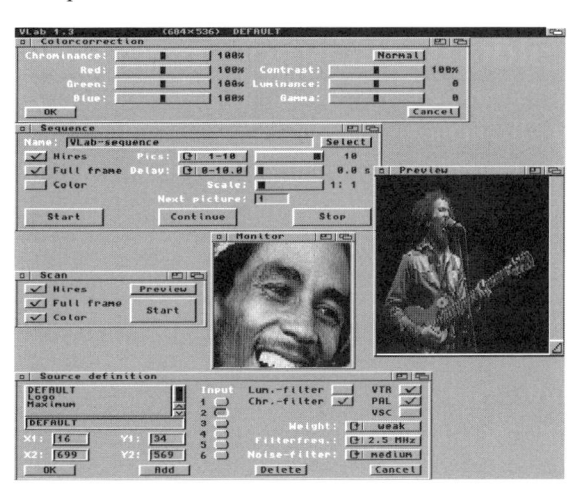

VLab is the top digitiser for serious use.

Get the most out of your Amiga 1993

overscan. An on-screen preview makes viewing easy and by hitting a key combination the frame is grabbed.

After grabbing an image has to be processed into something the Amiga can understand and VLab can convert the grabbed file to standard IFF, AA modes or (best of all) 24-bit for further use. This stage can take a while, depending on the size and format of the conversion.

Like Vidi-Amiga 12, VLab produces excellent quality grabs and images can be captured live from tape or camera. They can also be grabbed in sequences, though not continuously in real-time. For serious users, and those who need top quality, VLab is strongly recommended.

COMPOSITE VIDEO
Video signals which combine both colour and brightness portions into one signal for simplicity.

Changing your image...

Image processing tends to be thought of as a DTP application but it is equally important in pure graphics work. Changing the nature of an image is often necessary – scaling it, adjusting its colour balance, reformatting it into another graphics standard or compositing parts from one image with another are common events in an electronic artist's life.

The good news is that the Amiga is blessed with several excellent image processing programs which can handle many different tasks. The bad news (for beginners) is that the more 'professional' ones tend to use memory like there's no tomorrow and can be quite expensive.

But there are some simpler programs that even a novice can get to grips with, and a little time spent looking around the PD libraries should pay off handsomely.

GRAPHICS FORMATS
Other computer systems use different formats for storing images. A common one is GIF. With suitable software many of these formats can be converted to ones suitable for Amiga use.

Get the most out of your Amiga 1993

Painting, modelling, multimedia and DeskTop Video!

Traditionally, image processing software is used by DeskTop Publishers to adjust images for printing. But image processing is probably of equal value to electronic artists and video makers because it enables a whole range of special adjustments to be made to computer images. Programs like Art Department Professional and Image Master are extremely flexible and will let you manipulate images in ways you would never have thought possible.

✓ Image Master £175
GOOD BUY
From: Amiga Centre Scotland. Tel. 0896 87583
Minimum Requirements: AmigaDOS1.3, 512K chip + 3Mb fast RAM, hard drive (accelerator recommended)

A whole chapter wouldn't be enough to describe Image Master, so let me just say that it has extensive image processing features, a whole range of special effects tools, can assemble animations, has painting tools, compositing tools, converts between almost all available image formats and does a very nice morph into the bargain.

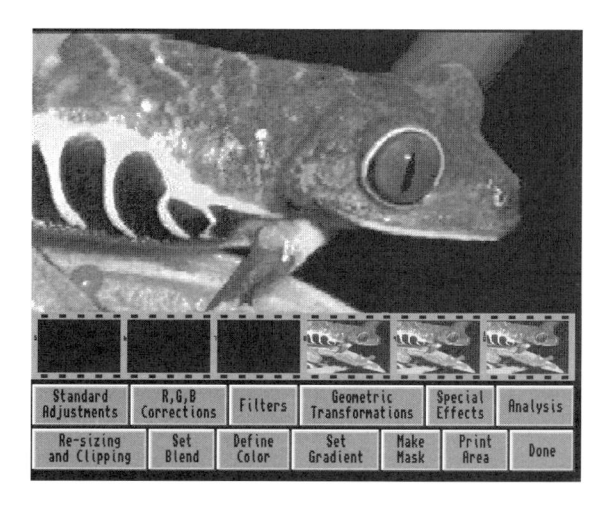

Image Master is a powerful image manipulation tool that can also carry out 'morphing'.

It can work with 24-bit images (though these obviously can't be fully displayed on a normal Amiga screen) and turn out some very nice quality results. It makes a very viable alternative to ASDG's Art Department Pro and Morph Plus combined.

Image Master is a powerful, integrated, image-processing and animation tool with very capable morphing feature as well.

COMPOSITING
Image layering using digital cut and paste techniques to achieve a wide range of effects.

✓ Art Department Pro 2 £211.50

From: Digital Marketing International. Tel. 0753 686000
Minimum Requirements: AmigaDOS2.04, 1Mb chip RAM, 2Mb fast RAM, hard drive (much more RAM recommended)

Like Image Master, ADPro has wide range of capabilities, from format conversions to image processing, rescaling, adding text, and compositing images together.

It is rather easier to use than Image Master but has fewer features overall and really needs Morph Plus to be added to match Image Master for power.

Art Department Pro 2 is easier to use than Image Master, but has fewer features.

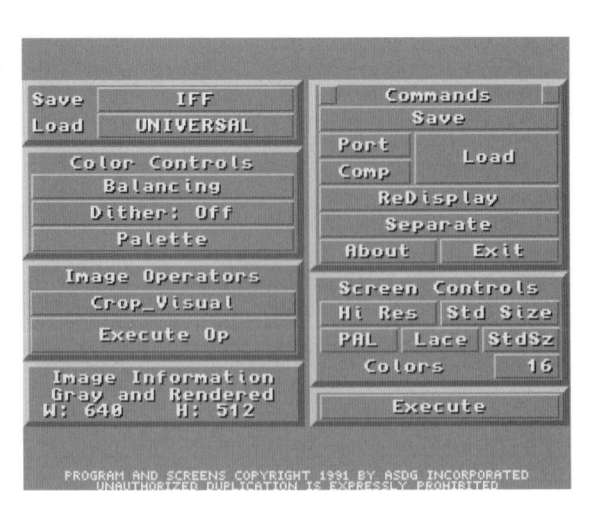

Nonetheless, ADPro remains a vital tool for many power users, particularly in the DTP profession. It provides great quality output in a whole range of formats, including 24-bit, standard IFF modes and AA graphics modes. A no-nonsense professional image processor with a wide range of capabilities.

Useful bits of software

Sometimes there are times when you need smooth-edged typefaces for that special look. And others when you have a a big sequence of images that you need to rename and renumber and you really don't fancy using the Shell (AmigaDOS) to do the job. Here are two excellent utilities to help you out.

AntiA £39.95

From: Zen Computer Services. Tel. 061 7931931.
Minimum Requirements: Any Amiga.

AntiA is a unique program which takes a normal Amiga bitmap font, or one of the newer scalable Bullet fonts, and not only produces a new range of smaller sizes from it but also smooths out its edges by using anti-aliasing techniques. The result – beautiful

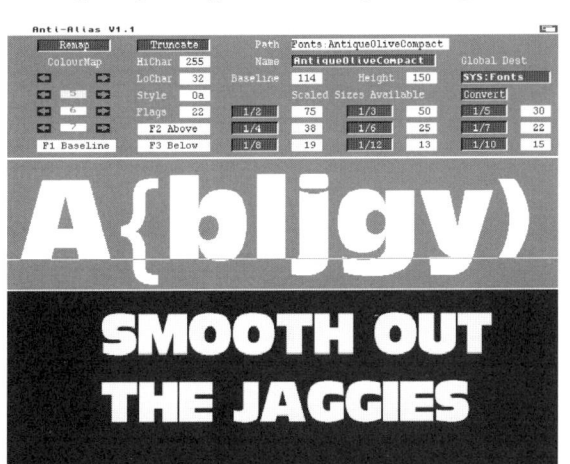

'Jaggies' are the scourge of bitmapped graphics. AntiA smooths them out.

quality Colorfonts which can be used in many Amiga graphics programs just like normal fonts.

Simple to use, effective software for smoothing out the jaggies from bitmap fonts.

✓ Reverser £10

GOOD BUY From: Alternative Image. Tel 0533 440041
Minimum Requirements: Any Amiga.

Many Amiga programs produce standard IFF image files but there seems to be no accepted naming convention when multiple files are the result. Some may be called MyPicture.XXX, others MyPictureXXX or MyPicture.XXXX. This can be frustrating when trying to use one set of files in a program which expects another naming convention, and animators in particular will be sick to the back teeth of this problem.

So for renaming batches of image files from one numbering system to another Reverser does the business. Easily, quickly and, above all, cheaply. This is a bargain for everyone who's ever

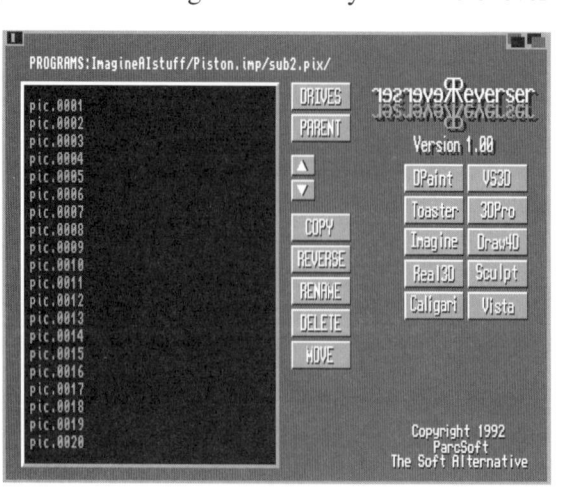

> **ANTI-ALIASING**
> A graphics technique for smoothing out the steppy edges of bitmapped graphics by introducing intermediate colours to soften edges.

Reverser is a priceless utility for those who have to handle large numbers of different graphics file types.

struggled with the Shell to do this job. Cheap, simple and efficient. Great value.

Where to get free (nearly) software!

Not surprisingly, there are a number of excellent utilities which have been made available for the greater good by their authors. Mostly these are display programs but there are others too. Here is a short selection of those that I find most useful and which should be in everyone's graphics toolkit.

✔ Rend24 $25 (shareware)

From: PD sources and bulletin boards
Minimum Requirements: AmigaDOS1.3 and enough RAM to handle your chosen images or animations.

Rend24 is an invaluable tool for animators everywhere. Principally designed for 24-bit work to convert a series of 24-bit files into an Amiga-viewable animation it can also use standard IFF files as well – and convert and save GIF and JPEG files to IFF ones.

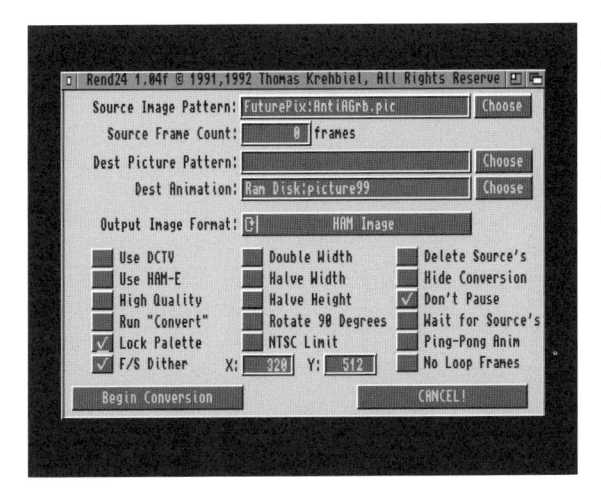

Rend24 is an excellent file conversion utility for Amiga animators.

With a whole host of massively useful functions such as dithering, palette locking, rescaling, DCTV output and much more. Rend24 is a very useful program.

Viewtek — free!

From: PD sources and bulletin boards
Minimum Requirements: AmigaDOS 2.04 or greater and enough RAM to handle your chosen images or animations.

This is a viewer program that will take a variety of image formats – including GIF, JPEG and IFF24 – and convert them to a form which can be viewed on a normal Amiga. It will also play back animations and display standard Amiga images. It can also display AA mode images and play back 256 colour AA mode animations!

It's nothing flash, and the user has no control over the quality of the results, but nevertheless a very useful program if you don't have any image processing software to hand – and it costs nothing.

View 3.0 — free!

From: PD sources and bulletin boards
Minimum Requirements: None, except enough memory to display chosen animations or pictures.

View 3.0 is an animation and IFF image viewer which can play back animations more quickly and more smoothly than Deluxe Paint and also handle animations with multiple palettes – which Deluxe Paint cannot. It is extremely easy to use. Recommended for lazy artists and animators everywhere. Add this to your viewer collection – you won't regret it.

GIF

Graphic Data Interchange Format. A 256 colour image format which has become especially popular amongst PC users.

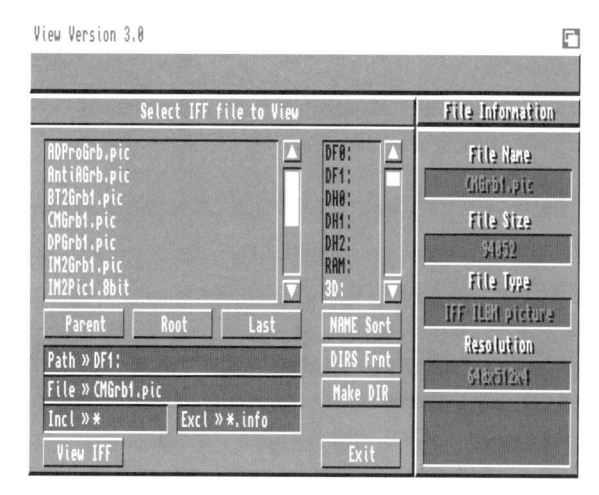

View 3.0 lets you view animations and IFF files quickly and easily.

Is that the lot? (No)

Well, I think that's scratched the surface deeply enough for now, though I would like to have been able to talk more about Amigas and video editing, monitors, flicker fixers, 24-bit and other display devices... but for all this and more, make sure you read Amiga Format every month!

Making music

Electronic music produced in the past has often been the domain of techno-boffins with huge wodges of cash. Yet these days anyone with an Amiga can produce marketable music in their own homes! The ability to link your Amiga to a whole music system or play back high-quality sampled sounds without any extra hardware makes the Amiga a powerful music tool. Music expert Maff Evans tells you what you need…

When most people think of electronic music, the image that springs to mind is of studios with racks of expensive sequencing, recording and synthesizing technology. With the arrival of affordable 16-bit computers, this position has changed quite drastically. The Amiga can be used as the centre of an entire music set-up – either controlling musical instruments using MIDI or producing sounds by itself – without adding any other hardware.

If you're thinking that you still need to splash out a load of extra dosh for a system, this isn't true at all. Sure, the Amiga can act as a sequencer for playing racks of advanced sound equipment, but it can also be used on its own to create some stunning pieces. After all, dance band Urban Shakedown managed to get a single in the charts that was created using two Amigas, a handful of samples and a PD music package – no synths were used! So you could be a pop star just using the superb computer that you own: the Amiga.

MIDI

Stands for Musical Instrument Digital Interface, which is the 'language' that electronic instruments use for sending messages to each other.

What's involved?

Producing music on the Amiga falls into three basic categories: Sampling, tracking and sequencing. Lets have a look at what these areas involve:

Sampling

Sound sampling is basically taking a recording of a sound and turning it into numbers that the computer can understand. This is done by rapidly taking a 'sample' of a sound's volume at a particular point and storing that volume as a number, then doing it again and again and again. By replaying these numbers in sequence (turning them back into specific volumes) the original sound is recreated.

Making music

SAMPLING

When sampling, only record short, percussive sounds at high sample rates, otherwise you will use up far too much memory. Voices often sound better a little 'grunged up' anyway!

So what can you do when you've recorded a sample? Well you can edit it for starters. You can chop sections out (to remove any unwanted bits), reverse it, change the volume or loop it (make it play over and over again). Once you've edited it to your liking, you can save it onto disk and load it into a tracker or sequencer to play it back, effectively using it to play a tune.

There are a number of sampling systems available in different price brackets. You do get what you pay for as far as sound quality and editing features go, but you can still achieve very good results with cheaper packages.

Audio Engineer Plus £204.30

From: HB Marketing. Tel 0753 686000
Minimum requirements: Any Amiga

For those who want the absolute best in Amiga sampling, this is the one. For your (not insubstantial) money, you get a version of the superb Audiomaster IV software (which can also be bought separately) and an absolutely cracking piece of sampling hardware (which is the bit that records the sounds).

The hardware has stereo microphone and line-level inputs, separate level controls for left and right inputs and a switchable printer through-port (so you don't have to unplug it to use your printer). The software is the best you can get, with loads of options available from fast and easy to use pull-down menus and excellent recording quality. There's even a time-stretch function, which enables you to change the speed of a sample without changing its pitch – something which is only usually found on studio samplers costing thousands.

The combination of the wonderful hardware and simple to operate, feature packed software makes this the Rolls Royce of Amiga samplers. Sure, it's expensive, but it's worth it! Top notch quality and bags of features make this the best Amiga sampler you can buy.

Technosound Turbo 2 £32.99
From: New Dimension, 0873 850028
Minimum requirements: Any Amiga

As far as starter packages go, Technosound Turbo 2 is a real winner. The package consists of a cartridge to plug into the back of your Amiga (which actually does the recording) and a disk containing the program. The package yields some very good results for a system at this price, and the program features loads of easy to operate editing tools.

Recording is simple enough – just get a sound playing into the machine and click on the record icon. The editing tools feature the usual cut, paste and copy commands along with a pretty good looping and special effects section. Although there are a lot of things in there, everything is laid out pretty simply, so it doesn't boggle the beginner. Even if you do find the software limiting after a while, you can always buy Aegis' Audiomaster IV software for some state-of-the-art sampling tools, since it can be used with the Technosound hardware without any problems.

For a cost-effective and simple to use starting system, Technosound Turbo 2 is a good bet. It sounds good, it's easy to use and you can buy new software if you want. A well laid out and good sounding sampler at a decent price.

> **LOOPING SAMPLES**
> When looping samples, always try to get the levels at the start and end of the sample to be equal, otherwise you will hear a click.

Making music

TRACKS

The Amiga's built-in sound hardware can play four different tunes or 'tracks' simultaneously.

Tracking

Trackers are programs that enable you to load in Amiga samples and use them to play a tune. The Amiga is capable of playing four sounds at once, so you effectively get four 'tracks' for reproducing music. Many of the tunes heard in games are created on tracker programs and saved as 'modules' to be loaded into the game code.

There are some programs that use some clever processing to play eight sounds at once, such as OctaMED and Oktalyser. These programs make it possible to make more complex tunes, but the sound quality does suffer a little, since two sounds need to be combined to double the number of sounds played at once.

To get round the problem of sound quality, Urban Shakedown use MED to create their tunes on four tracks, getting two Amigas to play in time to give them eight tracks. Given that they use such basic technology to create their music and still manage to get into the charts, it shows you that you can create great-sounding music at a very low cost for yourselves.

✓ MED V3.21 £1.25

From: Amiganuts United, 169 Dale Valley Road, Hollybrook, Southampton, SO1 6QX
Minimum requirements: Any Amiga

MED is pretty much the favourite tracker program for most purposes. The main part of the program involves playing notes using the Amiga keyboard into four columns (which signify the four tracks). You can use any Amiga samples to create your tune, or synthesize sounds within MED itself, enabling you to create some very original pieces.

Not only can you record notes, edit them and copy them around different blocks to arrange a song, but you can also add effects such as pitch bending, muting and volume changes, to make it sound even more professional. The note entry system isn't everyone's cup of tea, but it is the standard for tracker programs. Once you get used to the wealth of options on offer, it does allow for some very impressive musical pieces. A full-featured tracker with a good user interface.

SCORE WRITER
A computer program that enables you to print out full musical notation of your MIDI sequences.

✓ OctaMED Pro £22 (£32 + manual)

From: Amiganuts United, 169 Dale Valley Road, Hollybrook, Southampton, SO1 6QX
Minimum hardware: Any Amiga

To go that little bit further in tracking, you'll need to use an eight-channel system (either that or use two Amigas, but the first method is a lot cheaper). OctaMED Pro is pretty much the ultimate in eight-track sample tracking on the Amiga at the moment, since it takes all the options and capabilities of MED and adds the ability to use eight sounds at once along with a whole lot more.

The operating system has been improved, making it quicker and easier to move around the program, using large, clear screens and

OctaMED Pro – the ultimate in 8-track sampling on the Amiga.

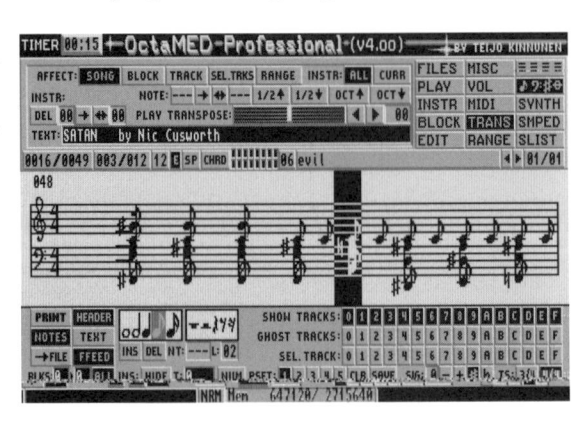

Get the most out of your Amiga 1993

Making music

MULTITRACK

A recorder that enables you to record a number of layers separately which can then be played back at the same time.

panels so that you can find all the options easily. As well as having the usual column-entry method for notes (as found on MED), you can enter and edit notes on a conventional musical score (which should please musicians).

An early version of OctaMED was available on the coverdisk of Amiga Format issue 29, so have a look to see if this is what you want. After some experimentation, you can get hold of the super-duper souped-up version later and get *really* stuck into tracking! Probably the most powerful tracker available for the Amiga, with loads of tools and a rapid editing system.

MIDI Sequencing

If you really want to get the maximum musical capabilities out of your Amiga, then you'll need to get into MIDI sequencing. A sequencer is a program that enables you to record, edit and play back music using external synthesizers, samplers and drum machines. A sequencer basically acts like a multitrack tape recorder, except that instead of recording sound, the computer records the information about what notes to play, how loud to play them, whether the pitch is bent up or down and other messages such as changing the sound to be used.

Most sequencers operate in a similar way to a tape recorder in that you can record the information by playing notes into the computer, rewinding and then playing them back. The difference is that you can then edit the individual notes, chopping out any mistakes, quantizing, changing the pitch or even speeding up and slowing down the tune – all of which is not possible with most tape recorders!

Get the most out of your Amiga 1993

Music-X   £199

From: Software Business. Tel 0480 496497
Minimum hardware: 1Mb RAM

For some time, the favourite MIDI sequencer on the Amiga has been Music-X. Currently in its version 1.1 incarnation, Music-X offers 250 sequencer tracks, a simple to use graphical editing system and a very flexible song arrangement method. You can put all your sequences into sections on individual tracks (for the intro, verse, chorus and so on) and call them up when they are needed, chaining and layering sequences to produce the finished song.

The editing system is a doddle to operate, thanks to the use of a piano-roll representation of the notes. All you need to do to add, delete and move notes is click on them with the mouse pointer and drag them where you want, copy them or delete them. Simple. There are also other points to note, such as the ability to load in up to 16 Amiga samples to add to your sequences, store MIDI sys-ex data for synth sounds and even set up keyboard splits for live performing.

QUANTIZE

A method used for correcting the timing of notes played slightly out of time.

Software business are also getting ready to launch Music-X 2, which will not only feature improved editing tools and options, but a full score-writing and editing package should be worth watching for! A flexible and easy to operate sequencer with a lot of useful and fast tools.

Making music

✓ Dr T's KCS 3.5 Level I £279
From: Zone Distribution. Tel 071 738 5444
Minimum hardware: 1Mb RAM (2Mb RAM recommended)

By paying a little bit extra, you can move up to something which is seriously professional! KCS was one of the first MIDI sequencers to appear on the Amiga, but this version has come a long way since then! All the usual recording, copy, paste and delete functions are there, but KCS 3.5 goes further than just offering you the features of a single program.

Level II is actually a complete suite of programs, including KCS itself, Tiger (which provides a graphical method for editing notes and other MIDI data), Quickscore (a score-printing package), Automix (an automatic MIDI mixing page) and the powerful PVG (Programmable Variations Generator, which is a system for generating songs in a particular style). All this adds up to a system which is aimed at the professional electronic musician (hence the higher than normal price for an Amiga program). It gives you all the tools and options that you'd expect to find on the machines in a studio, so beginners may find it a little overwhelming.

> **SYS-EX**
> System Exclusive data, which is a definition for the configuration of data used by a particular synthesizer. Syx-ex data can be sent via MIDI to an editing program on a synth.

> **SYNTH CONTROL**
> When playing a keyboard synthesizer to record into a sequencer, turn the synth's local control option off, otherwise you will be playing two sets of notes, which could cause your synth to 'stick' (leave odd notes playing).

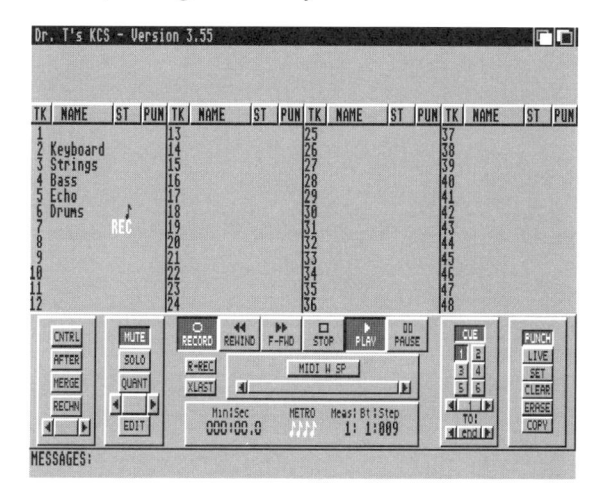

Dr T's KCS – the start of a seriously professional system?

Get the most out of your Amiga 1993

However, for those with a grasp of the workings of MIDI, it really is the bees knees as far as Amiga sequencing goes. The most powerful sequencer you can get for your Amiga.

Well, as you can see from our brief visit, the music world's full of its own jargon and exotic-sounding hardware, but don't be afraid to try it out. Who knows – your Amiga may be your route to stardom! (Just don't send us any demos.)

> *TRY BEFORE YOU BUY!*
> *When buying music equipment, ALWAYS demand to try it out first. Don't take the shop-keepers word for how good or bad something is. It could be just what you want, even if it is cheap!*

Getting down to business

It's hard to imagine how businesses ever got by without computers. From simple DeskTop Publishing in the marketing department to vast integrated accounting and stock control systems, the business world has been quick to exploit the considerable benefits and competitive advantage that computers can bring. Although traditionally all but ignored by the business community, the Amiga has many excellent software packages which offer a great deal of functionality for a very modest outlay, as Phil Gladwin explains…

One feature common throughout business collapse is the failure to keep a firm grip on the ebb and flow of the company's money. This point cannot be stressed too strongly – if you don't know who owes you money, or where you are spending your money – and why – then your business future will probably be short and relatively inglorious.

Whether they're used as simple book-keeping tools or full-blown management information systems, the modern databases, spreadsheets and the integrated accounting packages and other tools available on computers are sophisticated enough to make the control and analysis of information both simple and fruitful.

> **INTEGRATED SYSTEM**
> *A collection of commonly-used software tools in one easy to use package. It might incorporate, say, a word processor, a database and a spreadsheet.*

A system to start with

If you are new to computing, and you can't really see what the benefits might be as yet, then you should have a look at an integrated office system. Packages like this usually claim to provide the complete working environment for the business, and while that is often almost the case, that is also their undoing. It's always true that you get what you pay for, and if you can afford the extra and go for the components separately then you won't regret it.

If however, you are sceptical about what computers can do for you, or you are on a very tight budget, but have to have a degree of automation, then the better integrated packages are worth looking at. For a very limited outlay you could find yourself with perfectly usable spreadsheet, database and wordprocessor which you may go on to use happily for years to come.

What's a spreadsheet?

Along with word processing, the arrival of the spreadsheet was a dominant factor in the success of the personal computer. Starting

Getting down to business

A simple spreadsheet

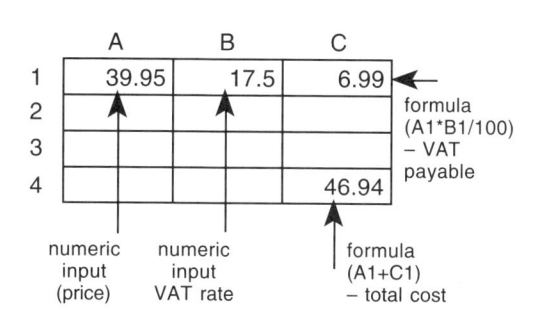

	A	B	C
1	39.95	17.5	6.99
2			
3			
4			46.94

- A1: numeric input (price)
- B1: numeric input VAT rate
- C1: formula (A1*B1/100) – VAT payable
- C4: formula (A1+C1) – total cost

A spreadsheet is an array of interlinking 'cells' Each cell has a unique grid position (e.g. A1 C2 etc.) and you can use the contents of each cell in calculations.

SPREADSHEET

A spreadsheet is a large, automated piece of ruled analysis paper. You fill in the figures, and describe how you would like them worked on, and the spreadsheet does the rest. Each cell is a 'box' where you can store a number, or carry out calculations based on the numbers in other cells.

just over ten years ago and coming on strong ever since, today's examples often do everything but go out and sell your products for you. The concept is simple enough, yet the effect is devastating, and there are many accountants today who simply refuse to remember how miserable life was before their first spreadsheet.

Imagine a massive grid, an array of little boxes, with each box being able to contain either a number or a formula. Each formula can take as its input anything from the boxes around it, so that repetitive and tedious calculations of the sort needed in any financial forecast can be completely automated.

When you are running a business, or thinking about setting one up, it's not hard to see how a spreadsheet could make a massive impact on the hard work of producing cash flows for the ever-cynical bank manager. With manual systems, one single alteration to any of the figures can mean the repetition of tens of calculations. A spreadsheet makes all this simple, letting your try out 'what if' calculations quickly and easily. Leaving you free to worry about the direction of the business, not arithmetic!

✓ K-Spread2 £59.99

From: HiSoft. Tel 0525 718181
Minimum requirements: Any Amiga

With K-Spread 4, the heavyweight of the Kuma spreadsheet range now off the shelves, I chose to look at its little brother, K-Spread 2, which comes packaged with K-Data – a flat file database of no mean ability.

K-Spread 2 has its problems: a slightly fussy user interface, relying on two different cursors and different combinations of shift and Alt keypresses, plus a free floating edit/entry window which kept getting lost on my Workbench, all combine to make less than a thrilling first impression. And in general it has a lack of attention to fine detail that keeps it separated it from the big boys.

However, apart from the usability issues, K-Spread2 packs no mean punch. Its apparently sparse menu system reveals all the usual logical, trigonometric and plain arithmetical functionality. It is able to import and export files in the .DIF format (used by,

K-Spread 2 is good value, particularly when you bear in mind the 'free' database.

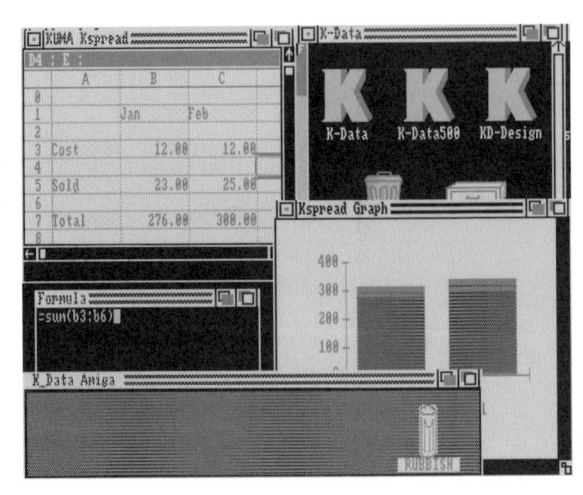

CASH-FLOW
A prediction of what money you will be making and and how you will be spending it over a period of, say, the next year.

K-SPREAD 4
K-Spread 4 is out of circulation undergoing redesign. It should be re-released later this year.

Getting down to business

MACRO
A sequence of keystrokes you have decided to make the system remember. This means you can activate a whole sequence of commands with a single keystroke, putting the machine on 'autopilot'.

among others, Wordworth), and it has a Macro editor that will let you create and store formula using up to 9 different variables.

Its graphing facilities are fairly sparse: two sorts of bar charts and a line graph only, but then again I've always wondered when it comes down to it what a pie chart tells you that a plain old bar chart can't. Not a classic, but a solid performer, at an excellent price when you consider the free database.

Professional Calc £160
From: Digital Marketing. Tel 0753 686000
Minimum requirements: 1Mb RAM, 2 disk drives

I used Advantage, Procalc's predecessor, for two years so I'm biased. But in my opinion, Procalc is far and away the best spreadsheet you can currently get for the Amiga. The 'advantage' of the original Advantage over slightly better specified opponents lay in its startling clarity of use, and Procalc has, with its new Workbench 2 style interface and toolbar, actually gained in this department, and raised the function count to around the 140 mark in the process.

CELL
Each square holding data in a spreadsheet is called a Cell. Think of these as being boxes containing numbers or formulae, or the results of other calculations.

It's the little things that count, and if the extensive, flexible graphing facilities, the style tags for text on the sheet, the ability to take multiple views of the same sheet don't convince you, what about the PostScript printer support, the ARexx support, the multiple screen resolution support?

Pro Calc can import files from Advantage, Maxiplan, and Lotus 123, and graphics can be saved as IFF, CAD and Prodraw. There is a macro language, naturally, and there is even Outline Support – more familiar from word processors.

So the frills are wonderful. What about the heart of the thing, the spreadsheet itself? Well, I'm glad to say there's not a lot to report – it does exactly what good, powerful software should do; reliably and quickly, with a minimum of fuss. Pro Calc is streets ahead of the competition – the nearest the Amiga has to a professional Spreadsheet.

Why you need a database

Like a card index system gone mad, a database provides information and insights simply unavailable before computers. Once the data has been entered, producing mailshots to thousands, even millions, of potential customers becomes a simple matter.

If your customer database is correctly set up then you can 'target' your mailshots with a high degree of precision, in terms of geography, social class, income, employment. Likewise, if your sales database is set up correctly then finding out about the performance of your salesmen, or areas to concentrate on, or products that are doing well or badly, is effortless. You can keep track of your stock inventory and you need never lose track of who has ordered what from you, or who owes you money!

OUTLINE SUPPORT
The condensing of sections of your data into a single heading line, useful for gaining an overview.

DATABASE UPKEEP
The computerised office is only as good as its input. If you have a database it will only be useful if it is kept up to date.

A simple card index-style database stores individual pieces of information in 'fields' on a 'record'. A collection of records is a 'file'.

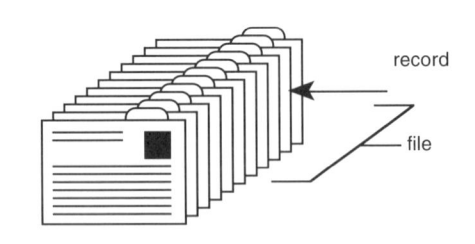

A card-index style database

Getting down to business

✓ Mail-Shot Plus £49.95
From: Digita International. Tel: 0395 270273
Minimum Requirements: Any Amiga

DIRECT MAIL
Also known as junk mail! Where you write directly to individuals to market your product, rather than relying on advertising.

Mail-Shot Plus is not a pretty program; it's six years old, and looks every day of it. Yet what it does it does pretty well.

A clearly laid out editing screen that looks and acts like a strip of labels means that the chore of entering your thousands of target addresses for direct mailing is made as easy as it ever could be. There are limited – but adequate – search facilities; you can create subsets of your data for particular mailshots; you can sort your addresses by any part of the address you want, and, importantly, with a bit of fiddling around, you can import data from other databases.

DO LOOKS COUNT?
Much of the business software on the Amiga looks a little old-fashioned compared to the very newest stuff. Don't be put off – if it does the job then who cares what it looks like?

Mail-Shot Plus is not really recommended for someone who has another database, as its one function could easily be duplicated by the Prodatas and Superbases of this world. However, if your business is low-tech, and has a large mailing list full of addresses and not much else – and you are feeling the pain of writing those addresses out each time you want to do a mailshot – then it's well worth having a look.

Mail-Shot Plus gets a mention here by virtue of its clear focus and simplicity. Most people won't find a use for it – those that can will be very glad of it. An easy-to-use address label printer cum small database. Great at what it does, yet not cheap.

Get the most out of your Amiga 1993

✓ ProData 1.2 £40
From: Arnor. Tel 0733 68909
Minimum requirements: 1Mb RAM (hard disk recommended)

This program comes from the quality stable of Arnor, whose wordprocessor Protext has been winning awards for years now. And it shows. Some would say that Prodata lacked speed around the curves, and they would be right, as its habit of writing every change you make to disk as you do it means that unless you have a hard drive you will spend much time waiting for the green disk light.

To be fair, Arnor are within their rights to expect a hard drive because Prodata is aimed fairly and squarely at the serious user. It is a flat file database, as opposed to relational, yet the power on offer puts it at the top of its field.

Each record can have up to 300 fields, and files may have up to five indexes, with supplementary sort fields available for real subtlety. When it comes to retrieving your data you can create and save your own filters, assigning them as a component of a pull-down menu.

There is a full data entry and display form editor which, while only consisting of fields and line drawing, is adequate for the job, and there are multiple layers of password protection, with the facility to protect specified screens.

All in all, Prodata is a fluent, powerful performer, at the top of the 'flat file' league.

> **FLAT-FILE DATABASE**
> A simple form of database which is easier for the novice user to handle, though not as powerful as a relational database.

> **MAIL MERGING**
> Prodata has built in compatibility with Protext, so performing those mail-merges for your direct mailing couldn't be easier.

Getting down to business

✓ SuperBase Pro (SBase 4)   £249.95
GOOD BUY **From:** Meridian Distribution. Tel. 081 543 3500
Minimum requirements: 1Mb RAM, 2 drives (more RAM and hard drive recommended)

RELATIONS
The data in a relational database is held in tables called Relations.

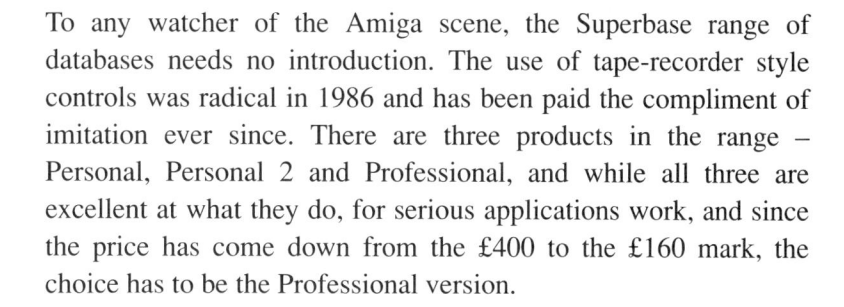

To any watcher of the Amiga scene, the Superbase range of databases needs no introduction. The use of tape-recorder style controls was radical in 1986 and has been paid the compliment of imitation ever since. There are three products in the range – Personal, Personal 2 and Professional, and while all three are excellent at what they do, for serious applications work, and since the price has come down from the £400 to the £160 mark, the choice has to be the Professional version.

DATABASE LANGUAGE
A small programming language present for those users who want the fine control to build power applications. Many users find databases 'off the shelf' do not provide exactly the features they want. This is an opportunity to 'fine tune' the software.

Relational databases are more complicated than flat-file databases, and you aren't going to get away without a fair bit of thought before you start implementing your staff record scheme. Yet the results will be more than worth it. Superbase is fully programmable, and includes an object-oriented graphical forms designer, to help create input forms that won't frighten your users.

As far as retrieving your data goes, you can select groups of records using a very flexible filter system, or for the masochistic who are intent on mastering the relational aspect of the database and making the full use of the power available there is the even more powerful Query option.

With the presence of the Database Management Language – a kind of cross between dBase IV and Basic – and the ARexx interface, there really is no doubt; this is the best database system available for the Amiga at the moment.

Get the most out of your Amiga 1993

Book-keeping made easy

In the race to stay alive, small businesses often neglect the less obviously urgent aspects of their work, like book-keeping, until chaos is knocking at the delivery entrance.

Well, even the Amiga can't turn the drudge involved in keeping the books straight into unmitigated pleasure, but there are packages around that, by guiding you through in a hand-holding sort of a way, take most of the headache and all of the confusion out of the process. When they then also have the ability to calculate your VAT liability, and to produce figures accepted by the Inland Revenue, then they are beginning to pay their way. Nowadays, when a human book-keeper costs around £6 an hour, it has to be worth looking at some of these packages for their ease of use and reliability.

BOOK-KEEPING
If you don't keep your books properly in the first place then the addition of a computer will make no difference to you – it could even make things worse.

✓ Cash Book Combo £79.99
From: Digita International. Tel 0395 270273
Minimum requirements: Any Amiga

Cashbook Combo is a very useful accounts package, but not really designed for beginners.

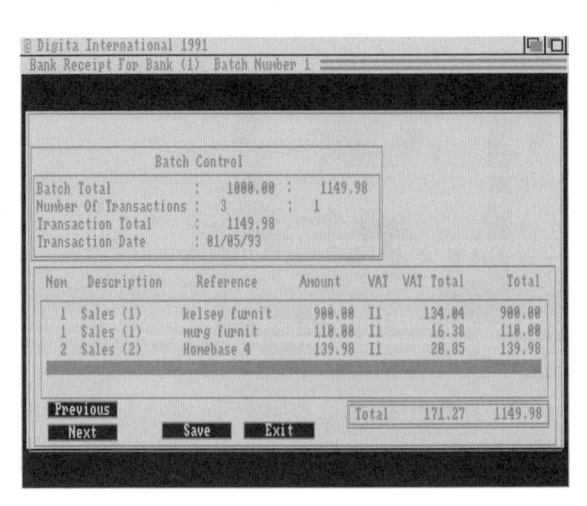

Getting down to business

CHANGING SYSTEMS?
Run your usual paper accounting system for six months alongside your Amiga system before you abandon it, leaving plenty of time for problems to emerge.

BACKING UP
Always keep full backups – at least one copy some distance from the office! Remember, you will have a disaster with your system at some point, and the Inland Revenue aren't noted for their sense of pity.

Cashbook Combo is actually two separate packages marketed together; Final Accounts is a report generator for information produced from Cashbook Controller and can't be used on its own.

Overall, Cashbook Combo is a very professional performer, doing just about all the book-keeping that a small business would need. It does require a certain amount of book-keeping knowledge, though, and the manual is on the terse side. But the package is well designed and possesses many of the features of systems from the IBM world that cost five times as much.

Some nominal ledger accounts are already set up for you; add to them and change these around to get the best set-up for your particular business. You have the choice of entering payments and receipts via the Sales and Purchase Ledgers, where the double entry is automatic, or working directly into the Journal.

Movements between accounts, receipts and payments can be handled individually, or entered in batch form. VAT liability is taken care of, and you can check each nominal account by the month and by the year.

The reporting facilities are generally very advanced without being pretty. Cashbook Combo will generate Trial Balances, Profit & Loss reports and Balance Sheets. If you want to get really clever and get into real Management Accounting there are different profitability ratios to help you with your business strategies. Simple to use and very effective, the Cashbook Combo could be used to great effect by all the small businesses I know.

System 3 £60

From: Digita International. Tel 0395 270273
Minimum requirements: Any Amiga

GOOD BUY

System 3 is an integrated package with three components, which handle between them Sales Invoicing, Stock Control and Cash movements. The user interface can be a real brute, while the Cashflow controller module is quite poor. However, the stock control and invoicing components could be very useful for those that want to generate any invoices while having stock levels adjusted automatically.

You have 99 customer accounts to play with, three levels of VAT, and a 1,000 stock items. There is an extended version of the system if these limits are too small, which effectively doubles these figures.

You are not allowed to raise an invoice on stock that you haven't currently got, and you are warned when you are in danger of running out. System 3 even warns you if you are selling your stock too cheaply!

RAISING INVOICES
You enter (or "raise") an invoice in the system, and System 3 will automatically deduct the items on the invoice from your current stock.

System 3 now looks a bit old-fashioned, but it performs well, and is simple enough to use.

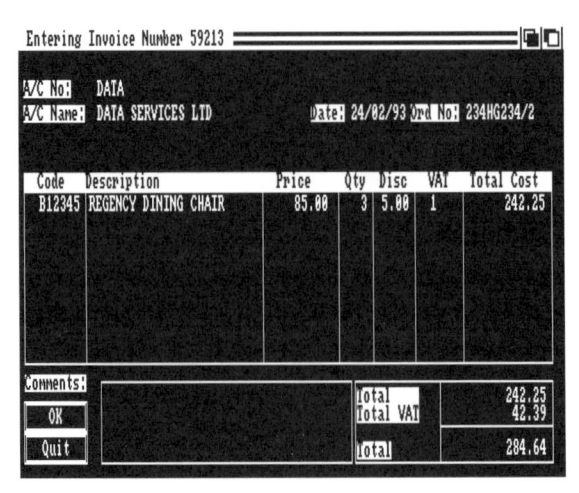

Getting down to business

> **BUY THE BEST!**
> Always buy the best products you can afford. All Amiga software is cheap when you consider its equivalents in the IBM world, and by lashing out that extra £30 you will make a considerable difference in the quality of the goods you end up with – in the long run making your money go further.

Reports printable include full stock breakdown, generation of price list, which of your customers owes you money, and to which of your customers you owe goods. End of month routines exist to create a VAT report detailing your output VAT for the period. Again, simple to use, performs OK, but a rather antiquated feel.

Who needs a PC?

In the last analysis, the real reason for investigating an Amiga-based office setup is the price. The Amiga has never made much of an impact in the world of corporate computing, and whatever the reeasons for that the fall-out as far as we are concerned is that the prices of software are very much lower than in the IBM-compatible market.

Of course, the lack of interest and the resultant lack of profits has deterred many companies from producing business software for the Amiga, and the quality of the software that has come out has sometimes been unacceptably flaky. However, there are enough good, solid products around to make setting up an Amiga-based working environment possible at a fraction of the price the IBM buyer will pay.

You won't have the straight power that, say, Word for Windows, dBase, or the more expensive Sage accounting systems, possess, yet on the other hand it would take a big business to stretch Sage to anywhere near its limit, and most businesses will take a long time to use a tenth of the facilities offered by dBase.

If there's no need for IBM-compatibility – if, for example, you don't already have a large amount of data on an IBM machine – then there is really no reason for not looking hard at the Amiga; the price and quality of some of the software available makes the cost-to-functionality ratio of this kind of setup extremely good.

Get the most out of your Amiga 1993

✓ The Works, Platinum £59.95

From: Digital Marketing. Tel 0753 686000
Minimum requirements: Any Amiga

The Works was the first integrated business package for the Amiga, and it is just about standing the test of time. Four program modules – database, spreadsheet, wordprocessor and a communications package – all for the price of two games can't be bad, and when they are all as good as these then there's no question about it.

Of course, just as in buying a CD/record/tape player, if quality was your primary concern, you would be better off buying separate components rather than a midi player. And what you are getting is cheap and cheerful all-round functionality rather than extended performance in any particular area. Having said that, although I want a HiFi system, I have lived with a music centre for ten years now and not really missed the difference! If your demands are not excessive – you want to type a lot of letters, keep a cash-flow or two going, and keep a customer records database going – then you have no need to look any further.

GET A MODEM

If you can afford it get a modem and get online to one or two of the business-orientated networks in this country. Make valuable contacts, hear rumours before they become facts, and discuss the state of the business world.

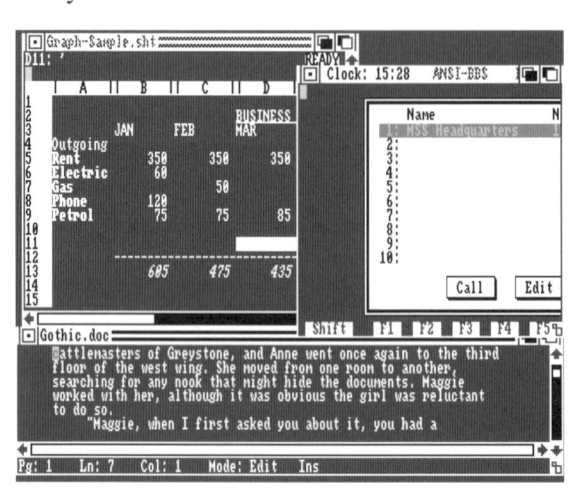

The Works, Platinum Edition could offer all the business software you need! It includes a database, spreadsheet, word processor and comms module.

Get the most out of your Amiga 1993

Getting down to business

THE WORKS

The Works is a smoothly integrated set of useful business tools for the user who doesn't demand too much.

Ease of use is the watchword. Installation of the program is the most technical thing you will be asked to do, and there is a windowing utility supplied which makes it easy. After that the four program modules are called from the same menu, and have a great deal in common in terms of the way they behave, decreasing the learning time on each of them. Good value for the beginner, or the business which doesn't have heavy computing needs.

The cost-effective solution?

You don't need a PC to run a business. And you don't have to pay a fortune to buy all the Amiga business software you need! The PC is still the machine to have if you need serious accounting and stock control power, but the Amiga is perfectly capable of running a typical small business.

From word processing to DeskTop Publishing...

You don't need us to tell you how great the Amiga is. Many of you, though, may be unaware that within that slab of plastic lies a hidden talent. That of publisher! Whether it be slushy piece of poetry to impress (or turn off) that new girl friend, or a magazine about your favourite subject. The Amiga can do it all – the only limit to how far you go is time… and money. Lawrence Hickmott is our Amiga expert on words

WORD/ -n a sound or combination of sounds forming a meaningful element of speech, shown with a space either side of it when written or printed...

So says The Concise Oxford Dictionary. Now you know what words are, let's look at the way your Amiga can help you use them.

The first thing you to have to consider is the content of what you want to write. Will it be just text or do you want to add pictures? The Amiga can handle the full spectrum, from simple letter-writing to advanced, professional-standard DeskTop Publishing...

Basic word processing

In order to communicate, we can use pictures, words... or both! With your help, the Amiga can take these two elements and combine them to produce professional-looking documents.

But before you go racing ahead, buying all the latest gizmos and word crunching software, take a moment to think about what you need. We all know the importance of thinking before opening one's mouth, well the same goes for word processing.

Until a few years ago, word processing was carried out on specialist machines. Now the Amiga possesses the ability to run software that will do the job better and with more flexibility. Whether it be a few lines of slushy poetry, or thousands of words for a book, you are going to need a tool which is going to help you mould your ideas into print. On the Amiga, there are three definitive types of programs:

1. Text-only word processors

The first type is the text only word processor, which is slowly becoming extinct. An example of this would be something like

WORD PROCESSOR
There are two types of programs on the Amiga which can be used for entering text into a document. One is a text editor, the other is word processor. Generally, a text editor is more of a programmers tool, while the word processor is more user friendly.

From word processing to DeskTop Publishing... 103

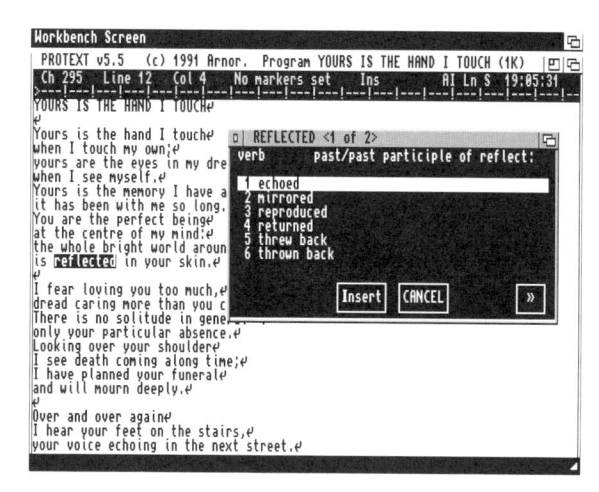

A thesaurus, like the one in Protext, is an excellent feature to have in a word processing program; it helps you find just the right word.

Protext, or Scribble! The main task of these programs is to let you type out your text in a presentable form ready for printing.

ASCII

Acronym for American Standard Code for Information Interchange. Text saved in this format can be used in any program that will load ASCII text. This accounts for the majority of programs on all platforms.

Text-only word processors are quick, allowing you to type out text as quick as your fingers can hit the keyboard. The only negative thing about these word processors is that they will, more times than not, be controlled by menus and their own control codes. This makes them rather more difficult to use. This has not gone unnoticed by the publishing houses, and bit by bit they are moving towards the type of interface which is controlled by icons and menus.

A major advantage of the text-based word processor is that its hardware requirements are not as great as the other types of programs. (That said, a program like Protext will run much smoother and more efficiently from a hard drive.)

Get the most out of your Amiga 1993

✓ Protext 5.5   £80
From: Arnor. Tel 0733 68909
Minimum requirements: 1Mb RAM

As far as word processors go, this program has no rival on the Amiga. Its fast, powerful and pretty much bulletproof. The word publishers may have their uses, but for sheer speed, give me a word processor/DTP package any day.

The only problem with Protext is that, because of its enormous power, learning it is a rather long process. But with the ability to type out documents quickly, formatting them using the extensive menu items, it comes out tops for sheer speed and efficiency.

Protext also comes with its own command language which you can type in direct to its command line. From here you can reformat text, print pages, and do many other jobs. The commands are short and, after a while, easy enough to remember.

The program comes with an English dictionary and powerful thesaurus. Its ability to pick up those silly typing errors is perfect

Protext is a text-only word processor; fast and efficient at handling text, but no facilities for graphics

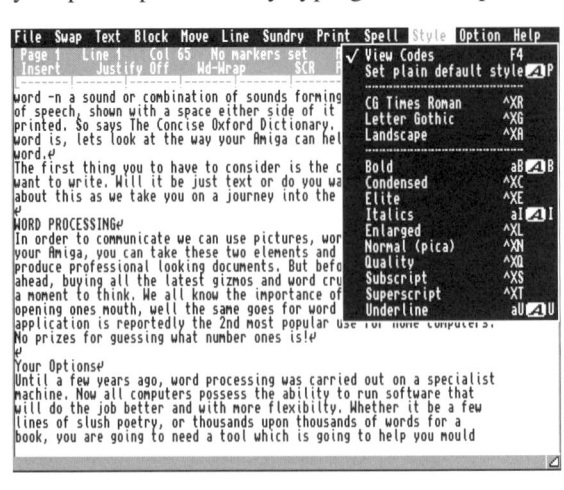

COVER DISK SOFTWARE
Although some word processors have come down in price to around £30, many magazines have had commercial variations on their cover disks. These can be back ordered for around a fiver. Also take a look in the public domain, there are many excellent packages to be had for only a couple of quid.

LATEST SOFTWARE
Try to get the latest version of any word publisher, as the old ones are rather slow and clunky. But if you want to save some bucks, then the older versions will still do the job. You get what you pay for, though!

Get the most out of your Amiga 1993

From word processing to DeskTop Publishing...

WYSIWYG

Acronym for What You See Is What You Get. Unlike a word processor, where all your text may be written in a standard screen font, in a word publisher and on a page produced by a DTP program, you can alter the size of text and see exactly what the output on paper will look like.

FONT

Another word for typeface. Its precise meaning is a typeface in one style and size. The word 'font', though, is used in most manuals and magazines to refer to a typeface such as Times or Helvetica.

for the typist whose fingers don't quite have the necessary accuracy…

Protext also provides the user with an extensive help screen which can be called up from within the program. You can open up more documents than you could possibly use and cut and paste between them all. And Protext also uses its own printer drivers, which cuts out preferences altogether.

Protext is best used with a hard drive although will it work from floppy. For sheer word-crunching ability, they don't come much better than Protext. If you don't fancy waiting around all day while word publishers refresh their screens etc, this will let you get on with the job. A cracking piece of kit – and check out version 6 when you can!

2. Word publishers

This type of word processor is a cross between the text-only word processor and a DTP (DeskTop Publishing) program. They allow you to mix the text with pictures, place text in columns and draw the odd line or two.

They also use icons in the form of tool boxes, to give the user a pictorial view of tools which carry out particular functions. Another word creeps in here – 'intuitive'. This basically allows the user to dive in and start creating documents.

The other big advantage to this type of program is that it gives the user an idea of just how each page is going to look. This is called a WYSIWYG (What You See Is What You Get) interface. You can type out your text, apply the attributes of typeface, size, and colour and see how it's going to appear on the paper.

Word publishers also let you place pictures in with your text. This is great – but there is a down side to this. All this extra work makes more demands on your hardware. For a program of this type, life will be more comfortable with a second drive or, even better, a hard drive. Along with this should be some extra memory. Don't underestimate the importance of memory! Amiga programs are so powerful these days that it is becoming more and more necessary to have upwards of 4Mb of memory for some tasks. A lot of problems with the more powerful programs can be solved by adding memory.

But what do you look for?

Before we move onto the final category, DTP programs, how about we look at some of the features that you should look out for in your word processor?

● **Ease of use:** Some, like Protext, take a lot of getting used to. Even smaller programs like Transwrite and Scribble can take a while to learn. If you prefer an icon-driven program, check out Wordworth 2 or Kindwords 3. These really are the pick of the bunch at each end of the monetary scale.

● **Spellchecking:** We all make mistakes, especially when our mind races faster than our fingers. A spellchecker is important, then, to make sure all those little typos (as we in the industry call them – ahem) get caught. Things to watch out for are that a program has an English dictionary, and even a Thesaurus, to suggest that word that you can't quite think of. Programs like Protext may also have added features, such as being able to catch typical errors (like a word written twice, or a sentence that doesn't start with a capital letter).

KINDWORDS 3

For those who aspire to Wordworth but can't really stretch the budget that far, try getting your dealer to show you Kindwords 3. It's far removed from the Kindwords 2 (which never got great reviews) and should suit the budget-conscious user.

From word processing to DeskTop Publishing...

SERIF

Take a look at the letters in the main column alongside. Many of them exhibit small 'blobs' or flourishes at the ends of the strokes. These are 'serifs'. Now look closely at the text you're reading now. There are no serifs – this is a 'sans serif' typeface. Broadly, serif typefaces are more 'classical' and – some say – easier to read. Sans serif typefaces are more popular at the moment, and are thought to be more 'authoritative' and precise, thanks to their cleaner, unfussy look.

● **Word Count:** Another important feature, especially for those who write professionally, or to fill a given space. For instance. When the editor says 1,000 words and not one word more, he means it!

● **Mail Merge:** For those with zillions of friends, or a business to run, this is a feature worth looking out. It lets you take a bog standard letter, add a few codes in strategic places, and then let the word processor insert names and addresses from a table, in place of the codes. Everyone gets the same letter, but with their own names and addresses at the top. You will usually only find this feature in a word processor/publisher. That said, Professional Page is one DTP program that I know has the ability to do mail merge.

● **Justification:** The method of aligning text against both the left and right hand margins.

● **Search & Replace:** A method of searching for a word like 'Macintosh' and replacing it with 'Amiga'!

● **Text styling:** Allows you to apply type styles such as italics or bold to your text.

● **Text runaround:** When you place a picture slap bang in the middle of your text, the text should go round it rather than through it! This is called text runaround. The most advanced form of runaround is 'irregular', which allows your text to follow the outline of your picture.

● **Fonts:** For word publishers, check out the type of fonts that they can use. Also, the format of pictures they can import. Most will allow you to use Iff ILBMs. Some may go further and allow you to use structured clip art.

Get the most out of your Amiga 1993

Wordworth 2 £129.99

From: Digita International. Tel 0395 270273
Minimum requirements: 2 disk drives, 1.5Mb RAM (hard drive, 4Mb RAM recommended)

Wordworth has certainly come along nicely since its early days. There is hardly a feature that it doesn't have. It will import IFF ILBM's graphics files, as well as others such as PCX and BMAP. You can also import EPSF but you can't view them.

Most writers who have reviewed it have been every positive about it. There's good reason for this. It is quicker than its rivals, although not as fast as a normal text-only word processor.

Like Protext, Wordworth 2 contains an English dictionary and a thesaurus, plus great features such as being able to generate a table of contents. The interface is very intuitive, and many users will be able to use the program without the (excellent) manual.

I personally do not like word publishers, but Wordworth 2 is certainly helping to change my mind! It now supports outline fonts

> **USE PICTURES**
> Pages that contain only text, will rapidly become boring and tiring to read. Use some pictures and white space to brighten them up.

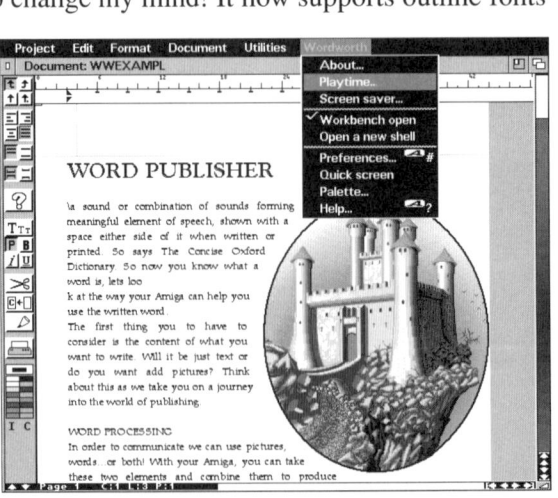

Word publishers are basically word processors with the added ability to handle graphics. Wordworth is currently the best on the Amiga.

From word processing to DeskTop Publishing...

STRUCTURED GRAPHIC
Although the bitmapped images from programs like Deluxe Paint have their place, if you want sharp images which can be stretched and scaled without loss of quality, then you need a 'structured graphic'. Basically, the image is described by mathematical formula and not a map of pixels. Examples are images in the `pro clip' and DR2D formats.

as well as a printer's own internal fonts. There are two modes to work in (for those in a hurry), and formatting your page is a breeze. It is PostScript compatible, which gives it that bit extra as a professional tool.

If you're in the market for a word publisher, then give Wordworth a try. It is the bee's knees of Word Publishers. The developers have added every power feature that is needed and it's also neat-looking. On a 1200 or above, it really zips along!

3. DeskTop Publishing

The next step, beyond word publishers, is to use a program that mimics the traditional method of arranging elements on a page – a DTP program. These elements can be text or graphics. Now while a word processor restricts you somewhat as to how you can place objects on the page, a DTP program allows you complete freedom.

Its akin to taking a blank sheet of paper, some text, a few pictures and arranging them on the paper so that they take on the appearance you want.

This extra 'freedom' can be a pain, though! You may know what sort of image or feel you want for your page, but unless you can turn that idea into a reality instinctively, you may find DTP rather frustrating. This is where design comes in.

Think about what you want

If you're using a word publisher or DTP program, you will need to think carefully about how your page is going to look. There are several things to do before booting your DTP program.

❶ Plan out what you want to say.
❷ Do some 'roughs' of how you want your page to look.

❸ Make sure you have all your elements (text, graphics etc.) prepared ready to place on the page.

❹ Finally, boot your DTP program and start laying out.

All that flexibility!

By using a medium-spec Amiga and some appropriate software, you can create many different printed effects that would very difficult to do using traditional layout methods. And the advantage the Amiga has over other hardware platforms is that this comes relatively cheap. Compare the price of QuarkXPress on the PC and Professional Page on the Amiga to see what I mean!

Given all this flexibility, there are a two little rules that are worth mentioning:

● Many desktop publishers, faced with hundreds of typefaces, will use far to many in a single document. For newsletters keep to two or three. Few layouts need many more.

● As a general guide, if you are using a serif typeface for your body text then use a sans serif for your headlines. If though you

POSTSCRIPT

A page description language developed by Adobe. It has many advantages over the normal method of printing artwork (bitmapping). One problem, though, is that it takes a programmer of considerable experience to sort out a rogue file that won't print. PostScript is now the industry-standard format in the publishing world.

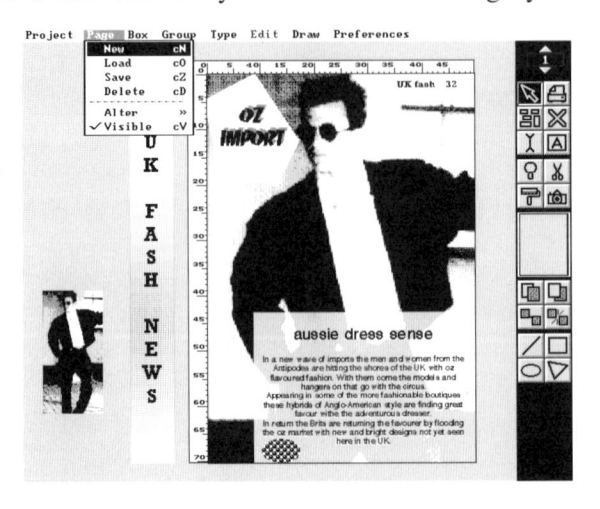

DeskTop Publishing is the ultimate mixing of words and pictures. This is PageSetter 3.0 in action.

From word processing to DeskTop Publishing...

have sans serif body text, then use a bolder version of that for crossheads etc.

EPSF

Encapsulated Postscript Format. A variation on the PostScript format. For example, you can save a Professional Page file out as an EPSF and import it into a program such as Pagemaker on the PC and print it out. Amiga users are unable to view raw EPSF files as yet.

Making sense of typefaces

Some typefaces come with many different styles, or 'weights'. So it is possible to have just one generic typeface but in many different styles and weights to give a page some variety.

As a guide, go out and buy ten different magazines and newspapers. Look at how they use type and then make your own mind up as to what looks good and what doesn't. The main point though is to make sure that, whatever you use, it's appropriate to what you're saying! It's just something you have to develop a 'feel' for.

The Amiga makes it easy to become a professional-quality publisher. But there is a disadvantage to being a one-person enterprise. Errors can creep through without you ever knowing – it usually takes a fresh pair of eyes to spot them, even real clangers. So the moral here is check (and double-check) everything, if possible get a second or third opinion.

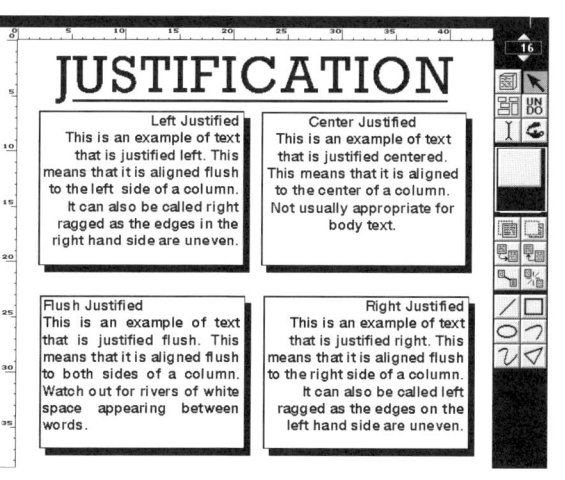

Justification is the term used to describe the alignment of the left and right-hand sides of a piece of text

Get the most out of your Amiga 1993

How to input the text

This will probably come from a word processor. This is because once it's on a page, text is difficult to write and edit. You also find that with a typical A4 document that you have to keep scrolling the page to read the end of columns and lines. This forces the screen to keep refreshing, which can take an age and slow you down immeasurably.

Professional Page and PageSetter 3.0 come with an integral word processor for this very reason. Soft Logik have also introduced Pageliner, which is hotlinked to PageStream. In here you can type out your text, spell check it, format it and generally get it ready to place on your page. Once finished you can send it back to the page.

In a DTP program you can take this text and apply many different attributes to it. This allows you to have one typeface for your main text and another for a headline. DTP programs these days allow you to create large headings, with eye-catching effects. Text does not have to be boring.

> **PRINTER DRIVER**
> *These are necessary to let your Amiga talk to your printer. On your extras disk you should find a printer driver that will be compatible with your printer. Most printers also have what is called an emulation mode. This allows them to behave like another brand of printer for which there is probably a more popular driver available.*

Serif is a term used in publishing to describe the blocks or blobs on the ends of the lines that make up letters. Some typefaces have them, some don't.

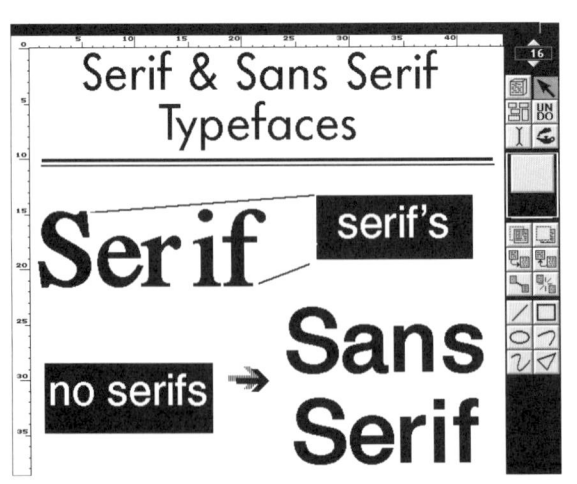

From word processing to DeskTop Publishing...

PRINTER UTILITIES
As preferences is limited for graphics output, if you intend printing a lot of pictures to a dot-matrix printer then you can get a special printer utility. These give you a lot of control over the image and the number of colours printed. Look out for the following in your retailer: Studio (Brill), True Print and Turbo Print.

By clever use of the text, you can produce school projects that will blow your teachers away – just make sure you tell them you did it on an Amiga!

A DTP program allows you to control many aspects of text preparation. Not only the typeface, but attributes such as leading (the white space between lines of text) and the style of the text (whether it be italicized, bold, or 'shadowed'). DTP programs at the top end of the scale give you powerful tools such as tags to control this more easily.

To give you an idea of the professional power and versatility of Amiga DTP, programs like Professional Page and PageStream will let you produce anything from a simple flyer to a book like the one in your hands now.

And now for the pictures...

We live in a very visual world. Everyone takes for granted that any published document will include some sort of image. But where can you get these images? How can you create them?

Well, for a start, many Amiga owners will already have a version of DPaint (Deluxe Paint), the Amiga paint program – this has formed part of various Amiga 'bundles'. This wonderful tool can be used to create a picture which can then be imported into your page and printed out with your text.

A point to remember here is that some DTP programs, such as PageStream, load all these into memory. Therefore if you plan to produce documents with lots of colour pictures in them, a program like Professional Page (which doesn't) may suit you better.

If, like me you lack that creative touch, the public domain libraries are full of clip art already drawn for you.

Another source of graphics is to scan something in. With the technology available to day you can scan pictures and text and place them into your computer's memory. From here you can manipulate it in hundreds of ways. Programs like Art Department Pro, Morph Plus, Deluxe Paint and many more, can do things you wouldn't dream of and make these images really awe-inspiring to look at.

Features to look out for

Just as with word processors and publishers, there are certain features you will need to think about when purchasing a specialized DTP program.

● **Hard disks:** Few worthwhile DTP or even word publishing programs are bearable without the storage capacity and convenience of hard disks. The budget-conscious can pick up small hard drives quite cheaply compared to previous years, though. Try to get at least a 40Mb drive, although a 20Mb one is better than none at all. If you're serious, go for a drive of around 100Mb!

EMULATORS

When is an Amiga really a Macintosh? Or a PC? When it has an emulator installed! With an emulator, you can use software from another platform, such as QuarkXPress on the Mac. Ones to look out for are Emplant (Mac), Amax (Mac), Golden Gate (PC), and Vortex ATonce (PC). There is also a software emulator called PCtask (PC) in the public domain.

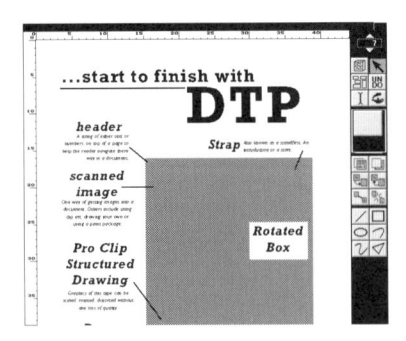

Raw EPSF cannot yet be viewed in Amiga DTP programs. One way around this is to create an IFF ILBM file solely for the layout work.

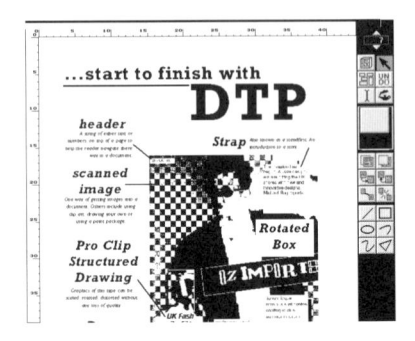

From word processing to DeskTop Publishing... 115

MULTISYNC MONITORS
With the advent of new screen modes for the Amiga has come the ability to use multi-sync and VGA monitors. If you're considering professional DTP, then look for a multi-sync that supports all the Amiga modes for flicker-free work.

● **Memory:** This plays a big part in deciding how productive your program will be. A starting point would a 2Mb upgrade, while for the higher-end applications, start off with an additional 4Mb. Most machines come with at least 1Mb, while the 1200 has 2Mb as standard.

● **Printers:** Will the program you're looking at work with your printer, or any printer you propose buying?

● **Tools:** Does this program hotlink to other programs to carry out modifications to text and picture files? Also, what steps are involved in this?

● **Multiple documents:** Being able to switch between two or more documents as you work can be very useful.

● **Typefaces:** Which types does it support?

● **Speed:** Find out how long it takes to load a picture file compared to its competitors.

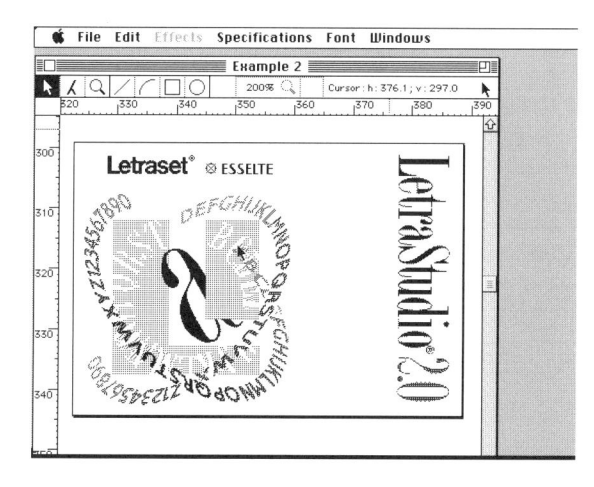

If you want to get really serious about DTP, you can even get a Macintosh emulator for your Amiga (the Macintosh is THE DeskTop Publishing machine).

● **Colours/display:** How many colours does it use when displaying a picture file?

● **Picture file types:** What type of picture files will it import, i.e. IFF ILBM, GIF, TIFF, PCX, EPS, Pro Clips, Illustrator etc?

● **Print quality:** What's the program's output quality like? Test it with rotated bitmaps as well as text.

● **PostScript output:** If you intend using a typesetting bureau, ask them what program gives the most reliable output using PostScript. Also whether the ability to save out files in EPSF is important. Being able to ouput in PostScript format is important – even essential – if you intend producing professional-quality pages.

● **Screen updating:** Does the screen refresh quickly? Test this with both picture files and text. Also try rotating a picture/text file and changing your magnifications.

A printer utility such as Studio (right), True Print or Turbo Print will give your graphic output a new lease of life.

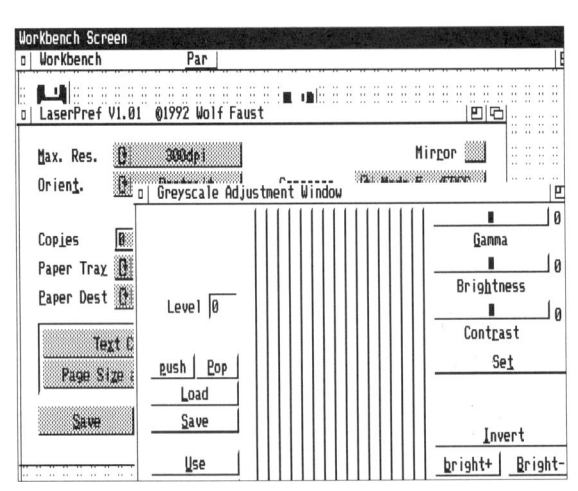

From word processing to DeskTop Publishing...

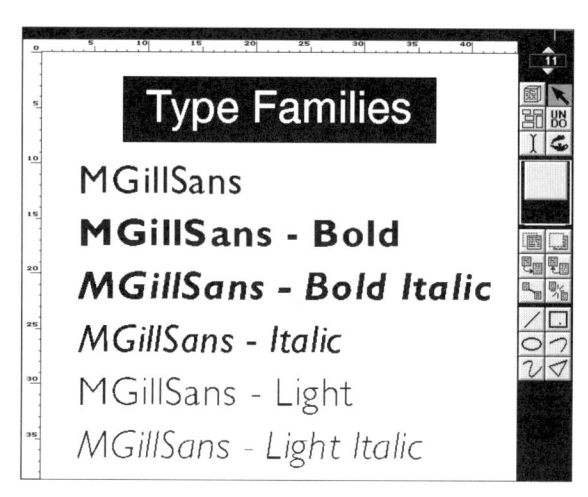

Typefaces tend to come in 'families' of different weights and styles – yet all share the same basic structure.

PageStream 2.2 — £200
From: Silica. Tel 081 309 1111
Minimum requirements: 2 disk drives, 1Mb RAM (hard drive, 4Mb RAM, monitor, accelerator recommended)

HOTLINK
Say you create a graphic that you use in several different documents. A 'hotlink' will automatically update these copies when you edit the original! Very useful, but use with caution...

PageStream has always been ahead of its rivals on features. It does, however, suffer from various niggling problems which limit its professional value and make it more of a tool for those who don't intend to push it too hard...

PageStream's main problem has been the fact that many of the major advantages it used to have over its chief rival Professional Page have been eroded as Professional Page has taken note of what the users want.

That said, PageStream is still a flexible tool for those who want a free-form publisher. Unlike Professional Page, PageStream allows the user to place objects on the page without the need for frames. This comes into its own, for example, with the ability to stretch text typed out onto the page.

The program probably supports more graphic formats than any other DTP program, including IFF ILBM, EPS Illustrator 88, Pro Clip, TIFF, GIF and many more. It will use PostScript fonts direct, as well as Compugraphic and Pagestream's own format.

Features worth noting are its guides, which help in aligning objects, and the ability to add fonts on the fly. You can also magnify a particular area of your page using the magnifier tool.

Problems include its slowness when loading bitmaps, and screen refreshes which take forever. It has also proved to be unreliable more than once. And PostScript output has a question mark hanging over it when using large 24-bit IFF files.

PageStream nevertheless has many devoted followers, and if in doubt get a demo disk and check it out against Professional Page. Do make sure you use the benchmarks earlier in this section to give you an accurate idea of which one performs best for your needs. PageStream doesn't feel a truly professional package. Many users, though, like its features. Ease of use is one of its strong points.

BUREAU

Printers capable of the extremely high resolution needed for top-quality professional printing are VERY expensive. Luckily, there are companies that will print out pages for you (usually charging you by the foot/metre).

PageStream 2.2 is popular with many home users, but still a little 'shaky' for professional use. Good user support, though.

From word processing to DeskTop Publishing...

✓ Professional Page 4.0 £200
GOOD BUY **From:** Silica 081 309 1111

Minimum requirements: Hard drive, 3Mb RAM, ARexx (for Genies) – 6Mb RAM, monitor, accelerator recommended

As the name implies, this is a truly 'professional' program. With the release of Professional Page 4.0, Gold Disk fulfilled many users' requests for certain features that fit the 'professional' tag. These include editable facing pages and support for EPS and other graphic formats such as TIFF.

With its powerful genies, reasonable speed and hotlinked word processor, this is *the* publisher on the Amiga.

Professional Page has always had the edge over its rivals, and when tested it performs solidly. With support for the AGA chipset, it also provides Amiga users with near true colour display.

The program is box-based, which means that everything you place on the page has to be placed in a frame. This is actually an advantage, as you can mark out where you want your element

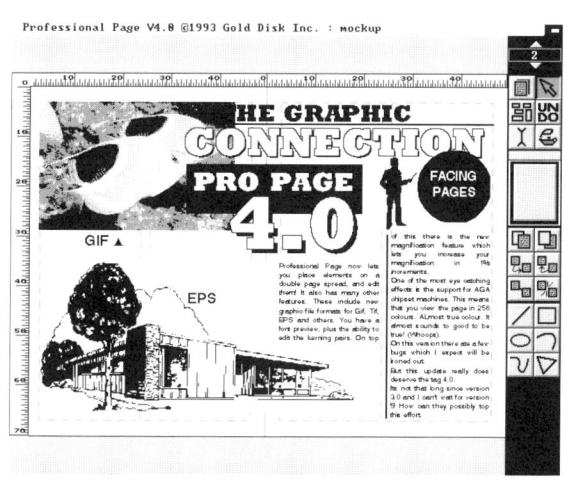

Professional Page 4.0 in facing pages mode, showing off its new graphic import filters for GIF and EPS files.

placed and then import it, knowing that it won't spill out into other areas.

The output from Professional Page is also more suited to professional use. Most bureaus prefer working with its files, as they cause fewer problems. As a publisher, I wouldn't be without it!

Professional Page has solid, reliable features that a professional publisher can rely on. It's not perfect, but the latest release (Version 4) has got pretty damn close! If you're on a budget, try its baby brother, PageSetter 3.0.

Yes, but how do you print it out?

Printing from a text-only word processor is a pretty quick job. A page from Protext on a average inkjet printer will come out in less than a minute or so. But if you tried to print a page containing pictures from a word publisher or DTP program you will notice that it takes substantially longer! A page from Wordworth with two bitmaps and compugraphic fonts will take about 20 minutes…

It's one thing having the ability to reproduce professional-looking documents on-screen, but most problems usually come about in the printing stage.

Your publishing software will give you certain controls over your final output. There will be times, though, when this output is limited by the Amiga preferences and your printer driver. The printer driver is one of the most constant source of headaches for an Amiga publisher! To get round this, make sure you ask your supplier what driver to use to get the most out of your printer. And make sure you read the Printers section in this book!

PS INTER-PRETER
Many desktop publishers use a 'PostScript interpreter'. This can take a PostScript file from your program and print it via your dot-matrix printer. The most widely used interpreter is Post, from Adrian Aylward. It is available in the public domain which means it's cheap. The advantage of it is that many programs offer more options when printing to PostScript and so those with ordinary dot-matrix printers can use this feature to take advantage of this.

From word processing to DeskTop Publishing... 121

Some programs (like Protext and PageStream) cut out preferences altogether, and you will have to make sure that you configure the program to use the correct driver for your printer.

Choosing a printer

As with the software, printers come in all sorts of sizes and price ranges. As a guide, if all you ever intend doing is the odd letter using a word processor then a dont-matrix printer will suffice. For around £175, you should get a pretty good one.

One of the most popular printer types, though, is the inkjet. The quality of these (on special paper, admittedly) is equal to that of a laser printer. The Canon series seems to be the best option at the moment, along with Hewlett Packard's Deskjets. If you want colour then the new Hewlett packard Deskjet 550c is a must.

For those with plenty of dosh to splash around, a laser printer is one of the best devices for output. These also offer a higher resolution – up to 600dpi.

When things go wrong with your PostScript files, a utility like Post 1.7 from Adrian Aylward, will help suss out what's causing the fuss.

Get the most out of your Amiga 1993

Lasers can be as cheap as £500 but a typical PostScript-compatible will cost £1,000 or more. A non-PostScript laser printer could be a false economy, though.

Your final option for printing your work is through a bureau. These will allow you to fully exploit the technology available to desktop publishers. There are a few around which cater for Amiga users, although even those without Amigas can help you (most cater just for the PC and Mac).

The advantage of using a bureau is that it can take your document files and produce the separations necessary for full colour copy. Don't be put off by how complicated it sounds – give a bureau a ring and find out how you can take advantage of what your program can do. Then bundle off your document file to them on a disk. For £15 or so you can get a high-resolution full colour copy of your work that will be the envy of everyone still struggling with their 9-pin dot-matrix printers.

More to the point, though, your Amiga will have produced a professional-quality layout indistinguishable from that from hardware costing five or ten times as much.

Indeed, this is typical of the Amiga as a machine – professional power, but at a fraction of the price!

ALFA HAND SCANNER
Your page is going to need more than text to make it attractive to the reader. If like me, you're not that artistic, them maybe a scanner will help. Take a look at the Alfa Scan hand scanner. This can also be bought with OCR software which enables you to scan text into a word processor. Another one worth a look is the Power scanner.

Going on-line

Comms is all about getting one computer to talk to another by using the telephone line, with the aim of exchanging information. That information can be anything from a private mail message, a picture, a program, or a plea for help with a problem. Comms tends to have a reputation for being a very mysterious and difficult area to get into... unless you get a helping hand from Dave Winder, that is.

Comms is one of the most fascinating areas of computing when you actually get involved in it. Although the public perception of a "hacker" breaking into a missile system isn't what it is all about, at least not for most people.

To get started in comms you will need three things:

- your Amiga
- a modem
- some terminal software

I guess you also need a fourth thing, and that is somewhere to call! For details of Bulletin Boards, keep an eye on the Comms Column in Amiga Shopper magazine, as the best ones are generally featured there.

As well as the free BBS systems, there are also larger commercial systems available. The Compulink Information eXchange (better known as Cix) is the best known and best of these. Many of the well known names in the Amiga world can be found on Cix – programmers, developers, Commodore themselves, and Amiga journalists too (me included).

So what's in it for me?

Lots. With a modem, you may never have to rely on the GPO again (at least not when swapping files, applications and even messages). You can also link up to a whole load of information services and many amateur bulletin boards to swap files, news and chit-chat. You also have access to a vast body of public domain and shareware software. Sure, you can get these by post, but why wait when all you have to do is dial up a bulletin board? These are just a few of the ways that comms can broaden your computing horizons.

Going on-line

BUYING A MODEM
Buy the fastest modem you can afford. Buying a slow modem is usually a false economy as the less time you spend on actually using the telephone, the cheaper your new hobby will be.

What is a modem?

And why do you need one? Well, computers talk in binary, a language of 0's and 1's, yes's and no's. A modem plugs into the serial port of your Amiga and converts this digital information into an analogue signal that the telephone line can cope with. You plug your modem into the telephone line and this converted information travels by telephone to the computer you are talking to. Once the signal reaches the other end of the link, another modem will convert the signal back into the digital form that the other computer can understand.

You need some software too

In order for your computer to talk to the modem, you will also need some software know as a Terminal Program. There are a number of these available, and all the best ones are in the Public Domain or Shareware. Comms is unusual in this respect – most of the really useful and best programs are free.

USING MERCURY
Another money saving tip is to use Mercury for long distance calls instead of British Telecom, and always make your calls during off peak times wherever possible.

A terminal program simply allows your Amiga to communicate correctly with the modem, and enables you to customise the way you will see the information received. As long as you read the documentation that comes with these programs, you should have no problems. Most of the trouble that people get themselves into when entering the world of comms is caused by impatience.

SupraFaxModem V32bis £269.99
SupraFaxPlus £139.99
From: First Choice. Tel 0532 637988
Minimum requirements: Any Amiga

I'm always telling people who ask about modems that they should buy the fastest that they can reasonably afford. This has always been a problem, as fast modems have always been very expensive.

Get the most out of your Amiga 1993

Well things have changed now, thanks to Supra. The SupraFaxModem V32bis is a top of the range modem, offering blistering performance at a price that is now affordable. One of its nicest features is an easy-to-understand alphanumeric status display. Most modems have a series of flashing LEDs on the front panel which report the status of the modem and any errors. These can be very difficult to interpret, even for an experienced old hand like myself. The SupraFaxModem V32bis, by contrast, reports its status in plain English. If the modem is ready to use it reports "OK" – simple as that!

This modem will actually save you money, as you will be spending less time using the telephone and therefore your phone bill will be reduced.

The manual is well written and easy to understand. To top it all, you even get a fax machine built in. Using this marvel of modern technology you can send and receive faxes via your Amiga, providing you have the relevant software. The only thing you should remember is that Supra modems do not currently come with BABT approval and are, like many phones and answerphones, not approved for connection to the telephone system.

If you really cannot afford the SupraFaxModem V32bis, at around £270, then the SupraFaxPlus is your best bet. Not as fast and not coming with the excellent alphanumeric display panel I mentioned, but none the less still excellent value for money. The SupraFaxPlus costs around £140.

BBS

A BBS is a Bulletin Board System. These are usually free and are a means of meeting and talking to new, and old, friends. Usually you can download a range of Public Domain programs, and many BBS's these days have online games as well.

Going on-line

✅ Term   free!
GOOD BUY   **From:** Public domain
Minimum requirements: WB 2.04 or above

V32BIS
This is a rating of modem speed, and refers to 14,400 bits per second (or bps in comms shorthand). It is simply the rate at which information is passed along a data channel.

Term is the latest in a long line of Public Domain and Shareware terminal programs that have dominated the comms scene. Term requires WB 2.04 or above to operate, and makes full use of the many enhancements this offers over WB 1.3

This program is highly configurable, down to the minutest of details, and this may make it seem somewhat complicated to set up. Provided you carefully read the comprehensive documentation, you should have no real problems.

This degree of flexibility is required because there are so many different types of modems and systems that may be used, and Term tries to ensure you will be able to cope with them all. Although Term does not have a script language of its own, it does have an ARexx server so you can execute scripts that way.

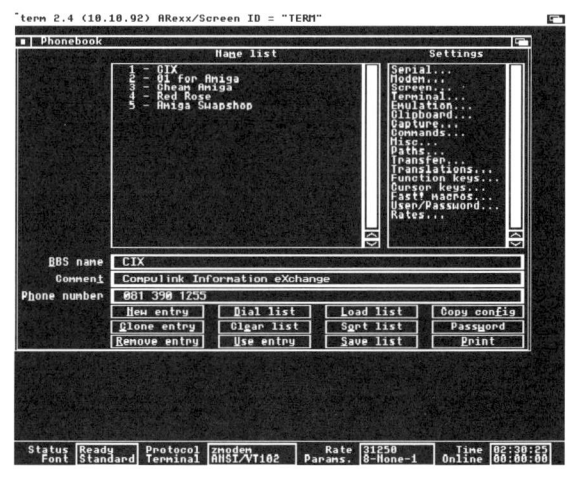

Term is just about the best comms software you can get – and it's in the public domain!

There are two features of Term I find very useful indeed. The first is the comprehensive phonebook. Each entry in the phonebook has its own configuration file, so you don't need to change system configurations when dialling completely different types of system. The other thing that I really like is the speech facility. Plus its implementation of the ZModem protocol. It really is comprehensive, and lets you get the very best out of your comms.

Term is so flexible and comprehensive, with its translation tables, different emulations, and almost endless configurability, that I doubt you will ever need another terminal program. Best of all it's 'giftware' – simply send the authors a gift if you like the program!

NComm   free!

From: Public domain
Minimum requirements: WB 1.3 or above

NComm has been the standard terminal program recommended by the comms experts for many years now. It's only the arrival of Term that has shaken its position as the number one terminal program.

NComm has now lost its number one spot to Term, but still boasts an excellent scripting system for automating routine tasks.

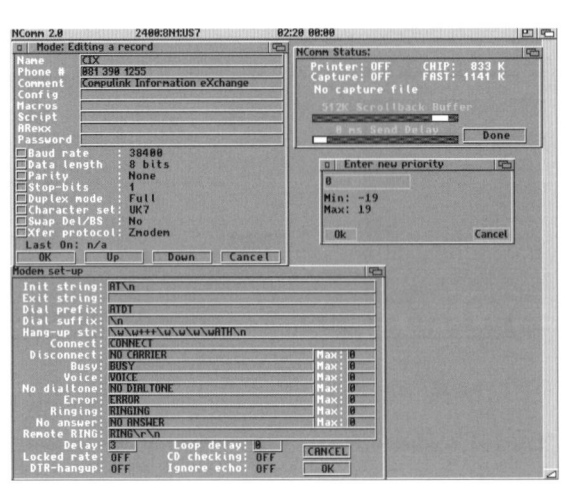

CAPTURE FEATURE
Save money by using the capture feature of your terminal software to grab the menus and file lists of BBS's you log into. You can then study them offline, learn the menu structure, see what files you want to download, all without paying telephone charges.

Going on-line

NComm's main attraction is its superb script handling – as well as an ARexx interface it also boasts its own script language. The use of scripts can automate many of the things you regularly do, and NComms script language makes this very easy to implement.

The protocols supported by NComm are extensive, but the all-important ZModem implementation isn't up to the standard of Term. NComm has excellent support for ANSI graphics, but while these may look very nice (and they do) they also slow down your comms session, which means you are paying more money!

The really big advantage of NComm is the fact it has been around for so long. This means there are thousands of people out there using it, which in turn means lots of good advice on the Bulletin Boards if you have any problems. There are also many utilities available for use with NComm, such as phone bill estimators, call loggers and so on.

NComm is a well tried and tested program, there are many happy users out there with a lot of knowledge to share. However, it has stiff opposition in the form of Term, which is constantly being updated and improved. NComm isn't free, it is a Shareware program that will cost $35 (US Dollars) to register. I think it has lost its number one spot to the free Term...

LhA and LhA-Win   free!
From: Public domain
Minimum requirements: Any Amiga

LhA is one of the quickest archivers available, and also one of the best at making files as small as possible. For these reasons it has become the default archiver in the Amiga comms community, and now dominates this field.

Get the most out of your Amiga 1993

LhA is an 'archiver', a program that compresses files into the minimum space – essential for saving on your phone bills when using comms!

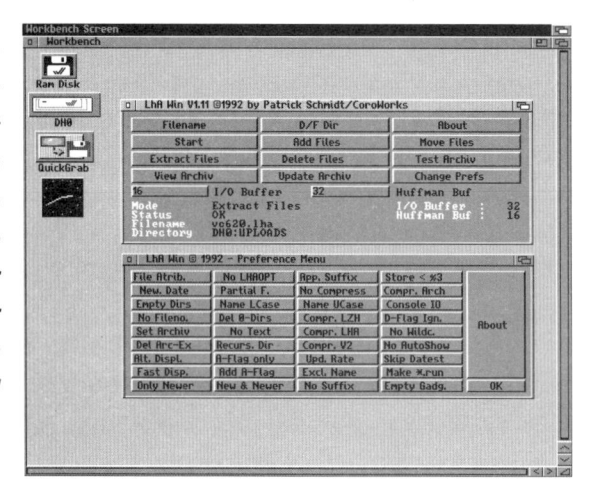

ARCHIVE
If you plan to send anything over the telephone line, you want to minimise the amount of time it takes. One way of achieving this is to archive the file before you send it. An archiver uses a mathematical formula to compress the file, thus making it smaller. The smaller the file, the less time it takes to transfer, the more money you save!

LhA is simple enough to use, provided you take the time to read the documentation, but its command line approach can be confusing for some people. To solve this problem there is a graphical front end available in the form of LhA-Win. This gives you a mouse controlled environment for all your archiving and un-archiving.

LhA is without doubt the only archiver you need to look at. It is fast and efficient, easy to use (especially in conjunction with LhA-Win). What more could you want?

ARCHIVING TEXT FILES
Don't archive text files as they actually transfer faster if they are left un-archived. The file will be bigger, but you still save money because of the increase in speed.

Get on-line!

Well, this has been a lightning visit to the world of comms, but hopefully it's at least pointed you in the right direction. Thanks to the comms support in the public domain, once you've paid for a modem, all you've got to worry about are the 'phone bills.

But look, don't just take my word for it – get a modem, and get on-line!

The top 25 Amiga games

The Amiga is NOT just a games machine, as the rest of this book shows! So why do so many people think it is just a games machine? Maybe because it just happens to be the best games machine in the world… Stuart Campbell picks the best 25 Amiga games of all time.

Sensible Soccer/v1.1 £25.99

✓ GOOD BUY

From: Renegade. Tel 071 481 9214
Minimum requirements: Any Amiga

Voted by the readers of the world's best-selling Amiga games magazine (Amiga Power) as the best Amiga game of all time, Sensible Soccer transcends all boundaries. Arcade game-haters, football game-haters, just plain old football-haters, all fall at the feet of this uniquely playable and impossibly entertaining game.

It's fast, it's instinctive (you can play this one within seconds of picking it up, unlike certain other popular football sims we could mention), and it's more fun in two-player mode than, ooh, just about anything in the world.

Sensible Soccer topped the all-price Amiga charts for an unheard-of four months back in the summer of '92, and the even-better updated version (improved goalkeeper, new rules, revised team and competition data) is still hanging on in there in the top ten to this day. Well on course to be the Amiga's best-selling game of all

SENSIBLE SOCCER
Sensible Soccer is still selling in huge numbers, so you shouldn't have any difficulty laying your hands on a copy whatsoever. If you do, have a word with Renegade.

Sensible Soccer is a football simulator that's easy to pick up and terrific fun – especially in two-player mode.

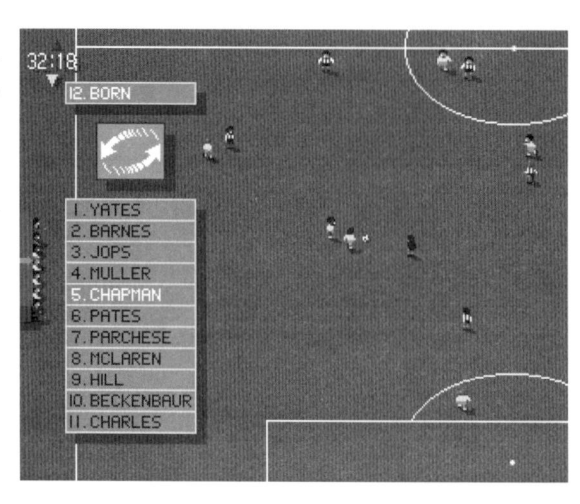

The top 25 Amiga games

time, this is to the machine what Mario and Sonic are to Nintendo and Sega.

You can't possibly call yourself a serious Amiga gamesplayer without a copy of Sensible Soccer in your collection, and that's all there is to it.

Rainbow Islands £7.99
From: The Hit Squad. Tel 061 832 6633
Minimum requirements: Any Amiga

RAINBOW ISLANDS
Rainbow Islands was released fairly recently on Ocean's budget label The Hit Squad. Most decent software shops should still stock it, but in the event of difficulty, call The Hit Squad.

This coin-op conversion isn't particularly accurate, and it wasn't a particularly good coin-op in the first place. Why, then, does it make such an astoundingly good Amiga game?

The cutesy graphics, perhaps? Nah, cutesy graphics have been done to death by the likes of Robocod and Rodland, and the ones in Rainbow Islands are, well, alright. Stunning sonics? Uh-uh. If you can listen to the jaunty rendition of 'Somewhere Over The Rainbow' much past the second level without grinding your teeth to a fine powder, you're clearly either deaf or insane.

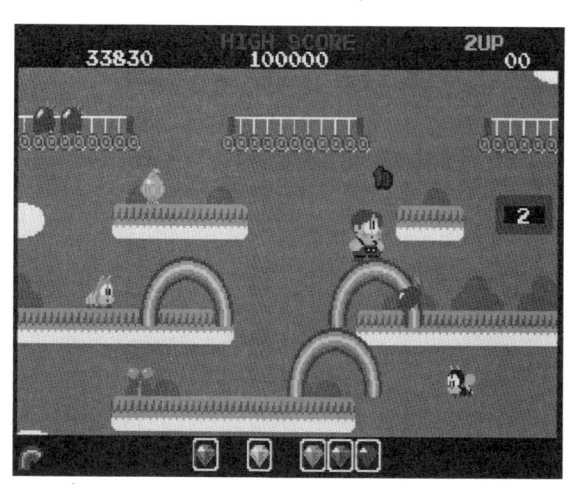

Rainbow Islands is simply the most playable platform arcade game ever produced.

Get the most out of your Amiga 1993

Maybe, then, it's just the unparalleled playabilit and perfect difficulty curve (with only four controls, anyone can play Rainbow Islands, but the number of people who've finished it can still be counted on the muddy fingers of a rugby team).

Or maybe it's the impossible addictiveness that comes from a game so simple to play yet so challenging to defeat that you just can't put it down? Yeah, that could be it.

✓ Formula One Grand Prix   £34.99
From: MicroProse. Tel 0666 504326
Minimum requirements: 1Mb RAM

Back in the days when the Amiga was born, if you could have taken a video recording of F1GP back through time from the future and shown it to the machine's owners and developers and said to them 'This is what Amiga games will look like in six or seven years', they'd have carted you off to the funny farm faster than you could say 'You can't do this to me, I'm Napoleon XIV!'

But veteran programmer Geoff Crammond went ahead and did it regardless, and the result is probably the Amiga's finest technical achievement to date.

F1 GRAND PRIX
Formula One Grand Prix is still a leading seller, but if you live in the Orkneys, call MicroProse.

Formula One Grand Prix is not just an amazing technical achievement, it's also a superb simulation of modern Grand Prix racing.

Minutely detailed, fantastically realistic, but most importantly supremely playable, F1GP is the only serious challenger to Sensible Soccer as Amiga owners' all-time favourite.

It's also *the* game for lucky purchasers of the A1200 – you've got to see it to believe it, speed fans.

Monkey Island £25.99
Monkey Island 2 £37.99
From US Gold. Tel 021 625 3366
Minimum requirements: 1Mb RAM (hard drive recommended)

MONKEY ISLAND

Copies of Monkey Island 1 are a little thinner on the ground than they used to be, but both games should still be easy to find. Or call US Gold.

Adventures used to be strictly a diversion for trainspotters when there were leaves of the wrong sort on the tracks at the station.

Despite the wit, complexity and diversity of the Infocom games to name just one branch of the genre, all that typing 'Go North' and 'Manacle Troll To Bathroom Cabinet' and so on was just too much trouble for your average R-Type devotee.

Nowadays, though, you don't have to have a beard to play adventure games, and the main reason is Monkey Island. Building on the user-friendly foundations laid down by the likes of Future

INDIANA JONES

Also see Indiana Jones And The Fate Of Atlantis, more of the same from the same authors, and also published by US Gold.

Monkey Island and its sequel are wonderful to look at, easy to play, very funny and a real challenge.

Get the most out of your Amiga 1993

Wars and Zak McKracken And The Alien Mindbenders, Monkey Island teamed lovely graphics with a razor-sharp sense of humour and a menu system that took all the pain out of adventure playing by taking the keyboard out of the equation altogether – Monkey Island is controlled entirely by a mouse point-and-click set-up that means even your granny can get into this in a matter of seconds.

Monkey Island 2 – LeChuck's Revenge was more of the same, only bigger (11 disks' worth) and better in just about every way, and both games are essentials for all but the most closed-minded zapping freak.

Speedball 2   £29.99 (compilation)
From: Image Works
Minimum requirements: Any Amiga

All these games are very fine and good and everything, but there's not much violence so far, is there? And what with horrible slaughter being the staple of about 80% of computer games since the dawn of Space Invaders, it's time we had some in this list.

Speedball 2 is fast, action-packed and supremely violent!

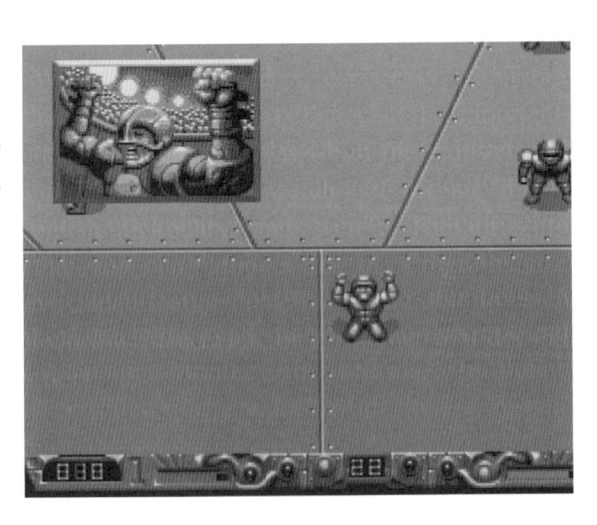

SPEEDBALL 2
With Image Works a casualty of the Maxwell Disaster, the only way to get a hold of Speedball 2 is on The Bitmap Brothers Volume 1, a compilation of games from the eponymous programming team released by Renegade (071 481 9214).

The top 25 Amiga games

JOHN MADDEN

John Madden Football from Electronic Arts (0753 549442) is another superb two-player violent sport sim, every bit as good as the Mega Drive version which many Sega pundits claim is the machine's number one game of all time.

Luckily, Speedball 2's got enough aggro for half-a-dozen games. Essentially a future update of six-a-side football crossed with ice hockey, Speedball 2 introduces a new rule to proceedings. This rule, in time-honoured fashion, is that there are no rules. Not only is it permissible in Speedball 2 to get the ball from your opponent by smacking him in the face and ripping the metal sphere from his grasp, it's actively encouraged – if you so assault one of the opposition players that he collapses, dead, on to the floor of the arena, you score as many points as you would do for throwing the ball into the goal.

The simple 'plot' and context-sensitive controls make Speedball 2 much more accessible than Sensible Soccer, and while the small area of the arena reduces the depth of play somewhat, it also ensures that the action doesn't let up for a minute. Fearsome and beautiful.

Sim City £25.99

From: Infogrames. Tel 071 738 8199
Minimum requirements: Any Amiga

SIM CITY

Sim City's gone through a few companies in its time, but for the best chance of getting yourself a copy today, call Infogrames.

The game that started the whole god-sim genre off, Sim City, mightn't at first seem like all that hot a concept. After all, how many thrills are there to be had from building a city, taxing the inhabitants and making sure the transport and fire departments are adequately funded?

You'd be surprised. Sim City takes its roots from the 'Kingdoms' games of prehistory, and as such shares the compulsion that made Kingdoms so enduring. Y'see, anyone who's ever looked at an urban apocalypse and said 'I could do better than this' won't be able to leave Sim City alone for a minute, because that's how long

Get the most out of your Amiga 1993

it takes for the imaginary city developing on screen to become a real place in your mind.

When citizens emigrate, protesting about high unemployment or excessive taxation, it feels like a personal insult to your new Utopia, and you redouble your efforts to create a paradise that no-one could ever want to leave. When a bit of bad planning causes traffic congestion, you actually imagine yourself stuck in the jam, and immediately resolve to do something about it.

And so on and so forth. And even when all this begins to wear thin, there are all the preset scenarios to cope with (handle a real-life city and solve its problems), or the little disasters you can inflict on yourself, just to see how your crisis management skills are. Fire? Plane crash? Godzilla attack?

All this and more is at your fingertips when you play Sim City. Never before was a genre so accurately titled.

Sim City was the first of the 'God-sims', but it'sstill one of the best. Can you manage a real, living city?

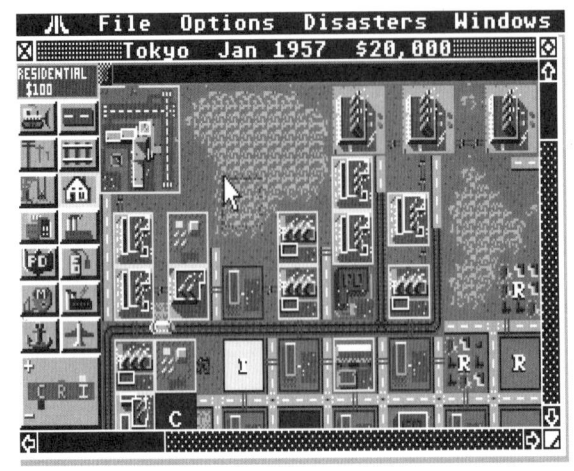

A-TRAIN

A-Train, recently released from Ocean, takes Sim City and crosses it with Railroad Tycoon and some lovely 3D graphics. It's a bit slow on an ordinary Amiga, but well worth a look all the same.

The top 25 Amiga games

Exile £25.99
From: Audiogenic. Tel 081 424 2244
Minimum requirements: Any Amiga

'Physics Is Fun', was the title of the textbook I completely failed my 'O' Grades with at school. I never believed it, but Exile changed my mind.

EXILE

Exile is not at all easy to find, and miniscule sales mean that there are very few second-hand copies floating around (and who, having bought it, would ever want to part with their copy of Exile anyway?), but you might find some joy if you ring Audiogenic.

Superficially unprepossessing, Exile looks not unlike a Commodore 64 game (indeed, its roots lie on the Acorn Electron, from which it hasn't progressed all that much visually), but probe a little beneath the surface and you'll find one of the most utterly gripping and enlightening experiences entertainment software has ever offered.

Your mission is an unremarkable one – to escape from a deadly planet by finding the means to power a spaceship free of the surface – but the way you go about it in Exile is revolutionary.

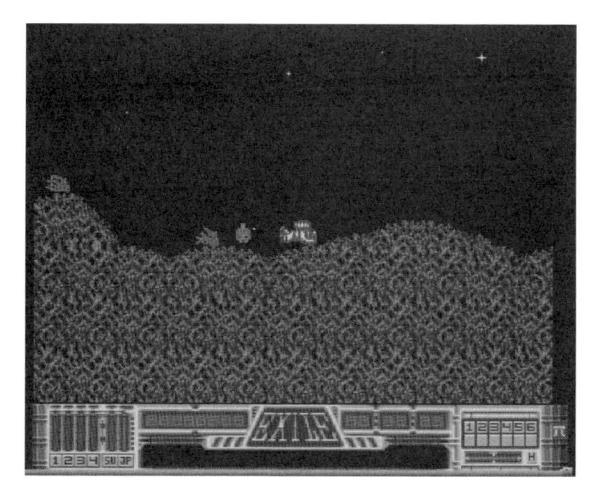

Exile doesn't really look much, but the gameplay is truly revolutionary.

Get the most out of your Amiga 1993

Jet-packing around a gravitationally-realistic environment, you find and interact with objects in a way that'll test your mental powers to their absolute limit.

Solving a problem might require the combination of four different objects or even creatures (the planet boasts many indigenous lifeforms which can help or hinder you, but in a totally believable way – they're not the evil slaves of some psychopathic madman, more just hostile natives like the venomous snakes or fierce predators you might find in any jungle), but the solution is always a flawlessly, perfectly logical one, which means the sense of reward you get from discovering it is one unparallelled in any computer game ever.

The exterior and a seemingly-unforgiving handful of keyboard controls mean that you have to make 30 minutes' worth of effort to get into Exile, but once you do you'll never come out again.

Probably the most criminally under-rated and under-selling game in the Amiga's entire history.

✓ Populous II £29.99
GOOD BUY **From:** Electronic Arts. Tel 0753 549442
Minimum requirements: 1Mb RAM

After Sim City, the other game that really defined the god sim genre was Bullfrog's Populous. Actually a far simpler game than Maxis' city-planning classic, Populous was basically a straight head-to-head battle between two all-powerful deities, indirectly controlling bands of followers like generals in a war.

Populous II is the same game, but updated and expanded at great length, so that the range of powers you can bring to bear in your

POPULOUS 2

Populous 2 is getting a bit long in the tooth now, but Electronic Arts should be able to point you in the right direction.

The top 25 Amiga games

In Populous 2 you can play god, battling against other deities and using who races of little people as pawns.

conflict with the computer opponent is far wider. Within a very simple framework, there's an ocean of depth to swim in, and in what's probably a unique tie-in, you can swap landscapes between Populous II and Sim City (with certain adjustments made automatically – no railway lines in Populous II, for example).

It's practically worth having Populous II for that feature alone, but it's got so many other great ones that you shouldn't need any extra persuasion.

KNIGHTS OF THE SKY
Again, it's getting on a bit in years, but Knights Of The Sky's lasting popularity should save you from ever having to phone up MicroProse.

Knights Of The Sky £25.99

From: MicroProse. Tel 0666 504326
Minimum requirements: 1Mb RAM

Of course, one of the main reasons people buy Amigas as opposed to the nasty Japanese console things is that Amigas are so much better at anything more complicated than platform games or vertically-scrolling shoot-'em-ups.

Get the most out of your Amiga 1993

Forget modern high-powered jets – one of the best flight sims on the Amiga has you controlling a World War One biplane...

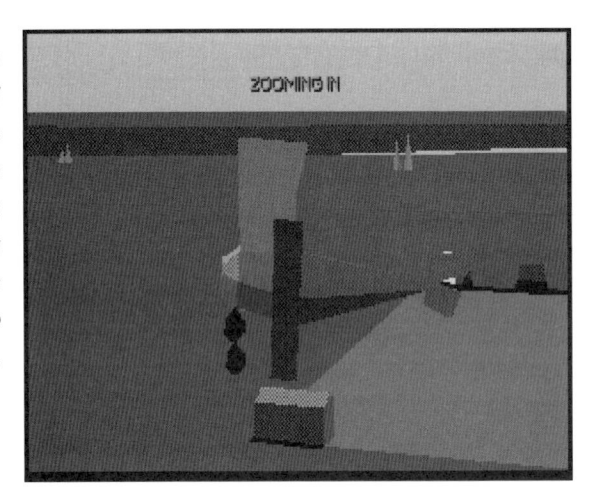

Chief among such genres is the flight simulation. The Amiga flight sim market is a crowded one, covering a strictly conflict-free area like piloting the A320 Airbus and the all-out, 'Never mind the aerodynamics, get the missiles in' side represented by the likes of Combat Air Patrol, and all points in between. But for us the peak has to be the sedate World War I action of Knights Of The Sky.

Presenting a huge, historically-correct variety of triplanes, biplanes and single-wings for you to choose between (you can play any of the war's combatants) KOTS captures the awestruck magic of the pioneer days of flying, where keeping your crate in the air was as much of a challenge as shooting down the enemy's equally-ricketty orange-box.

There's none of this dull modern firing a homing missile at an adversary three miles away who you can't even see – in Knights Of The Sky you have to get close enough to see the whites of the enemy pilot's eyes, and that makes for an unbeatable feel of noble jousting which is nurtured by the game's careful, all-round 'Tally-ho!' presentation.

The top 25 Amiga games

If losing yourself in another world is the prime purpose of escapist entertainment like computer games, then Knights Of The Sky is surely as close to perfection as you could ever desire.

✓ Jimmy White's Snooker/Archer MacLean's Pool £29.99
GOOD BUY

From: Virgin. Tel 081 960 2255
Minimum requirements: Any Amiga

WHIRLWIND SNOOKER
Jimmy White's Whirlwind Snooker is the kind of perennial which will go on selling quietly forever, while Pool is a very recent release, but Virgin will gladly help you out in the event of you not living near 'Any good software shop'.

Now it's all very well simulating future sports – they don't exist yet – or games like football, but the fact is anyone can go out and have a bit of a kick around pretty much any time they like.

Snooker and pool are different – after all, how many people do you know who have the room for their own snooker table?

Not everyone's old enough to go down the local pool hall or the pub, and they're not always open anyway, and these aren't the kind of games it's easy to simulate with ordinary household implements.

Jimmy White's Whirlwind Snooker and Archer MacLean's Pool are both stunning 3D simulations of favourite games.

Get the most out of your Amiga 1993

Three cheers, then, for the inventors of the home computer and for Archer Maclean, who's written a brace of games so like the real thing that with someone blowing acrid cigarette smoke in your eyes and someone else regularly removing large amounts of the folding stuff from your pockets, you wouldn't know you weren't really doing it.

Whirlwind Snooker and Pool both use the same 3D engine, an amazing piece of programming that allows lightning-fast 3D action to be viewed from practically any viewpoint imaginable in an instant.

But it's the attention to detail in the games themselves that make them such a joy to play. You can play pool to any set of rules currently in use anywhere in the world, or even to a custom set-up of your own choosing, and both games come complete with a set of difficulty-graded computer opponents which makes it possible to have anyone from your mate Spotty to Stephen Hendry or Joe Barbera round for a game at the touch of a mouse button.

You can even set up trick shots that'd put John Virgo and Jim Davidson well and truly in their place, or just hang around and watch the balls develop little faces and hold up amusing placards for a bit of a laugh. This game could put pubs out of business.

✓ Lemmings/Oh No! More
GOOD BUY **Lemmings** **£25.99 (twin-pack)**
From: Psygnosis. Tel 051 709 5755
Minimum requirements: Any Amiga

Almost certainly still the biggest-selling and most-loved Amiga game (if not computer game) of all time, Lemmings is also one of the most original ideas ever.

LEMMINGS

The aforementioned Lemmings double pack should be a fixture on retailers' shelves, but direct any doubting queries to Psygnosis.

There are no baddies to kill, no princesses to save, just hordes of furry little mammals on a mission of self-destruction. You can't control any of them directly, so instead you have to endow each lemming with some kind of power which, when used in the right place, will help to magically create a path to the safe lemming exit (as opposed to lemming entry, my dear Watson) in each level.

(There's a two-player mode too, where you can try to save your own lemmings while sending those of your opponent to their doom, but it's less popular than the simple brain-teasing of the solo version.)

It's amazingly absorbing and utterly addictive, as whole new generations are discovering to this day as the game effortlessly spans the great format divide, appearing on Spectrum, Game Boy, PC Engine, Mega Drive, Game Gear, Super Nintendo, NES, Master System and even the humble Atari ST.

Oh No! More Lemmings, a data disk which appeared as a stop gap between the original and the sequel proper (out any minute now and looking stunning), offers a hundred more levels but an inferior difficulty curve, and you're better off sticking to the first game, although both are available on a £30 double pack from Psygnosis.

Lemmings is basically just one of the most original and best-selling computer games of all time.

Dyna Blaster £30.99

✓ GOOD BUY
From: Ubi Soft. Tel 081 343 9055
Minimum requirements: Any Amiga

Way back in about 1985, a little-known development house called Hudson Soft released a Spectrum game on Sinclair's own label, by the name of Eric And The Floaters.

A frantic, compulsive and generally brilliant game, its simplistic graphics and apparent single-screen maze game plot denied it the success it deserved in an industry just beginning to be dominated by coin-op conversions and film licences. Hudson Soft weren't to be denied, though. Years later, via a debut on the PC Engine console and an appearance on the Game Boy, Eric And The Floaters came back as Dyna Blaster.

While essentially still the same game, Dyna Blaster boasted a number of significant advances on its parent. The mazes now scrolled around and there were a variety of power-ups to be found, but most importantly of all, Dyna Blaster was no longer a single-player game...

Dyna Blaster looks like a simple maze game, but it has brilliant gameplay and in multi-player mode is devestatingly addictive.

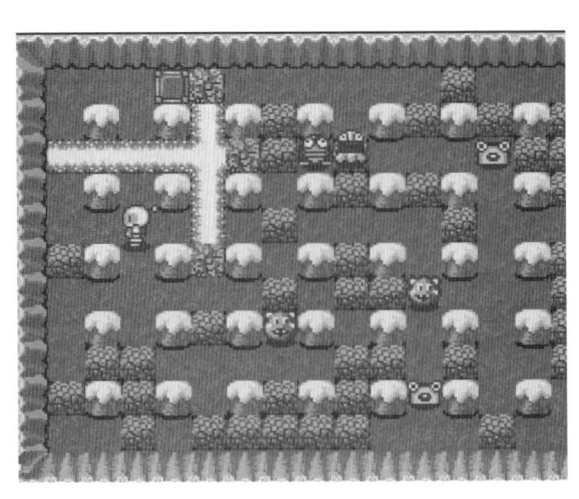

> **DYNA BLASTER**
> Dyna Blaster shouldn't be hard to find, but you can always call Ubi Soft, just to tell them how much you love it.

> **BUG BOMBER**
> Bug Bomber from DMI/Kingsoft (0753 686000) takes a very similar tack to that of Dyna Blaster, but mixes it with ancient Spectrum classic Chaos to excellent effect.

Get the most out of your Amiga 1993

With the aid of a joystick adaptor thoughtfully included in the package, up to five players at once could join in a single-screen 'Battle Mode', where the sole objective was to obliterate all your opponents.

With gameplay simple enough for anyone in the world to understand instantly, the multi-player mode swiftly became the only bit of Dyna Blaster most people bothered to play, and entire days disappeared at Amiga Format as AF staff, and those from other magazines at Future, picked up a joystick and found themselves mysteriously afflicted with an inability to put it down again until it was forcefully prised from their reluctant fingers by someone else desperate for a game.

Dyna Blaster is good fun, but Dyna Blaster Battle Mode is probably the best computer-related fun there is in the world.

Harlequin £25.99

From: Gremlin. Tel 0753 753423
Minimum requirements: Any Amiga

HARLEQUIN

Harlequin didn't sell as well as it should have and can consequently be elusive, but Gremlin can help.

Harlequin features not just breathtaking graphics and sound, but truly imaginative gameplay that lifts it head and shoulders above the competition.

Get the most out of your Amiga 1993

If you remember, a little while back we said that people buy Amigas because they can do so much more than platform games and scrolling shoot-'em-ups.

That's not to say, however, that they're no good at either of those things. For evidence, you shouldn't have to look any further than Harlequin. A bit similar to, but infinitely better than, the massively popular Robocod, Harlequin is an amazing rollercoaster ride through a gigantic dream world boasting over 20 interlinked worlds, from the Gates Of Heaven to the darkest pits of Hell, taking in Cutesy Land and history's biggest ever milkshake on the way.

Harelquin looks and sounds gorgeous, but it's the imagination that really lifts it above the competition – from start to finish it's full of little touches that leave you constantly slack-jawed and wide-eyed, and every time you think you've got it worked out, it pulls another trick out from up its sleeve and does it to you again.

One of the most emotionally affecting computer games ever, but even on a simple platforming level it's an absolute classic. Mario Schmario.

> **FIRST SAMURAI**
> First Samurai, available on a double-pack (with superb god sim Mega lo Mania) from Ubi Soft (081 343 9055) is another excellent platform game with particularly inspired use of sound and a level of imagination and invention not all that far removed from Harlequin's.

✓ Apidya £25.99
From: Blue Byte. Tel Kompart on 0727 868005
Minimum requirements: Any Amiga

And as for horizontally-scrolling shoot-'em-ups, well, can you honestly name a console one better than this? A vast and challenging blaster, Apidya takes everything good about console games (friendly options screens, customisable playability, ease of play) and transfers them into a game with the originality and imagination characteristic of computer products.

The top 25 Amiga games

APIDYA

Sightings of Apidya are rarer than the proverbial hen's teeth, so your best bet is to contact the UK distributor, Kompart, direct.

Apidya is strange, beautiful and simply terrific to play. If you can find it, buy it.

R-TYPE II

If you can dig up a copy of the now-defunct Activision's R-Type II from a mail-order house or classified ad somewhere, and you'll find Apidya's only serious contender for the crown of best-ever Amiga scrolling shoot-'em-up, in the shape of a practically-perfect coin-op conversion.

Covering wildly varied landscapes, from a Metropolis-like techno nightmare to a rat-infested sewer to the bottom of a country stream, Apidya puts you in the unlikely guise of a heavily-armed wasp with a wingful of power-ups.

Genuinely gorgeous graphics blend with soundtracks perfectly suited to each level (the one accompanying the first 'Techno' stage in particular is among the finest examples of the Amiga musician's art yet committed to disk), but a gruesome surprise is never far away (watch out when you kill the dead-rat boss of level three – it's gross).

It's not that which keeps you playing, though – the beautifully-judged gameplay and the near-perfect difficulty curve take care of that. Another disgracefully under-rated game, but one which will more than amply reward the effort it'll take to get yourself a copy.

Get the most out of your Amiga 1993

The top 25 Amiga games

✓ Crazy Cars 3 £25.99
GOOD BUY
From: Titus
Minimum requirements: 1Mb

Formula One Grand Prix isn't the be-all and end-all of driving action on the Amiga. There are plenty of people out there who find the technical accuracy and depth of the MicroProse title more than a little off-putting, and prefer arcadey, sprite-based games like the Lotus series.

Core Design's Jaguar licence challenged the Lotus games' long-held stranglehold on the sprite racing side of the market, but last year Titus unexpectedly came up with a game which, despite being a sequel to two of the worst games in the genre ever, left the Jag and the Lotuses eating dust. Crazy Cars 3 is a mad road-race across America, not entirely dissimilar in plot to Road Rash, or a reversed-roles version of Chase HQ, but the plot, while it gives the game far more atmosphere than its competitors, is by far the least important weapon in its arsenal.

Crazy Cars 3 is one of the best driving games ever – the cars are ultra-responsive and the sense of speed can be amazing.

CRAZY CARS 3
AVAILABILITY

Palace, Titus' UK distributor, recently folded, so your best bet for a copy of Crazy Cars 3 lies with companies like Special Reserve, or other mail-order houses found in the pages of Amiga Format and Amiga Power. Like Apidya, this is a game well worth the effort of finding it.

LOTUS ESPRIT
TOP TIP

Lotus Esprit Turbo Challenge, the original and best Lotus game, can be found on Gremlin's budget label GBH (0753 753423). While not up to Crazy Cars 3's standard, it's still a great game and boasts one advantage in the shape of the simultaneous two-player mode.

Get the most out of your Amiga 1993

The top 25 Amiga games

Where CC3 really scores over the older games is in playability – the ultra-high performance cars under your control handle absolutely beautifully, far more responsively than the Lotuses or the Jaguar, and the game's speed is always impressive, sometimes nothing short of breathtaking, especially as you hurtle down a narrow mountain canyon at a turbo-boosted 404 kilometres an hour with an impossible chicane waiting for you at the bottom of the hill. Play this for a day, and the competition feels like a fleet of milk floats.

Gem'X £7.99

From: Demonware. Tel DMI on 0753 686000
Minimum requirements: Any Amiga

GEM'X

Gem'X is newly released on DMI's fledgling budget label. Find out your nearest stockist by calling DMI.

It's not often you find a piece of software which can be truthfully described as 'sexy' (certainly not any of the pathetically sad strip poker games which are always doing the rounds), but Gem'X is Number One in the field. A puzzle game with some similarities to Klax and Columns (but not really very many), it's a brilliant game in its own right, but the beautiful oriental music played throughout, the seductive (but still cute and cartoony) hostess Kiki whispering

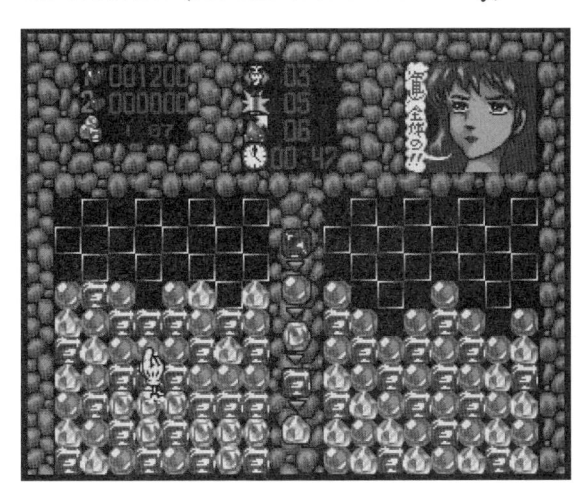

Gem'X – the 'sexiest' game ever written? Yes, but only in the nicest possible way...

Get the most out of your Amiga 1993

'I love you' as you start, and the gorgeous, er, 'babes' revealed as you complete levels give the game an erotic charge (in the sweetest possible way) that's pretty much unchallenged.

The sound in general, in fact, is a much-overlooked collection of cascades and twinkles (Not to mention shimmering shards of sepulchral majesty – Ed) that's almost enough to draw you into the game by itself, but even with the volume down and the lights on, Gem'X is compulsive enough to hold you in its grip for weeks.

✔ Asteroids   Free!
GOOD BUY **From:** Public Domain
Minimum requirements: Any Amiga (not A500+ or A600)

There aren't many coin-op conversions in this list (in fact, Rainbow Islands is the only true one, although other games like Dyna Blaster and Lemmings have appeared in arcades after their Amiga incarnations), but there's no way we could leave this out.

For one thing, it's the most perfect conversion the Amiga's ever seen – there isn't a pixel or a bleep of the original which isn't

Asteroids was one of the first arcade games ever written, and it's still one of the best.

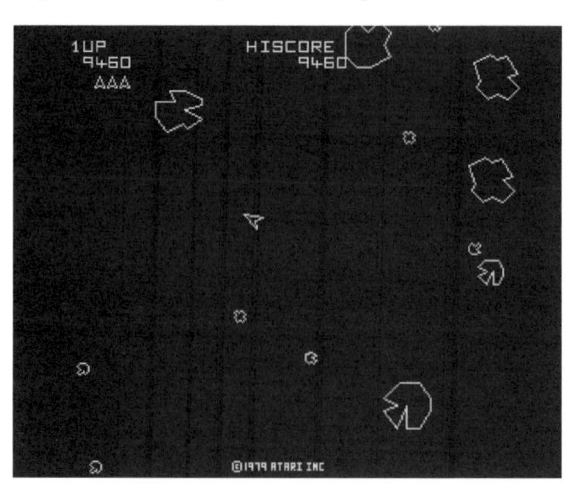

ASTEROIDS
AVAILABILITY

Most PD libraries should have Asteroids, or you can always pick up a back issue of Amiga Power, which gave away Asteroids on its issue 7 coverdisk.

The top 25 Amiga games

LLAMATRON

While you're ordering from your local PD library, don't forget to pick up a copy of Jeff Minter's Llamatron. A Robotron-inspired blaster, this is deservedly the most successful shareware game ever. Shame the concept still didn't properly catch on.

present in this version, and even the keyboard layout follows the same ergonomic design of the arcade monster.

For another thing, the original was an awesome, groundbreaking game which deserves a place in history for any one of several revolutionary concepts in its design.

The most important consideration, though, is that Asteroids is simply one of the greatest games of all time. Simple in concept but fiendishly difficult to master, it's one of the most addictive games you'll ever play – the control you have over your ship is so complete, and the hazards in the game so straightforward (some floating space rocks and the occasional flying saucer) that you can't believe you won't do better the next time you play it, and in such a way is obsession born. If a single game in this entire list deserves the label 'classic', Asteroids is the one.

✓ International Karate +   £7.99
From: The Hit Squad. Tel 061 832 6633
Minimum requirements: Any Amiga

IK+

Talk to The Hit Squad about IK+ if you can't 'persuade' your local shopkeeper to sell you a copy.

International Karate + is a beat-em-up from the very dawn of Amiga computing. But it can still cut it today...

Get the most out of your Amiga 1993

You know, there's another genre we forgot about when discussing the popularity of consoles a few pages back...

The beat-'em-up is probably the most popular gamestyle of all among the pre-pubescent boys who make up much of Sega and Nintendo's target audience, and despite the inherently limited nature of the genre, there's always a horde of eager punters out there waiting to snap up the latest, most brutal effort (witness the otherwise-inexplicable success of turkeys like Ocean's two WWF games, and the world-beating multi-million sales of the unremarkable in almost every way Street Fighter II).

The Amiga can spray blood and broken teeth around with the best of 'em, but for the very best in fighting action you have to go all the way back to the very first days of the machine, and to a game called International Karate +.

With three fighters at a time (one or two controlled by humans), a wide range of easy-to-use moves, great music and a truckload of brilliant touches and hidden features, IK+ stands up against all competition even today as being the beat-'em-up for people who don't like beat-'em-ups.

Terrific stuff, and if Street Fighter II doesn't agree it can step outside and discuss it.

✓ Pinball Dreams £25.99
GOOD BUY Pinball Fantasies £29.99

From: 21st Century. Tel 0235 832939
Minimum requirements: Any Amiga

Until last year, it was generally accepted that pinball games on computer didn't work. Where was the point, it was argued, in

The top 25 Amiga games

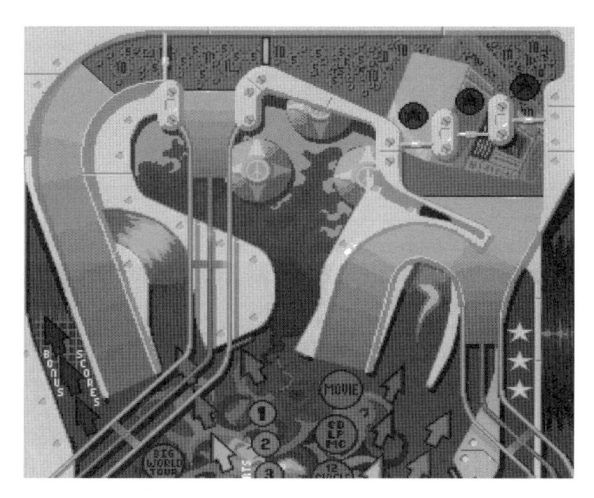

Can a computer really simulate a pinball table? Play Pinball Dreams or Pinball Fantasies and you'll never ask again.

PINBALL DREAMS

Can't get hold of a copy of either of these unmissable pinball games? Give 21st Century a call.

trying to simulate something that was as much about the physical feel as it was about the ups and downs of the actual gameplay? And besides, previous efforts had given the impression that realistic ball movement simply couldn't be done effectively on computer.

Then, all of a sudden, from the unlikely source of Sweden came a game so completely exquisite to play and so unputdownably addictive that no-one could be left in any doubt that computer pinball was not only possible, but a total necessity in any well-balanced life. Pinball Dreams and its superior successor Pinball Fantasies boasted four complete pinball tables each, every one of them an excellent game in its own right.

Ball movement was near-perfect, great features were in plentiful supply, and Amiga Format and Amiga Power lost days of work as everyone 'tested' the games thoroughly for themselves.

Get the most out of your Amiga 1993

✓ Putty £25.99
From: System 3. Tel 081 864 8212
Minimum requirements: 1Mb RAM

Even on the Amiga, one game release in about every three seems to be a platformer. While the majority are formula rubbish and the odd one is formula good stuff (there's nothing really new about, say, Harlequin, it's just exceptionally well done), original material is thinner on the ground than snow in Barbados.

When something like Putty comes along, then, it should be grasped with both hands and clasped firmly to the bosom of anyone who cares even slightly about the future of gaming. Although it's really just a simple platform game with elements of Rainbow Islands, Putty plays like nothing on Earth, with a bizarre, totally malleable central character who stretches, inflates, absorbs and even forms little amoeba-like fists with which to punch some of the most imaginative baddies in living memory.

With a superb supporting cast (including the soon-to-be-legendary Uncle Ted), Putty gives a game with a blue circle for a star more character than a hundred poor-quality Sonic The Hedgehog clones, and while it's not the world's hardest game it'll make you smile

PUTTY

Putty is new for '93, so System 3 will doubtless be most surprised if your local shop can't find a window in its stocking schedule.

For sheer imagination, cuteness and character, Putty is a star amongst platform games.

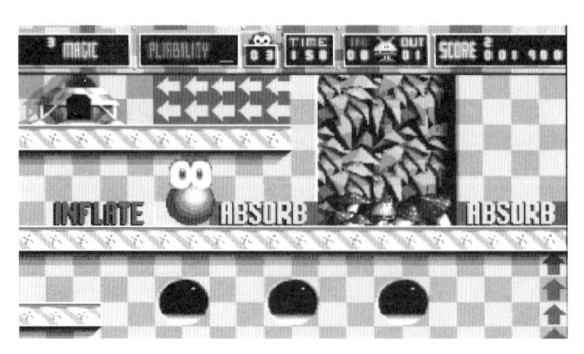

more than an entire day spent watching Have I Got News For You, and that's a lot of smiling.

✓ Wizkid £25.99
From: Ocean. Tel 061 832 6633
Minimum requirements: Any Amiga

The only competition to Putty in the originality stakes is this astounding tour de force of unhinged brilliance from the increasingly-wrongly named Sensible Software.

WIZKID

If you can't buy Wizkid, call Ocean and you'll soon be having a ball.

Defying any genre description save the extremely broad 'arcade game', Wizkid has you playing another ball character (a green one this time) in a game mixing shoot-'em-up, puzzle-solving, exploration and juggling (yes, juggling) with a sense of humour so far off-beam that it could well be the product of some alien civilization.

It also shares with Putty a user-friendly training section and near-terminal addictive qualities, not to mention more hidden features ('cos if we mentioned them, they wouldn't be hidden any more)

Wizkid is another platform game with real imagination.

than an Alan Moore comic. The kind of game that could only happen on a computer (for many reasons), and the kind of game that makes you glad you've got one.

✓ Hunter £25.99
From: Activision
Minimum requirements: Any Amiga

Who needs Virtual Reality?

Activision gave you a solid-polygon man walking through a stunning contoured landscape shooting things and solving puzzles (not to mention hijacking lorries and stealing bicycles) two years ago, and it still looks and moves better than most of those arcade efforts that you have to wear those horrible, hair-disfiguring helmets to play.

Even now, Hunter is one of the Amiga's finest technical achievements, doing for walking along on the ground what Knights Of The Sky did for flying a WWI biplane only more so, and more importantly it's a fabulous game as well, blending

HUNTER
Activision no longer operate in the UK, so you'll have to, er, hunt around in the mail-order pages and second-hand bins for Hunter.

Is virtual reality new? Hardly – Hunter was out two years ago, and it still looks and plays amazingly today.

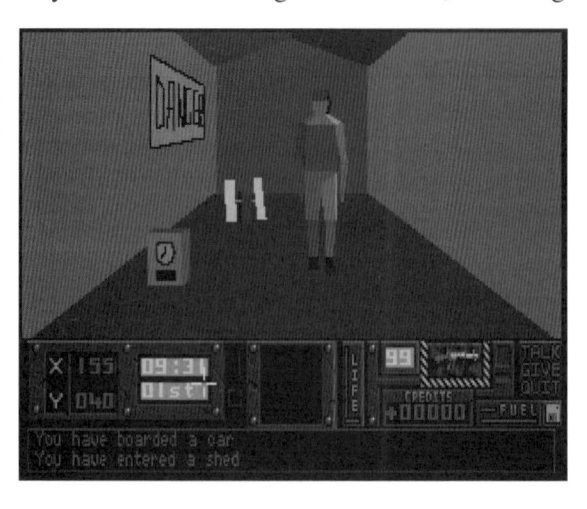

The top 25 Amiga games

atmosphere, action and adventure to breathtaking effect. It's a crying shame that more people don't own a copy of it, so if you stumble across one, don't hesitate for a second.

Vroom £25.99

From: Lankhor
Minimum requirements: Any Amiga

VROOM

Our best efforts couldn't come up with a contact number for Lankhor, so it's back to the classifieds for Vroom, I'm afraid.

Just to complete your racing game collection, there's a missing link between Formula One Grand Prix and Crazy Cars 3 – it's this.

Vroom actually has two separate modes of play, a straight arcadey sprite-based racer and the same thing but with more of a technical simulationey bent. It's extremely fast and very pretty-looking, and while it lacks the supreme accuracy of F1GP or the conflict and atmosphere of CC3, it's as much fun to play as either of them, and a must for completist race lovers. Get these three and you'll never need another driving game again.

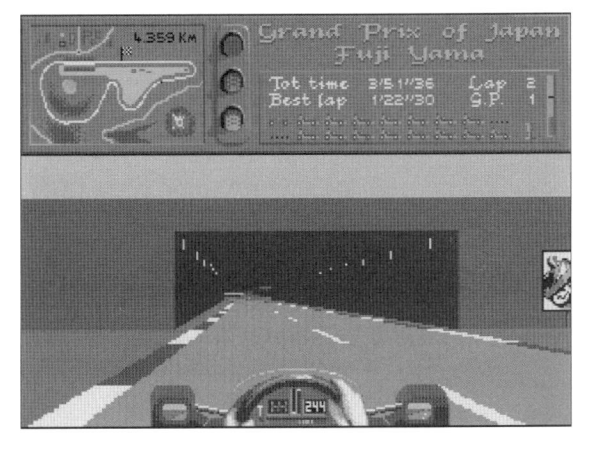

Vroom is a fast, playable racing game that lacks frills but is still up there with the best.

Get the most out of your Amiga 1993

✓ Zool £25.99
From: Gremlin. Tel 0742 753423
Minimum requirements: 1Mb RAM

If you really want to compete with the consoles on their own ground, you don't have to look any further than Zool. Star of a big, bold, brash platform shoot-'em-up, Zool the Ninja of the Nth Dimension is the Amiga's closest shot yet at a Mario-and-Sonic-style brand identity character, and the game copies the consoles' no-messing all-action ethos perfectly.

The only fly in the ointment is a bit of a bleak look to the ordinary A500/A600 version, but the recently-released A1200 update takes care of business in that department with some beautiful parallaxing backdrops, and loads of extra sound effects into the bargain.

Zool is a game that should be in everyone's collection, but if you've got an A1200 it's the best demonstration of your machine's new power yet.

ZOOL
Most of the software shops round our way have entire shelves devoted to Zool, but if yours are different, call Gremlin.

Zool is a Ninja of the Nth Dimension, and has more character and appeal than any number of Marios, or Sonics...

The top 25 Amiga games

✓ D/Generation £14.99
From: Mindscape. Tel 0444 246333
Minimum requirements: 1Mb RAM

If Zool is the game that shows the Amiga's strength as a console imitator, D/Generation is the one that shows its strength as a descendant of the 8-bit computers of the '80s.

D/GENERATION
Now one of Mindscape's mid-price £14.99 games, which might mean a between-two-stools shop-stocking scenario, in which case call the D/Generation Emergency Fix Helpline (well, Mindscape, anyway).

At heart it's a simple enough arcade puzzle game, but the presentation, plotting and atmosphere, linked to the superb design of the actual puzzles themselves, lift it into the stratosphere.

The isometric 3D graphics aren't everyone's cup of tea – some players think they look gorgeous, others seem bizarrely to reckon they 'don't make full use of the Amiga's capabilities' (whatever that means), but whichever way you swing, they're the least important aspect of this unfailingly gorgeous game. And in a recession-hit industry where the biggest single complaint of customers is one of extortionately expensive software, Mindscape's decision to put out Premier-division software at an

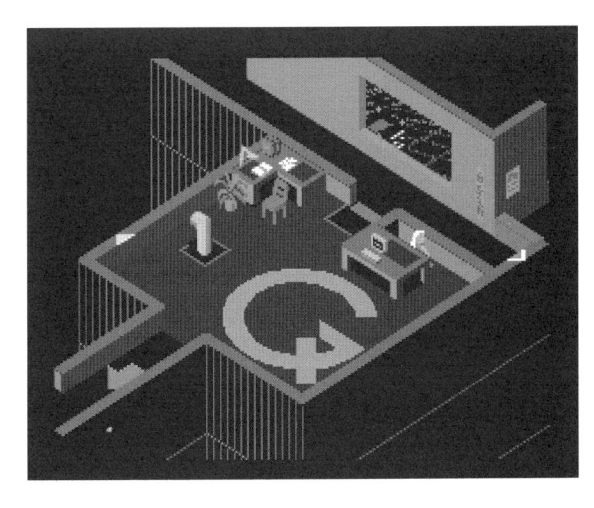

D/Generation is a brilliant arcade puzzle game, descended from the great isometric 3D epics of the '80s.

affordable price is one which we simply can't applaud often enough or loudly enough.

Cheap but not nasty, D/Generation should be at the top of your shopping list. And you'll still have enough cash left over for some cornflakes.

Essential game tips

The finest games machine in the world also boast some of the most challenging, frustrating and generally nadgery games in existence. Luckily, Jonathan (cool as a frozen cucumber) Davies is here to help...

Another World
From: US Gold

The game's spilt into eleven sections – these are the access codes:

Section 1: EDJI **Section 2:** HICI **Section 3:** FLLD
Section 4: LIBC **Section 5:** CCAL **Section 6:** EDIL
Section 7: KCIJ **Section 8:** ICAH **Section 9:** FIEI
Section 10: LALD **Section 11:** LFEK

BATMAN THE MOVIE
Type 'JAMMMM' on the title screen for infinite lives. You'll also find that pressing F10 will skip to the next level.

Fancy being able to switch your immunity on and off in Carrier Command?

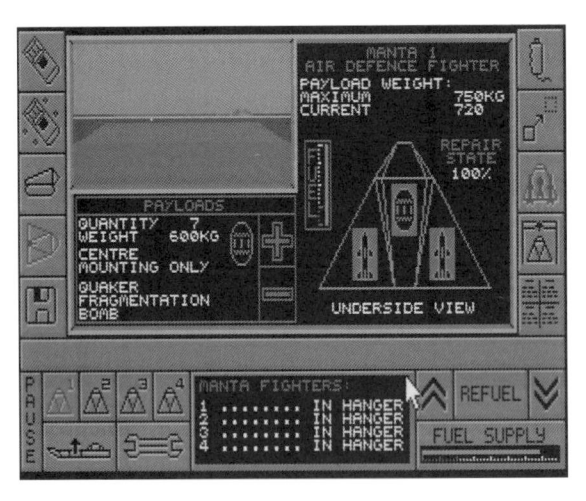

Carrier Command
From: Rainbird

Pause the game and type 'GROW OLD ALONG WITH ME'. You'll now be able to switch immunity on and off with the '+' and '-' keys.

Essential game tips

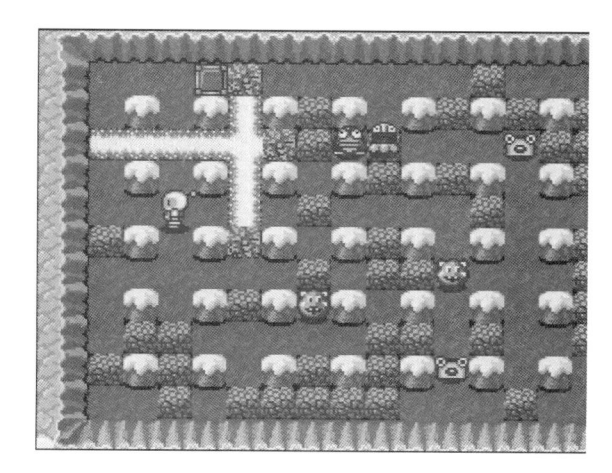

Check out the passwords (below) to Dynablaster.

Dynablaster
From: Ubi Soft

Here's a selection of haphazardly-chosen passwords:

2-5 – ROVEWTPC	3-1 – MXVCLSAH
3-6 – MXCCLIZY	4-2 – ROCEGMPU
4-7 – ROOCLWEL	5-1 – ROLCLSEW
6-1 – ROFVWBNL	6-7 – MXREPVNM
7-3 – MAREWGKP	7-7 – MXREVQNM
8-2 – MXAEPMYH	8-6 – MAHEGSLN

TOP TIP — DEFEND. OF THE CROWN
Hold down K until the game has loaded. You'll kick off with 2048 knights, which ought to be enough.

E-Motion
From: US Gold

During the intro sequence a picture of Einstein will appear. When it does, type 'MOONUNIT' to activate the cheat mode. Having done that you'll be able to use the following keys:

F1 – Go forward a level **F2** – Go back a level
F3 – Go forward 10 levels **F4** – Go back 10 levels

Get the most out of your Amiga 1993

Having an 'Epic' struggle? These passwords should make life easier.

Epic
From: Ocean

Here are all the passwords you'll need:

Mission 1 – Tracking Station: AURIGA
Mission 2 – CPU/Space ports: CEPHEUS
Mission 2 – Mining Complexes : APUS
Mission 3 – Glory: MUSCA
Misison 4 – Magma Cannon: PYXIS
Mission 5 – Galactic Storm: CETUS
Mission 6 – Command Centre: FORNAX
Mission 7 – Mother of all Battles: CAELUM
Mission 8 – Command Ship: CORVUS

Don't forget that you can press Enter on the keypad at any time to rearm and refuel your ship.

F-29 Retaliator
From: Ocean

- On the duty roster screen, enter your name as 'THE DIDDY MEN'. You'll then find that pressing Enter will land the plane for you.

FALCON

If you're running low on ammo, press and hold 'CTRL', 'Shift' and 'X' to replenish all your weapons.

Essential game tips

TOP TIP — FANTASY WLD DIZZY
Enter your name into the high score table as 'IMMORTAL' to give Dizzy infinite lives.

- Or try 'CIARAN' instead, which will give you unlimited missiles and ammo.
- If you get killed on a mission, it's possible to avoid your pilot's record getting scratched off – just reset the computer on the 'Service Terminated' screen rather than restarting the game.
- When setting up your mission, don't enter the weapons selection screen and you'll find you're given unlimited Thunderbolts.

Fire and Ice
From: Renegade

Try typing in 'COOL' and pressing Return.

If things are getting a little too hot in Fire and Ice, just try to keep cool...

Gem'X
From: Demonware

Some level codes:

Level B – EARTHIAN   Level C – KENICHI

Get the most out of your Amiga 1993

You can get to higher levels in Gem'X with these password codes. Isn't cheating wonderful?

Level D – INOKUMA
Level F – BADMAN
Level H – YOKOHAMA
Level J – X68000
Level L – REDMOON
Level N – MAGAMANN
Level P – FMTOWNS
Level S – ZAWAS

Level E – BURAI
Level G – NETWORK
Level I – EXACT
Level K – TURRICAN
Level M – CAMPAIGN
Level O – SYVALION
Level Q – GAMERION

Future Wars
From: Delphine

The numeric door lock baffles many people, but using it is quite simple. Just Operate each button individually – quickly, mind.

Gobliiins
From: Tomahawk

Here's the code for every single level. (Except the first one, obviously.)

Essential game tips

! **FLOOD**

For instant access to all 42 levels, use the password 'MEEK'.

Level 2 – VQVQFDE
Level 4 – ECPQPCC
Level 6 – HQWFTFW
Level 8 – JCJCIHL
Level 10 – LQPCTJU
Level 12 – FTQKULD
Level 14 – EWDGONK
Level 16 – TCUQQPL
Level 18 – KKKPTRD
Level 20 – NNGWSTN
Level 22 – TQNGEVB

Level 3 – ICIGCAA
Level 5 – FTWKFEN
Level 7 – DWNDFGU
Level 9 – ICUGBGS
Level 11 – HNWVFKA
Level 13 – DCPLPMG
Level 15 – TCNGSOU
Level 17 – IQDNJQN
Level 19 – NGOGJSO
Level 21 – LGWFFUR

Hook
From: Ocean

Rather than a complete solution (complete solutions are for wimps), here's what to do in some of the game's trickier bits:

Q How can I dig up the clock at the beach?
A You'll need a spade. There's one buried on the beach, at the spot marked 'X'. But to retrieve it you'll need a metal detector, which can be bought at the shop for three gold coins.

Q Okay, so I've got two gold coins, but I need one more. Where is it?
A It's in the jacket, which is obtained via an enormously elaborate process. Get the washing line pole and the anchor from behind the

Here's some clues to get you past the trickier bits in Hook

square and use the anchor on the anchor rope. Then go out through the door in the upstairs of the Bait and Tackle. Use the anchor and the rope on the piece of wood above the clock three times, whereupon you'll find yourself swinging across to the pirate. Get his hat, swing back, swing to the closed door and knock on it. (Tricky, isn't it?) Then quickly go down the stairs, and use the washing pole on the jacket behind the square. You'll then be able to take the gold piece from it.

Q What should I do on the cliff edge?
A First of all, make sure your life isn't in danger by using the piece of elastic on the slingshot. Then repeatedly jump off the cliff edge by 'using' the corner of the fence on the cliff edge.

There's also a bug in the game which can be exploited to your advantage. Enter the Bait and Tackle and pick up the mug next to the candle. Then keep 'picking up' in the space where the mug was and you'll get all the items you need to complete the game.

Humans
From: Mirage

Are these strange, unintelligent, ugly prehistoric creatures really human beings...

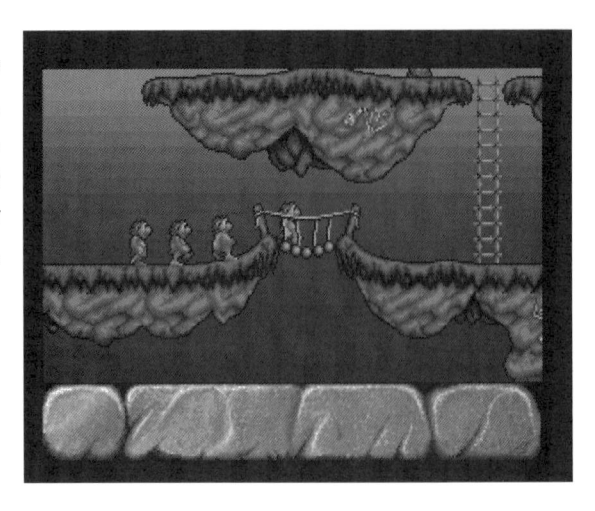

Essential game tips

Here are – as you might have guessed – all the level codes:

1 DARWIN	**2** ANDIE PANDY
3 GET A LIFE	**4** CARLOS
5 HOWIE	**6** MOOBLE
7 CSL	**8** THE HUMBLE ONE
9 PIXIE	**10** MILESTONE
11 WAR WAR WAR	**12** J MCKINNON
13 UNLUCKY	**14** BLUE MONKEY
15 RED DWARF	**16** BAD TASTE
17 THE KITCHEN	**18** CJ
19 SORT IT OUT	**20** SMART
21 VILLA3BORO2	**22** EARLY MORNING
23 BORO4LEEDS1	**24** EASY LIFE
25 JIMS TIES	**26** PARKVIEW
27 NICENEASY	**28** GREEN CARD
29 COOKIE	**30** MALCY MALC
31 RAVING BURK	**32** YOU GOT IT
33 SGNIMMEL	**34** MINISTRY
35 MAD FREDDY	**36** BIZARRE
37 FREE SCOTLAND	**38** APPLE JUICE

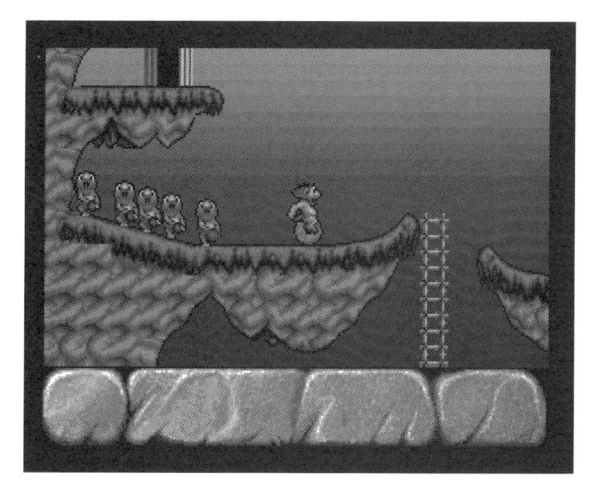

...But that's enough about Amiga Format. Here are the level codes for Humans.

39 PAYDAY
41 BONUS
43 NO MONEY
45 VISION
47 FAST FASHION
49 RAB C NESBITT
51 RAINBOW
53 MIGHTY BAZ
55 CONSOLIDATED
57 AMERICA
59 ISOLATION
61 DAEMONSLATE
63 MIAMI VICE
65 A34732473
67 THE EXILES
69 WINE AND DINE
71 TECHNOPHOBE
73 TIME IS
75 LORDS OF CHAOS
77 IM OUT OF HERE
79 BETTER LIFE

40 BANANA MOON
42 BOUNCING
44 A S F
46 SISTERS
48 CARGO
50 RANGERS
52 DOODY
54 TIRED
56 STAY HAPPY
58 ANOTHER DAY
60 PROMISED LAND
62 BIG RAB
64 MARGARET M
66 HELP ME
68 EIGHTLANDS
70 NIN
72 GETTING THERE
74 RUNNING OUT
76 NOW ITS DONE
78 HERES TO A
80 BYE BYE BYE

KICK OFF 2

While playing against the computer, run your fingers along the function keys and 'S12' or 'S14' will appear in the corner of the screen. You'll now be able to substitute the computer's goalie with one of your own players. And if you keep pressing R while a penalty's being taken, you'll be able to see where the ball's going.

Hunter
From: Activision

The first thing you'll need to do is locate someone we'll call the First Man. Use either a rocket boat you'll find near headquarters, or the helicopter at X-181 Y-107. He'll tell you where to find the Old Man (at X-181 Y-197). For fourbags of money, he'll tell you that the Master Key is at X-164 Y-061.

TheSecond Man should be next on your list – he's at X-099 Y-061. He'll send you on to the professor, who's to be found at X-049 Y-

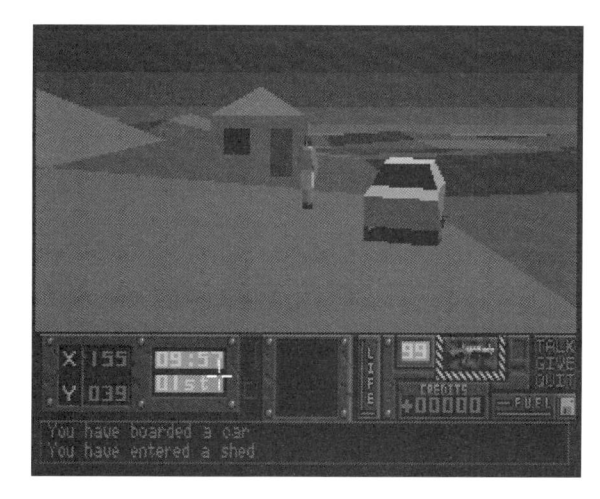

Is that the First Man? Maybe it's the Second? It could even be the Third... (You'll only know what we're talking about if you've played Hunter.)

115, and who wants the nuclear device which you'll find at X-028 Y-227.

Then find the floppy disk at X-100 Y-225 and the Third Man at X-195 Y-119. There's a computer at X-224 Y-199 for which you'll need the security pass that's to be found at X-090 Y-153. Then rescue the prisoner from X-135 Y-239 by taking him the hacksaw from X-151 Y-121, and take the monk at X-085 Y-174 some food (which consists of rabbits and birds).

The injured soldier at X-010 Y-036 will give you directions to the general's bunker at X-135 Y-239, which should be laid into with everything you've got.

And remember – many parts of the game are a lot easier if you disguise yourself with an enemy uniform.

Interceptor
From: Electronic Arts

- Qualifying is a lot easier if you do it like this: Take off from the carrier, switch on the afterburner and pull back on the joystick until you've done a half-loop, and you're flying upside down, but DON'T touch the left or right directions on the joystick. Fly along upside down for a while, and then push the joystick forward so you're flying the right way up again. You'll find yourself lined up for a perfect landing. (You did do that bit about getting the right way up again, didn't you?)
- There's no need to get too close to enemy planes. Instead, fire AMRAAM missiles from maximum range, causing your opponent to break and leaving him vulnerable to your cannons.
- The submarine mission gives many Interceptor players nightmares. Approach low, from an angle of around 320 degress, and hit the conning tower with all six missiles.
- There are some extra missions you might want to try, too. Press 2 to get into free flight, and then, before choosing your plane, press 6, 7, 8 or 9.

KID GLOVES
Pause the game and type in 'RHIANNON'. You can then press F6 to take you to the shop, F8 to top up your cash, and F9 for immunity.

Only James Pond could face end-of-level 'pipes'. Here's how to cheat your way past them

James Pond
From: Millennium

Type in 'JUNKYARD' while playing. You'll then be able to press D to remove the locks form the end of level pipes, and Return to toggle the cheat mode on and off. While in cheat mode, the bottom row of keys can be used to access the game's various levels.

The Last Ninja 3
From: System 3

The codes for all six levels:

Level 1 – SUSS	**Level 2** – IMED	**Level 3** – URTI
Level 4 – BASD	**Level 5** – NOUS	**Level 6** – REOO

Lemmings
From: Psygnosis

Here's a (very nearly) complete set of codes:

Fun Level:
- 02 – IJJLDNCCCN
- 03 – NJLDLCADCY
- 04 – HNLHCINECV
- 05 – LDLCAJNFCK
- 06 – DLCIJNLGCT
- 07 – HCAONNLHCX
- 08 – CINNLDLICJ
- 09 – CEKHMDLJCO

Can't get past this Lemming level? You don't need to when you've got all the passwords!

Essential game tips

	10 – MKHMDLCKCX	11 – OHODHCGLCU
	12 – HMDLCINMCY	13 – MDLCAKLNCS
	14 – DLCIJNMOCM	15 – LCAOLMDPCY
	16 – CINLOLOHQCW	17 – CEJHLFLBDX
	18 – KKHLNHCCDT	19 – NINNHCADDQ
	20 – HLFLCINEDS	21 – NNCAJNFDT
	22 – FLCIKLLGDV	23 – LCAOLLFHDS
	24 – CMOLNNHIDV	25 – CEKIMNHJDW
	26 – IJHMFLCKDV	27 – NJMFLCCLDW
	28 – JONHCKNMDV	29 – MFLCAJLNDU
	30 – FLCMKLMODS	
Tricky:	01 – LCANLMFPDK	02 – CMOLMFNQDK
	03 – CAJJLDMBEV	04 – OKILDMCCEU
	05 – NJNLMBEDEY	06 – JLDICINEEQ
	07 – LLICCJLFER	08 – LICOJLNGEQ
	09 – MCEOLLDHEW	10 – CINLLDMIEK
	11 – CEKJOLIJEJ	12 – IKHMDMCKEW
	13 – OJMLICALEJ	14 – JOLICOOMEK
	15 – MDMCAJLNEU	16 – LMBIJNOOEY
	17 – KCCNOMLPEV	18 – CINLMDMQET
	19 – CAKINNIBFO	20 – KJKLFOCCFN
	21 – OHLFMCADFN	22 – JNNICONEFT
	23 – LFMCAKMFFQ	24 – GICKKOLGFK
	25 – OCGNLLFHFM	26 – BIOMNFIIFM
	27 – CAJJMGMJFS	28 – MKKONKCKFY
	29 – OIMFOCGLFP	30 – IMFMCMOMFU
Taxing:	01 – MFMCGKLNFO	02 – FMCKJOMOFV
	03 – MCENLMFPFR	04 – CINNMGMQFJ
	05 – GEKKNMJBGJ	06 – OJJLLHGCGN
	07 – OHLEHGCDGO	08 – ILDLGKOEGL
	09 – LDLGCJOFGV	10 – ELGIJOLGGN

> **LOTUS CHALLENGE**
> Enter player one's name as 'FIELDS OF FIRE', and player two's name as 'IN A BIG COUNTRY' to qualify every time. Alternatively, try 'MONSTER' and 'SEVENTEEN'.

Get the most out of your Amiga 1993

Essential game tips

	11 – LGCNNLDHGK	12 – GKNOLDLIGU
	13 – GCKHOMHJGL	14 – OKHMDNGKGT
	15 – OIMDNGALGL	16 – HMDLGIIOMGR
	17 – MDLGGJLNGP	18 – DLGKJLMOGU
	19 – LGANLMDPGP	20 – GKNNOMHQGT
	21 – GGKHNNHBHY	22 – KJKLFLGCHJ
	23 – NJLGNGADHW	24 – KNOHGOOEHL
	25 –	26 – GNGKJNLGHT
	27 – NGANOLFHHO	28 – FINLLFHIHN
	29 – FAJHMFHJHP	30 – IJHMFLGKHN
Mayhem:	01 – NJMGLGALHN	02 – JOOJGKOMHR
	03 – OOJGCKNNHK	04 – FHFIJLMOHQ
	05 – LGANNMGPHV	06 – GOOOMOHQHK
	07 – FAJHLDIBIW	08 –
	09 – NHLDIFADIN	10 – HLDIFINEIV
	11 – LDIFAJLFIO	12 – DIFIJLLGIX
	13 – MGCNNLEHIO	14 – FINLLDIIIN
	15 – FAJHMDIJIP	16 – IJHMEMGKIO
	17 – NHMDIFALIV	18 – HMDIFINMIO
	19 – MDIFAJLNIX	20 – DIFIJLMOIQ
	21 – IFANLMDPIN	22 – FINLMDIQIW
	23 – FAJHLFIBJJ	24 – IJHLFIFCJS
	25 – NHLFIFADJP	26 – HLFIFINEJY
	27 – LFIFAJLFJR	28 – FIFIJLLGJK
	29 – IFANLLFHKX	30 – FINLLFIIJQ

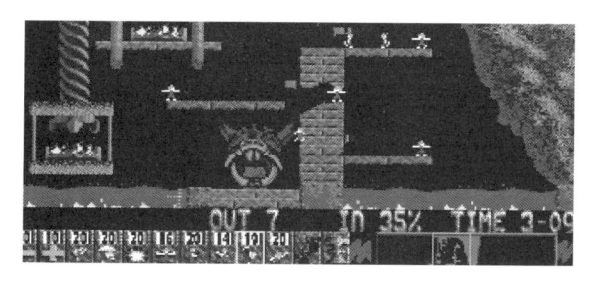

Oh, you got some out then? (Yawn)

Get the most out of your Amiga 1993

If Lotus Challenge II is driving you round the bend (ha ha) then you need these passcodes.

Lotus Turbo Challenge II
From: Gremlin

The codes:

TWILIGHT – Night Course
PEA SOUP – Fog Course
THE SKIDS – Snow Course
PEACHES – Desert Course
LIVERPOOL – Motorway Course
BAGLEY – Marsh Course
E BOW – Storm Course
Plus: 'DEESIDE' will let you qualify in every race whether you win or not, and 'TURPENTINE' will stop the timer. And try using 'DUX' to access a secret built-in extra game!

Essential game tips

Lotus III
From: Gremlin Graphics

Again, the codes:

TOP TIP — MIDNIGHT RESISTANCE
If you type 'ITSEASYWHENYOU KNOWHOW' on the title screen, you'll find you've activated the cheat mode.

Easy Level:	1 PWRWUWHNM-30	2 XMQIYSKAS-80
	3 UVQSNPBCM-70	4 CWVBQPCAV-50
	5 SFXUXXXXP-60	6 HSYWYSKGC-50
	7 IVVEMMKOZ-50	

Medium Level:	1 ANNSMQLPN-60	2 VSVDOPHCY-50
	3 RTLMYJKHB-60	4 ERRURV——67
	5 NSSSXXXXS-60	6 WSVUQPCSJ-70
	7 OUNDEFACG-99	8 GXWDYPACV-68
	9 BZ-ZF-BAT-90	10 LWNJWKACN-90

Hard Level:	1 IYVVNVEQR-35	2 KAZZNIKAI-45
	3 FGQLJGDAF-65	4 MFFSRPYDU-60
	5 PLQTZQDPE-80	6 ZKZGKJKKK-50
	7 TGGJGGTTT-63	8 AFZYBQCJT-70
	9 JBOUKJHKA-99	10 DASICOTET-80
	11 XDNVSEECE-85	12 QDSCJVEBT-75
	13 SKGYXXXXK-57	14 YKGJWVNAK-92
	15 WJMEGMEQH-60	

And try 'GAMESMAST' to access a special course.

There's more than one way to the top in Mega Lo Mania. There's the long, hard, honest way... and then there's this one.

Mega Lo Mania
From: Image Works

The level codes are as follows:

SQUCIGQEKNS – Epoch 2 **PHQCICHVTNG** – Epoch 3
FIAACVOFZNA – Epoch 4 **FUCAESCSXHS** – Epoch 5
PVNCSZGYRHG – Epoch 6 **IFIBUIRHPTM** – Epoch 7
CGRCEEQXJNM – Epoch 8 **OMXCQKJYONE** – Epoch 9
WNKAFKFCNMR – Mother of all battles

And bear the following tips in mind:

- Save plenty of men for the three islands in the last epoch – they need about fifty each.
- Once nuclear weapons enter the arena, put all your efforts into manufacturing them, as it's really just a race to see who gets there first.

Essential game tips

PREMIERE — TOP TIP

On the title screen – the one where it says 'Press Fire to roll cameras' – type 'SPARKPLUGS'. You should then get a cheat screen. Start the game and you'll be able to skip levels by pressing the grey '/' key on the pad on the very right of your keyboard. (Although Amiga 600 owners might come a cropper at that point...)

- You can only put one castle into suspended animation on each island so make sure it has a maximum of 999 men in it when you do.
- If one of the computer players attacks your castle with a force containing only unarmed men, return your men in that sector to return to the castle. The computer player's men will then leave the sector, as there's nothing they can do there.

New Zealand Story
From: The Hit Squad

Type FLUFFY KIWIS on the title screen for some extra lives.

Kiwis are flightless birds. They're also clueless. Just as well this New Zealand Story Cheat gives you a few extra lives.

Oh No! More Lemmings!
From: Psygnosis

Here (deep breath) are all the codes:

Tame Level:	02 IISTEHCCAQ	03 LRTDLCADAO
	04 RTDLCILEAH	05 TDLCAHTFAO

Get the most out of your Amiga 1993

06 DLCIHVTGAJ
08 CILVTDLIAP
10 IHRUDLCKAK
12 RUDLCILMAQ
14 DLCIHTUOAG
16 CILVWLHQAO
18 IHRTFLCCBE
20 RUNLBIMEBE

07 LCALVTDHAG
09 CAHRUDLJAR
11 MPVDLCALAG
13 WDHCAHTNAF
15 LCALVUDPAP
17 CAHRTFLBBL
19 MRVNLBADBL

> **ROBOCOP 3**
>
> Hold down the right shift key and type 'THE DIDDY MEN' to activate a cheat mode.

Crazy Level:
01 TFLCAHTFBR
03 LCCLWTFHBM
05 CAHSUFLJBF
07 LRUFLCCLBM
09 WNHCGHWNBJ
11 LCCMUUGPBF
13 CCIPTEMBCN
15 LQTDMCADCQ
17 TEMCCHVFCG
19 KCCMVVLHCE

02 GLCIHUTGBM
04 CKLTTGLIBD
06 IHSUFLCKBO
08 RUFNCKLMBH
10 FLCKHVUOBW
12 BMMTWFHQBL
14 KHRTDMCCCG
16 QTDMCKLECL
18 DMCKIUTGCO
20 CKMTVMKICM

Wild Levels:
01 CGHPUDIJCE
03 LRWEICELCN
05 UEMCCHWNCQ
07 MCALVUEPCD
09 CAHRTGMBDP
11 MRTNICEDDN
13 TGMCAHTFDF
15 MCELUTGHDQ
17 CCHSUGMJDL
19 MRUNICCLDE

02 MIQWMICKCI
04 PUMICIMMCH
06 LICOIWUOCR
08 CKLWUEMQCP
10 KHRTFMCCDJ
12 QTFMCIMEDN
14 NICMIVVGDK
16 CKLVTOKIDO
18 KHSUFMCKDD
20 QUFMCOLMDL

(continued overleaf)

Essential game tips

(The longest tip in the book)

Pinball Fantasies
From: 21st Century Entertainment

After pressing F1 to load a table, but before pressing F1 to Start, type EXTRA BALLS for – that's right – some extra balls, and DIGITAL ILLUSIONS to block off the hole at the bottom of the screen.

(And the worst joke)

184

Essential game tips

Wicked Levels:
- 01 VFOCCHTNDR
- 02 NICIHTWODM
- 03 OCCLVUGPDK
- 04 CKLWUFMQDR
- 05 GCHSTLHBEW
- 06 KHRTDLGCEL
- 07 MPTDHGEDEF
- 08 RVMHGILEEG
- 09 VMHGAHWFEQ
- 10 DLGIHTTGEP
- 11 NGALUTDHEP
- 12 GIMWVLHIEP
- 13 GEHQUELJEN
- 14 KIQWMHGKEL
- 15 MPUDLGCLEQ
- 16 PWMHGIMMEO
- 17 VLJGGIUNEN
- 18 DLGKHUUOEL
- 19 HGELVUMPEQ
- 20 GKLTWMJQEJ

Havoc Levels:
- 01 GGHPTGNBFK
- 02 KIPTFLGCFN
- 03 LPTGLGADFI
- 04 STFNGILEFF
- 05 TFNGCHVFFP
- 06 FLGKHWTGFH
- 07 LGALWTFHFS
- 08 GOMVVOHIFI
- 09 GAIQUFLJFM
- 10 KHRUFLGKFH
- 11 MSWFJFALFD
- 12 SUGNGILMFP
- 13 UFNGAHWNFH
- 14 FLGMHTUOFP
- 15 LGALWUGPFM
- 16 GILTUNJQFH
- 17 GCIRVLKBGO
- 18 KIPTDOGCGP
- 19 LPTDMGEDGL
- 20 RTEMGKLEGF

2-player Levels:
- 01 JAHPTDIBKE
- 02 IHPTDIJCKN
- 03 LPTDIJADKK
- 04 Out PTDIJILEKD
- 05 TDIJAHTFKM
- 06 DIJIHTTGKF
- 07 IJALTTDHKS
- 08 JILTTDIIKL
- 09 JAHPUDIJKN
- 10 IHPUDIJKKG

> **SILKWORM**
>
> *Make sure you're holding down HELP when your press fire to start the game. That way you'll get infinite lives.*

Get the most out of your Amiga 1993

Essential game tips

You'll never make it through Populous without some divine intervention... here's some passwords.

Populous
From: Electronic Arts

> **SHADOW OF THE BEAST II**
> That legendary cheat mode: When you get to the first pygmy, ask him about 'TEN PINTS' and you'll become immune to damage.

Here's a handful of passwords:

Level 050 – Hobozjob	**Level 075** – Nimlopill
Level 100 – Caleold	**Level 125** – Futdimar
Level 150 – Binqueme	**Level 175** – Alpapal
Level 200 – Eoampmet	**Level 225** – Hurtogodar
Level 250 – Veryoxt	**Level 275** – Buginond
Level 300 – Bilquazout	**Level 350** – Suzdiehole
Level 400 – Badmeill	**Level 450** – Josymar
Level 500 – Shadwildon	**Level 999** – Killuspal

There's a (sort of) cheat as well. First, load the Conquest Game as usual, and click on the Game Setup icon. Then select Custom Game and go to Game Options, changing anything you like. Finally, click on Evil, then Two Players, and then Cancel. The enemy will now be unable to alter the landscape, preventing him from making any progress.

Populous II

From: Electronic Arts

As the chances of you wanting to read through all 1000 passwords seem pretty slim, we'll just give you every tenth one:

0 DOEGAC	**10** UMHEAB	**20** NGAF	**30** GHTHAG
40 ATNEAF	**50** ERTUAK	**60** INUNAD	**70** OOOMAC
80 QUWIAB	**90** UXII	**100** ADPEAT	**110** FEAMAG
120 PIABAF	**130** LOLYAD	**140** UBNGAC	**150** MMUPAB
160 LDOO	**170** ALDOAT	**180** EGTIAG	**190** JIERAF
200 OPEMAK	**210** TUADAD	**220** DDLLAB	**230** AFMN
240 PEQUAT	**250** ISUXAG	**260** OMLOAF	**270** UGIMAK
280 VEEGAD	**290** ABFEAC	**300** MEAGAB	**310** IILDAT
320 DONEAG	**330** UMTUAF	**340** NGUNAK	**350** GHOMAD
360 ATJIAC	**370** ERSIAB	**380** INPE	**390** OOAMAT
400 QUABAG	**410** UXLYAK	**420** ADCCAD	**430** FEUGAC
440 PIWOAB	**450** LODO	**460** UBTIAT	**470** MMERAG
480 LDEMAF	**490** ALAKAK	**500** EGGHAC	**510** JIMNAB
520 OPQU	**530** TUUXAT	**540** DDLOAG	**550** AFINAF
560 PEITAK	**570** ISFEAD	**580** OMAGAC	**590** UGLD
600 VENEAT	**610** ABTTAG	**620** MEUBAF	**630** IIOWAK
640 DOJIAD	**650** UMSIAC	**660** NGPEAB	**670** GHAM
680 ATACAT	**690** ERDDAF	**700** INCCAK	**710** OOUGAD
720 QUWOAC	**730** UXDOAB	**740** ADIS	**750** FENEAT
760 PIMEAG	**770** LOAKAF	**780** UBGHAD	**790** MMMNAC
800 LDQUAB	**810** ALUM	**820** EGHOAT	**830** JIINAG
840 OPITAF	**850** TUFEAK	**860** DDAGAD	**870** AFAAAC
880 PEUX	**890** ISTTAT	**900** OMUBAG	**910** UGOWAF
920 VEJIAK	**930** ABPIAD	**940** MEETAC	**950** IIALAB
960 DOAC	**970** UMDDAG	**980** NGCCAF	**990** GHUGAK
999 WOITAB			

> **SPINDIZZY WORLDS**
> There's a cunningly-hidden level editor built into the game, which you can use if you know how. Load the game, and select a cluster of planets. Then type 'E', 'd', 'i', 't' (holding down Shift to type the 'E'). After reading the warning screen about possible damage to your copy of the game, you'll be given a brief summary of the commands available, and a blank landscape ready to let your imagination run riot on.

Essential game tips

THE SIMPSONS
Type 'COWABUNGA' on the title screen for infinite lives.

Alternatively, try this code, which will give you maximum everything: ADKIUCKBZNZEFIWX

And try typing MUSIC on the special codes section.

Rainbow Islands
From: The Hit Squad

While the title screen is displayed, type any of the following sequences on the keyboard:

BLRBJSBJ	Activates permanent magic shoes.
RJSBJSBR	Permanent double rainbows.
SSSLLRRS	Permanent fast rainbows.
BJBJBJRS	Activate Hint A.
LJLSLBLS	Activate Hint B.
SJBLRJSR	Activate Hint C.
LBSJRLJL	Activate the Book of Continues, allowing you to continue after Doh Island.
RRLLBBJS	All hidden bonus objects become money bags.
RRRRSBSJ	Activates both the above cheats.
SRBJSLSB	Sets your score to 100,000,000 points.

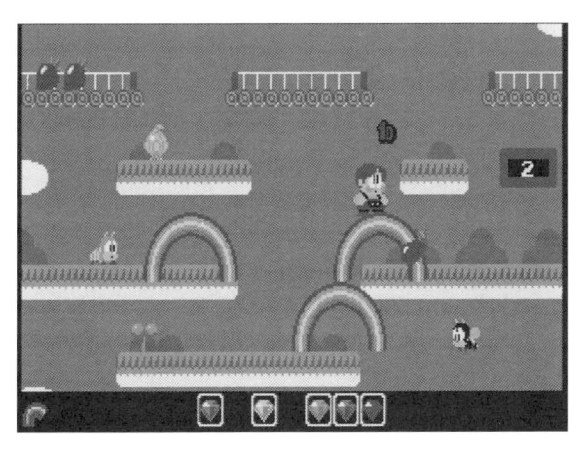

Magic shoes, special rainbows, extra continues, bonus money bags, ultra-high scores – just a few of the cheats for Rainbow Islands.

Robocod
From: Millennium

- Walk along till you get to the first ramp (jumping over the doors as you go) and jump up to a roof on your right. Walk left and you should go into the side of the building, leading you to the secret room.
- Finish the bath levels, and as soon as you come out of the door run straight to the golden snowmen in the bottom far left outside the castle. Jump onto these snowmen and you'll float upwards to the top of the screen where you'll be met by a door. Getting through this door is tricky, but it's worth it. Inside are loads of extra lives and energy stars.
- Go to the same place after finishing the circus room (the last room before the end-of-game baddy) and stand on the golden snowmen again. A platform made of two bonus blocks should float upwards, revealing a secret tunnel. At the bottom of this tunnel are even more extra lives and stars.
- There are a couple of cheats that are activated by picking up certain objects early in the game. On the first roof you come to, above a sign saying 'Arctic Toys', is a row of five objects: a tap,

SWITCH-BLADE II
Hold down the fire button before turning on the Amiga, and keep holding it until the game has started. You'll then be able to play with infinite lives.

For all you folks who though Robocod tips were a bit 'fin' on the ground, here's a few to get you 'hooked' (Sickening, isn't it?)

Essential game tips

STARGLIDER 2

Start the game, press F and slow your ship to a halt. Then pause by pressing DEL and type 'WERE ON A MISSION FROM GOD' and press 1. You'll then be able to re-arm your ship by pressing 1.

a cake, an earth, an apple and a hammer. Their initials are T, C, E, A and H. Pick them up in the following order: cake, hammer, earth, apple, tap. You'll then be invulnerable for the first three levels. Additionally, on the sports equipment level, after the second spike pit, are some lips, a violin, an earth, an ice-cream and a snowman – initials L, V, E, I and S. Pick up the lips first, followed by the ice-cream, the violin, the earth and the snowman. As the more anagram-minded reader will already have guessed, this will give you infinite lives.

- On top of all that, there's a comprehensive cheat mode built into the game that's activated by typing 'LITTLE MERMAID' (with the space) after the game has started. The following keys can then be used:

F – wings
Return – invincibilty (toggles)
B – bath
S – save position
K – commit suicide

X – jump straight to exit
P – plane
C – car
G – restore position
M – map selector

Try pressing the function keys, too.

The Secret of Monkey Island
From: US Gold

You'll never find out the Secret of Monkey Island without some help...

Get the most out of your Amiga 1993

As explaining the whole game would probably fill up the rest of the book (and then some), here are the answers to some commonly-posed questions:

Q How do I beat the Swordmaster?
A Training – that's what you need. First, get Captain Smirk to give you a few lessons (you'll need to be persistent). Then wander around the island a bit, taking on the pirates you'll meet.

Q How can I get hold of a file to get into the mansion?
A You'll be able to get one from the prisoner (who's in the prison!). You won't be able to talk to him until you've given him the breath mints from the hardware store. He'll swap the gopher repellant from the mansion for a cake, which contains the file.

Q How can I raise enough money to buy a boat?
A There's no need, if you're unscrupulous enough. Go to the shop and ask for a credit note. Watch the sequence of turns the shopkeeper uses to open the safe. He'll refuse you credit and, if you ask him about the Swordmaster, leave. Use the same sequence to open the safe and then buy a boat from Stan's.

Q How do I get off the boat and on to Monkey Island?
A Fill the cannon with gunpowder, and light the fuse (made from the rope in the hold) using the business card, after setting it alight in the fire under the cooking pot. Put the pot onto Guybrush's head, hop into the cannon and you'll be there before you know it.

Q How do I get the monkey to follow me to the Monkey Head?
A Give him five bananas – some from the tree on the beach, and some from the fruitbowl in the village.

Q Where will I find the root the cannibals want?

SUPER HANG ON
On the high score table, enter your name as '750J' to give you something of an edge over your fellow riders.

Essential game tips

TERMINATOR 2

Pause the game by pressing P, and then press all the function keys. After unpausing, presing Escape will skip from level to level.

A It's in the glowing box. To open that, you'll need the tools from the room with the squeaky door on the pirate ship.

Q All right, but what can I oil the squeaky door with?
A How about the cooking fat?

Sim City
From: Infogrammes

Type 'FUND' in capital letters while playing to rack up an extra $10,000. Do it more than three times, though, and you'll trigger an earthquake. It's also worth remembering that taxes are only calculated at the very end of the year. So what you want to do is keep them at 0% for most of they year, so that loads of people move into your city, and then sting the population for as much as you can get in December, reducing them back to zero before people have a chance to react.

You sure you can afford that stadium? With this Sim City cheat you can raise as much cash as you want...

In Street Fighter II you can fight yourself! Well, your own character, anyway.

Street Fighter 2
From: US Gold

It's possible to play a two-player game where both players control the same character. To play with Guile vs Guile, for example, what you've got to do is start the game and select a two-player game. Let Player 2 select his control method first. Then Player 2 should select Guile. (He must select his character and press fire first.) Then Player 1 selects any other character. Let Guile win. Then repeat the process, but with Player 1 selecting a different character, also letting Player 2 press his fire button first and win. Repeat this so that Guile wins four consecutive matches over four characters. Player 2 should then select Zangief, pressing fire first, and Player 1 should select Guile. When the match begins you should both be Guile.

Titus The Fox
From: Titus

Here's a set of level codes:

1) ON THE FOXY TRAIL – 2625
2) LOOKING FOR CLUES – 8455
3) ROAD WORKS AHEAD – 2974

SWIV
Pause the game and type 'NCC-1701'. That'll give your infinite lives. And if, after destroying a Goosecopter, you fire continuously at one of the tokens that appears, after 32 hits it'll turn into a star. Pick that up and you'll be equipped with the absolute ultimate in weaponry.

Essential game tips

And as Titus the Fox rides majestically into the sunset, we here the sound of distant level codes.

TREASURE ISLND DIZZY
Type 'EGGSONLEGGS' for invincibility, and 'ICANFLY' to allow Dizzy to – yes – fly.

4) GOING UNDERGROUND – 4916
5) FLAMING CATACOMBS – 1933
6) COMING TO TOWN – 0738
7) FOXY'S DEN – 2237
8) ON THE ROAD TO MARRAKESH – 5648
9) HOME OF THE PHARAOHS – no code
10) DESERT EXPERIENCE – 8612
11) WALLS OF SAND – 4187
12) A BEACON OF HOPE – 1350
13) A PIPE DREAM – no code
14) GOING HOME – 5052
15) JUST MARRIED – no code

Troddlers
From: Storm

As with Lemmings, the inspiration behind this game, there are an awful lot of level codes...

1 PREMIER **2** BUILDIT **3** NOSWEAT

Troddlers are trouble... unless you've got all the level codes, of course.

4 PYRAMID	5 CLEAROUT	6 SPHINX
7 QUARET	8 CENTRIN	9 REDGEMS
10 CROSSED	11 SKIPAROUND	12 PACKEDUP
13 PILLARS	14 BZZZZZ	15 FIVEROWS
16 TIGHTTIME	17 EASYONE	18 TWOTRIBES
19 DONTMIX	20 HELPEMOUT	21 MEANONES
22 NOPROBLEMS	23 TREASURES	24 STOREROOM
25 UPANDDOWN	26 TECHNO	27 ONEONONE
28 SIXROOMS	29 THETOWER	30 GOFORHEART
31 NEWTHING	32 BOULERO	33 CRUELWORLD
34 CRUELCUBES	35 SLIPNSLIDE	36 KEYX
37 GOLDCROSS	38 STONEM	39 HARDROUND
40 FIRSTGUNS	41 CROSSFIRE	42 RUNFORIT
43 NORULES	44 NOFARWALL	45 RUNAROUND
46 BADBIRD	47 COVERTHEM	48 SAVEBLOCKS
49 GLAMOUR	50 HACKBACK	51 ALOTTODO
52 UPSIDEOUT	53 DROPEMIN	54 POSSIBLE
55 CLOSEUP	56 FOOLSRUN	57 JEWELPUSH
58 GUIDETRY	59 WOTAWSGO	60 LOOSEM
61 YOURSOR	62 SACRIFICE	63 BOOMPARADE
64 WAITFORIT	65 ROCKBLAST	66 NOWASTEALL
67 FROMABOVE	68 SMASHHITS	69 CRUSHRUSH
70 FIRSTFIRE	71 BURNOUT	72 RUMBLEHOT

TOP TIP — VAXINE

To activate the cheat mode, type 'WILDEBEESTE' during play. F1 and F3 will then skip one and ten levels respectively, while F2 and F4 will do the opposite.

Essential game tips

XENON II

Pause the game and type in 'RUSSIAN AIR'. After unpausing, you'll be able to press N to skip from stage to stage.

73 COCKTAIL
76 SPINAROUND
79 BOUNCEIT
82 SLOWBURN
85 SOLOMAN
88 GOODLUCK
91 NOPULLPLUG
94 BRIDGEMIN
97 AUTOFIRE
100 TWEAKY

74 BUGGINHARD
77 LETITOUT
80 RAINDROPS
83 STALLEM
86 HELLSDITCH
89 TIMEHUNTER
92 GUNZONE
95 FALLOUT
98 SWEATHEART

75 MOREFUN
78 ALLABOUT
81 FIREANDICE
84 BADBOMBS
87 FIRSTFIRST
90 NODELAY
93 BELTZENRUN
96 COLOURUN
99 HEAVYDUTY

Wizkid
From: Ocean

Go to the shop with all five stars and over a hundred quid, and buy another star. You'll get an extra hundred pounds. You can achieve the same buy getting the balloon back to the shop and buying another star. This can be done as many times as you want.

Cute, isn't he? This is Wizkid, and you can help him accumulate loads of stars by cheating mercilessly.

There's cheats galore PLUS a secret game to be discovered in Zool.

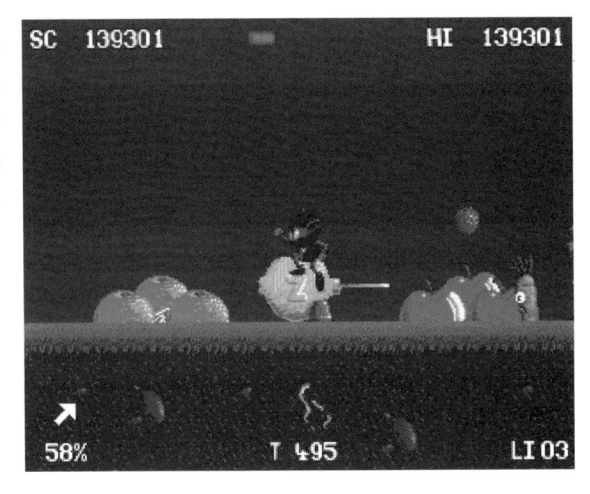

Zool
From: Gremlin Graphics

- Typing 'GOLDFISH' on the title screen accesses a cheat mode. You can then press F1 to F6 to skip from world to world. Additionally, press 1 to make yourself invincible, 2 to skip to the next level, 3 to jump to the same level in the next world, and 4 to, er, kill yourself.
- Value for money fans will be delighted to hear that there's a secret shoot-'em-up section on Level 2-1. To get to it, you'll need to get past the first two crumbling platforms with spikes underneath. Just after the second one, if you drop down to the floor next to the spikes you'll see a platform above your head and to the right a bit. Jump up into the corner underneath and all will be revealed.
- A common stumbling block is the piano on level 2-2. The sequence you'll need is Red, Yellow, Light Blue, Dark Blue.

Programming

Not content with the software that's out there? Need a program to do a specific job that no-one else has catered for? Or maybe you just want to tinker about with your computer? There are lots of reasons why people take up programming. But never mind 'why', Toby Simpson explains 'how'...

Programming

Computers are simple beasts. Their sole job in life is to do as they are told. They read a list of simple binary instructions and act on them, one after the other, until you switch the computer off. This list of instructions, consisting of simple operations such as add, or subtract, is called a program. Writing the list is called programming, and the simple binary instructions are "Machine Code".

In the beginning, programming was done on switches and buttons. You'd have to set up the switches to point to a part of your computer's memory, then set the switches for the instruction you'd want, and perhaps even have to press a button to make it happen. It would be even more complex to actually run your program, and if you made even the smallest error the likelyhood is that you'd have to start all over again

Programmers, in the search for an easy life, soon invented quicker and more efficient ways of getting this simple binary information into the computer. It was not long before you could key in your instructions on a small keypad, and view the results on teletype printers.

BINARY

Computer chips, at the most basic level, understand only two things: 'on' and 'off'. These are represented by the numbers 0 and 1. We use decimal notation for our counting system (i.e. 'base 10') – binary is 'base 2' (only two different digits, see?)

HEXA-DECIMAL

To make their lives easier, programmers now give computers instructions in 'hexadecimal' (mathematically, 'base 16'). This means programming is much more quick and easy. What's not so quick and easy is converting decimal numbers into binary or hexadecimal!

Take the number 43, say. Subtract 32 (the next highest number in the left column) then the next highest etc, adding the binary equivalents to get 101011!

DECIMAL NUMBER	BINARY EQUIVALENT
1	1
2	10
4	100
8	1000
16	10000
32	100000
64	1000000
128	10000000

Converting decimal to binary

Get the most out of your Amiga 1993

Programming

SOURCE CODE
Assembly language is the closest you can get to programming your computer directly. Even then, the code you write (source code) has to be translated into a form the computer can understand – object code (see below).

OBJECT CODE
Object code is code the computer can act on directly. However, it's almost impossible for a normal human to write! Hence the need for 'Assembly language', which is a kind of half-way house between human and computer understanding.

The techie basics

The real breakthrough arrived when they thought "Why type in all these long binary numbers?" Why indeed? A new number system, where four binary digits could be represented by one new digit was created. Hexadecimal made things much easier, the amount of information that would have to be inputted into the computer was quartered. This reduced the chances of error, and sped up the programming process.

This was soon taken a stage further. Computer programmers were still typing in long strings of numbers to make things happen. 'Assembly language', as it was called, was a neat solution to the problem. Why attempt to remember a number to mean 'add', when you might as well write "add" on the computer and get *it* to work out what you mean. And hence the first programming language was born. Programmers created programs called "Assemblers" which turned words like "add" into the binary instructions that the computer understood. This meant that if the program didn't work, it was possible to make small changes, add new bits, and simply "re-assemble" the program to run it again.

Assembly language is called a "Low Level Language". This is because it's a simple translation from the words that the programmer writes (The source code) to the program which the computer can run (The object code). One word in the source leads to one binary instruction.

Programming for mortals

Programmers are always convinced there is an easier way of doing something, and even if finding that easy way takes twice as long as actually doing it the harder way, they will do it!

Get the most out of your Amiga 1993

It was thinking along these lines that created the first higher level languages. High level languages are much easier for a human to understand and program, but bear little resemblance to machine code. In a high level language, one instruction typed may involve many machine code instructions to perform the action.

For example, a command to print your name on the screen may take a hundred machine code instructions, but only be one in a high level language, such as 'C' or BASIC. Programmers wrote vast, complex programs, such as compilers and interpreters, to convert high level languages into the machine code which a computer could understand.

Compilers converted the entire source code of a program to machine code in one go, and then the programmer could run his program and try it out, fixing bugs in the source code and re-compiling if necessary. This approach is good, because the object code generated is machine code and can be run on the computer without the compiler being present. Another advantage is that it is reasonably fast, depending on how good the compiler is at converting source code instructions into good combinations of low level machine code instructions.

Interpreters, on the other hand, run the program as they go along. Every instruction is simply converted and run on the spot. No separate object program is generated, so the source code cannot ever be run without the interpreter. Also, because the program is converted as it goes along, it is much slower that a compiled program.

Languages have evolved considerably since the first efforts in the late '50s and early '60s. As time has gone on, compiler technology

COMPILER

A compiler takes a program written in a high level language and 'compiles' it into machine code to make it run faster. It still won't run as fast as a program written in assembly language, though, but it's better than nothing.

INTER-PRETER

This is a program that, like a compiler, takes high level programs and converts them into machine code. Unlike a compiler, though, it converts them as it goes along – it's therefore much slower. (But still not as slow as running the high level program directly.)

> **MULTI-TASKING**
> Most computers can only carry out one set of instructions – or program – at a time. The Amiga can carry out a number simultaneously. Hence 'multitasking'.

> **C**
> A high level programming language (i.e. instructions that ordinary humans can understand) that is used extensively for professional programming. The advantage of learning C is that it's used widely on other computers too.

has improved, and languages have got better, easier to use and easier to understand.

The Amiga is a very advanced home computer, there is no other computer remotely near its price range that offers true multi-tasking. With a machine this complex, with all those goodies inside it, you'd expect programming it to be very hard. This is simply not true! These days, there is a programming language for everyone.

If you're seriously interested in programming your Amiga, there are some things you'll need, and some things you'll need to know. There are a number of books you'll need, and depending on the language you choose, you'll need to buy an interpreter or compiler too.

C – the professionals' language

C is a compiled high level language. It can be quite difficult to learn, but the experience is very rewarding in the end. Almost all of the programs built into your computer and supplied on the Workbench disks are written in 'C'.

'C' doesn't stand for anything, incidentally! In the early '70s there was a language called BCPL (The effects of which we're still feeling to this day. It was a bit of a pain, and AmigaDOS was first written in it. These days, AmigaDOS is in 'C'), which spawned a language simply called B. Then two chaps, Brian Kernighan and Dennis Ritchie came along and created C.

C compilers tend to be large programs requiring a lot of system resources (hardware, to you and me). As a general rule, unless you're very very patient, you should not take up C programming seriously unless you've got a hard disk and 2Mb of RAM.

SAS C 6.2 £299.00
From: HiSoft. Tel 0525 718181
Minimum requirements: 1Mb RAM (2Mb RAM, hard disk recommended)

This expensive package, is the best single buy if you're serious about programming in C. Firstly, its huge. The manuals are clear and easy to understand, and are supported by documentation on disk which works in a hypertext format. (You see a page, and certain key words are highlighted. Clicking on the highlighted words brings up further information. This way, armed only with small snippets of information you can quickly find out more detail on what you actually need to know.)

SAS C, incidentally, is what the people at Commodore use to write new Workbench versions and Kickstarts! The package comes with a compiler, lots of debugging tools, and a text editor together with other utilities to help make programming easier.

DICE C about £2.50
From: Public Domain
Minimum requirements: 1Mb RAM (2Mb RAM, hard disk recommended)

This is a shareware C compiler. It's written by Matt Dillon, and does the job fine. As it's not a commercial package, it's not officially supported – so if things go wrong with it, don't expect to get any help! Also, its documentation is not as good as SAS C, and it takes a lot longer to get it to work.

DEBUGGING

Unless you're a genius, any program you write will have mistakes, or 'bugs', in it which stop it working properly. Finding and removing these bugs is called 'debugging'. A good programming language will make this job a lot easier, by means of various handy little 'debugging tools'.

Get the most out of your Amiga 1993

Programming

BASIC

This stands for 'Beginners All-purpose Symbolic Instruction Code'. Anyone who's ever owned a computer will have come across it. It's a simple high level programming language that's easy to pick up and is available on all machines. However, BASIC programs are dead slow, so it's definitely an 'amateur' language.

Back to BASICs?

Everyone who's ever owned a computer will have used, or at least heard of BASIC. It's everyone's 'first' programming language, and there are versions available for every machine under the sun.

Unfortunately, although it's easy to understand and learn, the programs it produces are not terribly fast. In fact, compared to machine code programs, they're dead slow. It may also not be possible to use all of the machine's hardware potential.

AMOS £39.95
From: Europress Software. Tel 0625 859333
Minimum requirements: Any Amiga

AMOS is sold as an Amiga 'games creator', but it can produce 'serious' utilities too. It is like BASIC too use, but the results are much faster. With AMOS around, there's not much point buying a BASIC package for the Amiga.

PUBLIC DOMAIN

Many programmers write software for their own needs, then decide to 'donate' it to the world at large. This means anyone is welcome to copy and use it.

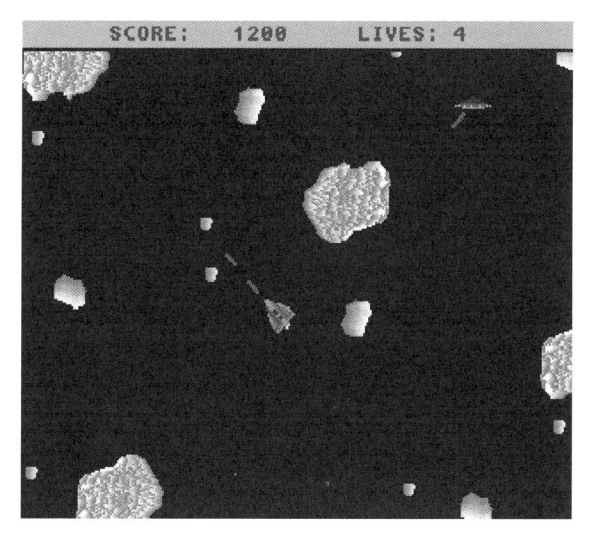

AMOS is based on BASIC, but has extra commands and features to take advantage of the Amiga's special capabilities. You can also get an AMOS compiler.

Get the most out of your Amiga 1993

AMOS is very easy to understand and well-documented language. It's also powerful. Its an interpreted language, although a compiler is available now to make the results even faster still. It's an excellent introduction to programming, although if you're thinking of writing large Workbench applications, such as a word processor for example, then consider 'C' instead.

AMOS is probably the Amiga's most popular programming language. It's also been given away on the cover of Amiga Format (January issue). And to find out how to get the best from it, look out for an Amiga Format AMOS book soon…

The dreaded Assembly language

Assembly language is the closest you can get to programming the microprocessor inside your Amiga itself. The commands you use are converted directly into machine code, and the resulting program is very fast and efficient. It's very much harder to understand and learn than the other languages, and unless you're thinking of writing computer games, you'd be much better off with a language such as C.

✔ DevPac 3 £69.95
From: HiSoft. Tel 0525 718181
Minimum requirements: Any Amiga

This is pretty much the best you can get. Its an excellent product, fully integrated. It comes with a powerful text editor to allow you to write your source code, a fast reliable assembler and some great debugging tools to help you to find out why your program didn't work when you ran it! The documentation is superb, and it comes with a handy little pocket-sized programming guide describing each of the instructions you can use. It is supplied with two versions, one for Workbench 1.3, and one for 2.0 and above.

SHAREWARE

Shareware is subtly different to public domain software. You can try it out free of charge but, if you like the program and want to carry on using it, you are meant to 'register' for a fee (still much lower than ordinary commercial software).

MACHINE CODE

Ugh. Nasty stuff. It produces the fastest-running and most efficient programmers, but it's almost impossible for humans to understand directly. That's why we need assemblers and high level languages as a kind of go-between.

Programming

KICKSTART

This is the Amiga's permanent internal memory. It holds all the instructions that tell the Amiga how to work. Without it, it would be an inert slab of plastic.

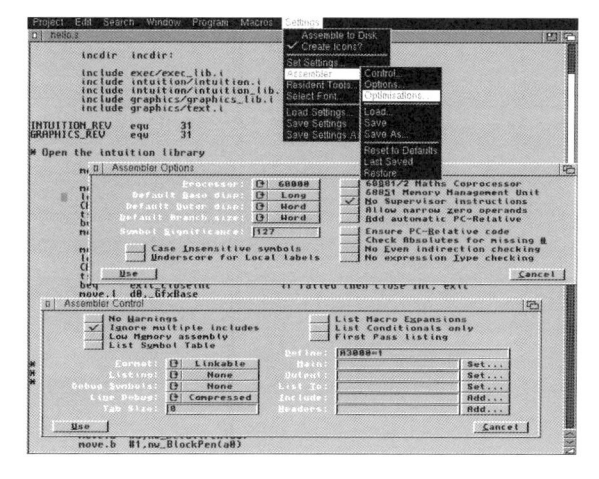

Devpac 3 is for serious programmers who fancy getting to grips with assembly language.

68000

The name (OK, number) of the Amiga's central processor. Learning how to program this chip will also help you program other computers that use the same chip (e.g. Atari ST, some Apple Macintosh models).

Time for some book-learning!

The best books you can get are the RKMs (Rom Kernel Manuals). These are official Commodore books which show you what everything does inside the Amiga's Kickstart. But they don't teach you how to program. For that, you'll need other books.

✓ C Programming Language £24.00
GOOD BUY **By:** Kernighan and Ritchie
From: Prentice Hall Software Series

This excellent book is written by the designers of C itself. An excellent C tutoria, but it may prove hard work initially.

✓ Amiga Assembly Language £24.95
GOOD BUY **From:** Bruce Smith Books

This book (best bought with the HiSoft DevPac Assembler) will teach you how to program in 68000 assembly language. It's comprehensive, easy to follow and packed with examples.

Get the most out of your Amiga 1993

Get the most out of your Amiga 1993

Public domain and shareware

Before you go out and spend hundreds of pounds on commercial applications, it's worth checking out what's available in the PD ('public domain') and shareware market – often you'll find that you can get exactly what you want for the price of a blank floppy disk. Too good to be true? Ian Wrigley explains how it works…

There is a wealth of PD and shareware software available on the Amiga – it's one of the reasons for the computer's popularity. Just about every kind of program you can imagine is available as PD or shareware – and many that you would never have dreamed of, too.

PD stands for 'public domain'. PD programs are programs which the author has made available to anyone who wants them. They are distributed on computer bulletin boards, via user groups and by PD houses – of which more later. If you have a PD program, you can copy it and give it to other people with no qualms. Indeed, doing this is actively encouraged, because that's how the software gets widely known.

Strictly speaking, much of what is described as PD software is more correctly called 'Freeware'. This is because if software is truly in the public domain, then the author has no control over it – anyone can alter it, pass it around with no documentation and even sell it as a commercial program. If an author releases his or her program as freeware, on the other hand, then what they are saying is: "You can copy and freely distribute this program, but I retain certain rights over it." Normally these are a basic copyright, and restrictions such as only allowing the software to be distributed as long as the documentation files are included.

FREELY DISTRIBUTABLE
PD and shareware programs are often lumped together under the title 'freely distributable software' – because that's exactly what they are. But the copyright may still reside with the author, and there may be conditions regarding the software's use.

Try before you buy

Shareware is similar to freeware, in that it can be passed around to anyone. However, there is a difference: shareware authors expect you to pay them if you find their programs useful. The idea is that you try a program out for a while – a week or two, say – and then decide whether you want to keep on using it. If so, you are expected to pay a 'registration fee' (or 'license fee') to the author.

Public domain and shareware

> **DON'T SEND STERLING**
>
> Many shareware authors are American or European. Don't send them normal cheques in Sterling unless they specifically state that they want this – it can often cost more than the value of the cheque to have it cased at a foreign bank. Send an International Money Order or similar.

> **KEEP THOSE DEMOS**
>
> Even when you've registered a shareware program, don't throw away the unregistered version – keep it so that you can pass it on to friends. Remember, passing on a registered copy of a program is software piracy.

This is normally in the range of £5 to £20, so it's far less than you'd pay for a glossily-packaged commercial program.

To encourage you to register, many shareware programs have Requesters which pop up every so often telling you that you're using an unregistered version – and some even have features disabled in the freely distributable version. When you register, you get a new version of the program which doesn't have these limitations, and often added goodies such as a printed manual or a version of the software with extra functionality.

Once you've received your registered version, you should treat it like a normal commercial program – don't copy it and pass it on to friends, since this is software piracy. You can only distribute the unregistered, trial version. Often the registered copy is personalised with your name – so if you pass it on to other people, it's easy to trace it back to you.

So why should you register? Well, even if the unregistered version isn't limited in any way, it's your duty to pay the license fee if you use it. Don't just say, "Oh well, other people will be paying so I won't bother." It's only registration money that encourages shareware authors to keep distributing software in this manner – if no-one registers, they may well give up. After all, it takes a lot of work to write a good program, and much shareware and PD software is just as good as that available commercially. In the past, disillusioned shareware authors have taken to selling their work commercially because of the lack of registrations – and the result is a program which costs you, the user, far more.

There is one category of software closely allied to shareware: licenseware. This is essentially shareware which only certain PD houses are entitled to sell. Licenseware normally costs somewhere between £3 and £10, and a portion of the selling price goes directly to the author – a rather surer way of getting financial reward than shareware. Unlike PD and shareware, you are not allowed to copy and give away licenseware programs – they must be purchased from authorised dealers.

Why do programmers do it?

An obvious question is why on earth people spend so much of their time writing programs which they then release as freeware, with no obvious gain to themselves?

There are a couple of answers to this, depending on the programmers themselves. Some people program for the sheer fun of it: the enjoyment of setting themselves a programming challenge and then beating it. Some do it for the fame. And for some people, writing PD programs is a good way of advertising themselves to any potential employers. A number of the documentation files that go with PD programs include a sentence along the lines of: "I graduate next July; if you need a programmer then, please get in touch with me." And often this can work: a number of people who started out programming demos (see later) have found themselves being employed by companies as games writers, because their skill at graphics, sound or whatever has been noticed.

Getting hold of PD and shareware

As mentioned above, there are a number of ways to get hold of PD and shareware. Downloading from bulletin boards is a good way if you own a modem (see the comms section in this book), since you can be fairly sure that you are getting the latest version of a piece of software. You can also chat to other users of the programs – so you'll be warned of any bugs or limitations in advance.

SHOW OFF YOUR WORK!
If you write a PD or shareware program, send it to as many PD houses as possible – that way it will be widely distributed. Also send it to magazines such as Amiga Shopper and Amiga Format, which regularly review freely-distributable software.

Public domain and shareware

BULLETIN BOARD
A central computer which others can link up to using modems. You can store ('upload') and retrieve ('download') files, leave messages and electronic mail for other users and take part in on-line discussions on a wide range of topics. See the comms section of this book for a fuller description.

Next come user groups – and, of course, just swapping software with friends. At many user group meetings, people swap their favourite PD and shareware, and resident software wizards are normally on hand to solve any problems you might have. To find out the location of your nearest user group, check your local library for any notices, or look in Amiga Shopper magazine, which prints a listing of user groups every month.

Finally, you can purchase disks of PD and shareware from companies known as 'PD houses'. Basically, these are organisations which exist solely to distribute software.

Strictly speaking, they shouldn't make a profit from the sale of this software – it is, after all, supposed to be freely distributable. What normally happens is that the company will, instead, add a charge per disk for duplication, materials, time, expertise, collation of the software and so on.

PD houses normally charge between about £1 and £3 per disk. Often the disks are jam-packed with software, but sometimes you can find that you've paid £3 or more for just a couple of small programs, with inadequate documentation. Our advice if you're going to buy software from a PD house is to check out a few, and then regularly purchase from the one you're most happy with. Later on we've printed a list of some of the larger companies, but you should also check the adverts in magazines like Amiga Format and Amiga Shopper.

An American called Fred Fish has devoted a great deal of time over the last few years to collecting as much freely-distributable Amiga software as he can find and sending it to PD houses and user groups all over the world in batches of disks commonly called Fish Disks. Although the disks aren't 'themed', they are well

Get the most out of your Amiga 1993

worth getting hold of – they always have the most up-to-date versions of software on them, and they're about the best way of getting hold of the latest PD releases. Many PD houses sell Fish disks, and often also sell disks containing a full catalogue of the contents – amazingly, there have been well over 800 Fish disks released so far.

So what's the best stuff?

The variety of PD and shareware available is so great that it's an almost impossible task to produce a definitive listing of the best available – especially since new programs are being released all the time.

So instead, we've listed some of our favourites in a variety of different categories. Remember, when you're looking for a program to do a specific job, that you should try to get the latest possible release; get hold of an up-to-date Fish disk catalogue and find the latest release through that, or write to the program's author if you suspect that you're not using the latest version.

Almost all software authors are happy to receive comments on their programs, and often you'll find that they'll reply with a wealth of additional information – and sometimes they'll even send you other projects that they're working on.

You will notice that we haven't given sources for the software that we review here. That's because all of the programs should be available from most PD houses (with the exception of licenseware).

And remember to pay your shareware fees!

CD-ROM SHAREWARE
If you have a CDTV or a CD-ROM drive connected to your Amiga, there are a couple of CD-ROMs available which contain large collections of PD and shareware. You'll find them at your local computer dealer.

Public domain and shareware

DEMO
A demo is a program which matches great graphics with – usually techno-style – music. They're written by programming 'crews', who often go on to work for games software companies.

Demos and games

We haven't reviewed any demos or games here. Why? Because things move so fast that whatever we look at now will be out of date by the time you actually read this!

For totally up-to-date information you should check out Amiga Format, which reviews the latest programs each month. Or look at the adverts in magazines like Format or Amiga Shopper. Suffice it to say that many demos put full-price commercial games to shame, animators like Eric Schwartz produce absolutely stunning work and many of the PD and shareware games you can get from libraries wouldn't look out of place on the shelves of your local software dealer.

Twilight Zone — Freeware
GOOD BUY **By:** Rainer Koppler

Screen blankers, or savers, were invented because people became concerned about the possibility of 'burn in' – that is, the danger that if you leave your computer displaying one image for a long

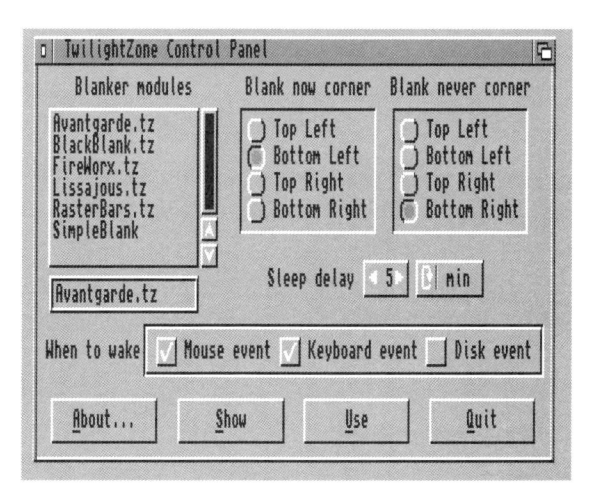

Could Twilight Zone stop the dreaded phosphor burn-in?

time, that image may become 'burned in' to the monitor's phosphors, and so show as a permanent ghost of the image.

The original screen saver programs simply turned the screen black after the computer was left untouched for more than a few minutes, but people soon started to write screen blankers that display pictures or messages on the screen. Twilight Zone is about the best screen saver available on the Amiga. It's modular, which means that you can choose from a range of different displays which will appear on the screen when your Amiga is left alone, and it is very configurable.

The author has obviously used the Macintosh computer, because Twilight Zone is very similar in many respects to Mac screensavers such as After Dark and Pyro. Control of the program is via a Control Panel, from where you set how long the program should wait before it blanks the screen, which module to use, and what user actions will restore the screen to normal. You can also define 'blank now' and 'blank never' corners of the screen. Move your cursor to the former and the screen saver will start work immediately, move it to the latter and Twilight Zone won't blank the screen however long you leave it for.

The beauty of a modular screen saver is that other people can write programs which display patterns or whatever, and don't have to do the donkey-work of actually deciding when they should go into action – this is all done in the main body of the program.

Twilight Zone comes with instructions for writing your own module (assuming that you can program in Assembly language, of course), and a number of people have already written add-in modules. It's an excellent screen saver – certainly the best available for the Amiga at the moment.

COMPRESSION
If you're sending files to someone who doesn't have an Amiga, don't use a compression program. Most aren't compatible across platforms, and even those that are will give you more trouble than they're worth.

LhA — Shareware ($20)
By: Stefan Boberg

(Good Buy)

Everyone will need a file compression program at some time, and LhA is about the fastest (and best) around.

Compression utilities 'shrink' files, creating an 'archive' that's often several times smaller than the original. This can be useful in a variety of situations: for instance, putting a large program or database on to a floppy disk as a backup, or uploading a file to a bulletin board, where the smaller the file size, the less time is taken to upload, and so the smaller your phone bill.

There are two considerations when looking at compression software: speed, and final archive size. Both are important: you don't want to wait hours while your file decompresses, but similarly there's no point having a fast compressor if the archive is only a couple of K smaller than the original file.

Of the several compression programs around (such as LhArc, LhA, LZ and Zoo), LhA is by far the best. It's extremely fast, produces small archives and can even decompress archives created with three other archiving programs – LhArc, LhArcA and LZ. If you send in your shareware registration fee, the program's author, Stefan Boberg, will send you an improved version which allows you to create archives split across several volumes – so if you've an archive which won't fit on one floppy, you can split it across two or three.

The program comes with copious documentation, and a wealth of options – although most people will just use the basic compression and decompression commands. It's a Shell-based utility (no pretty

Intuition display, sadly) but the manual is fairly easy to follow, and you should have no problems getting to grips with it.

If you need a file compression utility (and everyone does from time to time), LhA is the one to go for. It's fast, produces small archives and even copes with files produced by its rivals.

VirusZ — Shareware (DM10)
By: Georg Hörmann

GOOD BUY

Viruses are a fact of computer life: for some reason, there are plenty of idiots out there who think that it's clever to write a program that trashes your hard disk. Fortunately, there are some people, such as Georg Hörmann, who don't agree.

Georg has written an anti-virus program called VirusZ which should go a large way to keeping your Amiga healthy. The program recognises hundreds of bootblock and file viruses; it sits in the background and scans the bootblock of any new disk that you insert, checking to see that it's virus-free.

It will also periodically scan your Amiga's memory to make sure that no memory-resident virus is lurking.

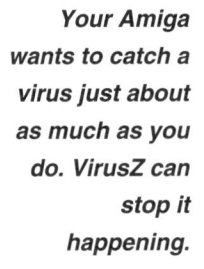

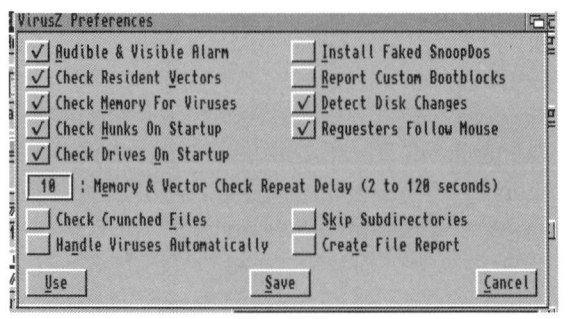

BOOT BLOCK

The bootblock of a floppy disk is an area which contains instructions that help the computer to 'boot up' (start). Unfortunately, it is also a good place to put a virus.

Your Amiga wants to catch a virus just about as much as you do. VirusZ can stop it happening.

It's very important that you have a virus-checking program on your Amiga: otherwise you're running the risk of losing all your files at a stroke. Don't think that it won't happen to you – that's a recipe for disaster. It's equally important to realise that new Amiga viruses are being created all the time, so don't trust to an old detection program. You should update to the latest version as soon as you can, and make sure that you've constantly got the newest release.

There are plenty of prophylactic programs around, but VirusZ is one of the best. It works unobtrusively in the background, and you'll only notice that it's running if you should happen to insert an infected disk.

Every user should have an anti-virus program. VirusZ is one of the best, and is constantly being updated to take account of new viruses. Get it now!

Arestaure   Freeware
By: Jean-Yves Proux

If you've ever emptied the Trash or issued the Delete command from the Shell, only to immediately realise that you've thrown away the wrong file, help is at hand in the shape of Arestaure. This program will attempt to recover any recently-deleted files on Fast Filing System (FFS) and Old Filing System (OFS) disks – that is, just about any Amiga disk, floppy or hard.

The program has a simple user interface, with messages displayed in any one of French, German or English. You simply click on the button corresponding to the drive you want to search, and the program goes off and finds as many recently deleted files as it can.

You thought that file was lost and gone for ever? Arestaure may be able to get it back.

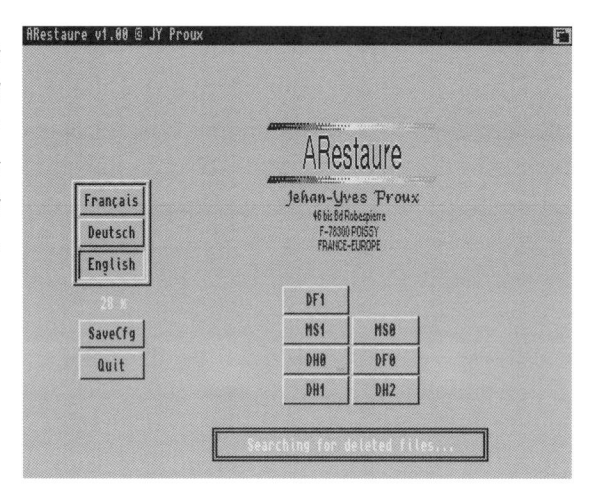

You are presented with a list of their names, and clicking on them restores them to whatever drive you've defined as T: in your Startup-sequence (normally the RAM disk).

The program doesn't claim to work miracles – it's very unlikely that files deleted weeks ago will be found. But if you run it within a day or two of deleting a file, there's a fair chance that you will be able to recover it.

Arestaure does a good job of finding deleted files, although it can be rather slow – especially if you run it on a large hard disk with a lot of files. It's still an invaluable program to have in your collection, though.

SID Shareware ($25)
By: Timm Martin

SID is the de facto standard hard disk navigation program. It comes in three versions: Personal, for those without much RAM; Trial, which is the version distributed by PD houses and bulletin

Public domain and shareware

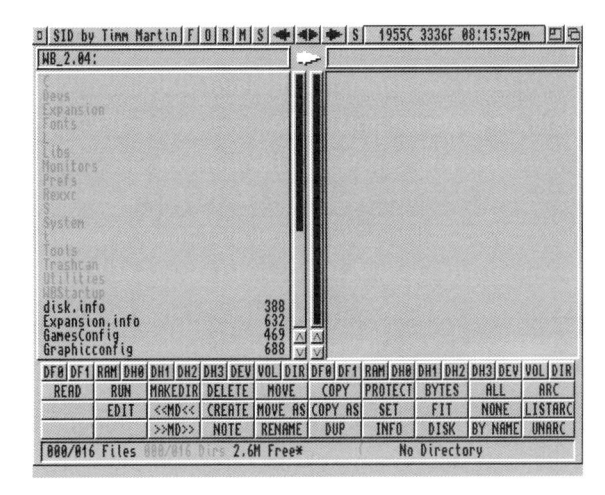

Having trouble navigating round your hard disk? SID is the answer!

boards; and Professional, the registered version customised with your name, which allows you to save your Preferences settings and so customise the program to your own requirements.

Disk navigation programs abound (we look at another one below), but from its earliest days SID has had a large band of devout followers. It was one of the first utilities of its kind to offer the sort of power that people wanted, and it's still going strong.

The basic appearance can be a little daunting at first, but you'll soon get the hang of the various buttons and options available. There are two main windows, each of which can display the contents of a different directory; from these you can select files to move, copy, rename, delete or whatever. The program also has built-in links to programs such as Arc and More, so you can decompress archives and view text and graphics files without leaving the program.

You can customise the Trial version of the program by altering the Preferences settings, but it's only after you have registered that you will receive a version which allows you to save these settings – and with a program this fully-featured and complex, that's vital.

SID 2.0 is still widely respected as a disk navigation tool, but there are many pretenders to the throne, and this program may well be just too complex for the novice.

FileMinder   Shareware ($10)
By: Joel Swank

Anyone who's used XTREE on the PC will soon feel at home with FileMinder, another disk navigation program. Compared to SID, this program is a dream to use – after a few minutes the sophistication and simplicity of FileMinder is bound to win you over.

The main display takes the form of a tree diagram showing the directory layout of any specified disk, while underneath the contents of any highlighted drawer are displayed. Files can be 'tagged' for mass copying, deleting, moving or whatever, and

Fileminder's another disk navigation program. It's not as sophisticated as SID, but it's wonderfully simple to use.

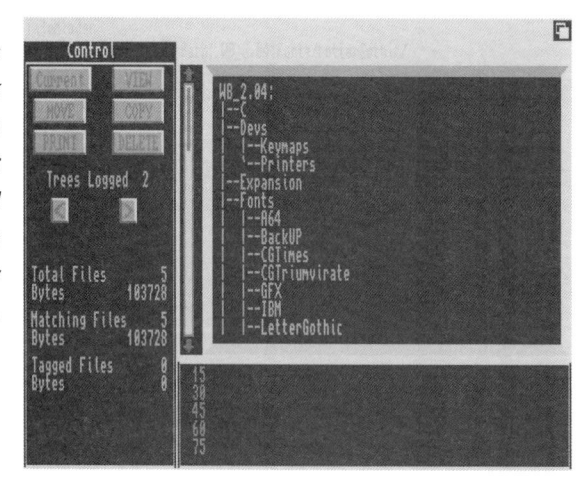

Get the most out of your Amiga 1993

Public domain and shareware

things like directory creation are simple. The program is fully customisable, and there's even a built-in Find File utility.

It's true that FileMinder doesn't have all the bells and whistles of SID, but for many people – beginners or power users – this is the utility of choice. Highly recommended.

FileMinder is powerful, easier to get to grips with than SID and does everything that you want from a disk navigation program.

Text Plus — Shareware (£8)
By: Martin Steppler

GOOD BUY

Text Plus is a shareware word processor which rivals many commercial packages. It's a measure of the thought and work that's gone into this program that almost any feature you can think of has been implemented: for instance, not only can you perform the normal block operations like copy and move, but you can also print and save just the specified block. Tab stops can be selected and moved just by clicking in the ruler. Date and time can be auto-

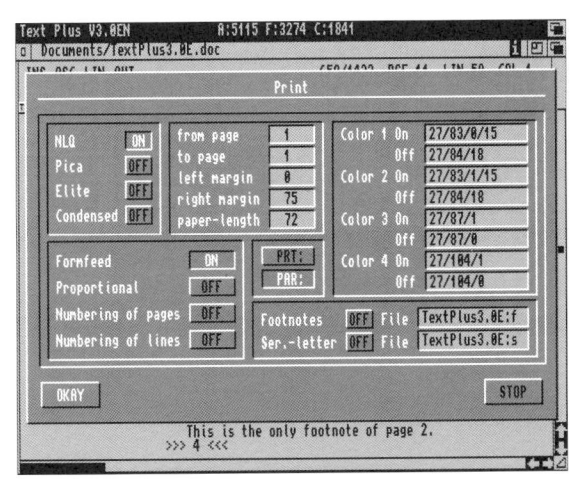

Should you really buy a commercial word processor before checking out Text Plus? Not if you've got any sense...

Get the most out of your Amiga 1993

inserted into the document from a menu option. Mail merging is supported. And on and on.

Text Plus really is one of those programs that demonstrates just how impressive PD and shareware can be. The only criticism (and it isn't really a criticism at all) is that until you register the program, a Requester appears every few minutes telling you that you're using a shareware program. Annoying? Yes. But a good incentive to get you to send off the £8 fee.

If you need a word processor, check out Text Plus before you buy a commercial package. The chances are that you'll find this great piece of shareware does everything that you want at a fraction of the cost.

Where to get PD and shareware

We haven't quoted suppliers for the programs above, simply because there are lots! There are many PD and shareware libraries around and they all stock dozens (often a lot more) of favourite Amiga software. Here are a few libraries to start with:

Amiganuts United
169 Dale Valley Road, Hollybrook, Southampton

AMOS PD
1 Penmynydd Road, Penlan, Swansea SA5 7EH

Anglia PD
115 Ranelagh Road, Felixtowe, Suffolk, IP11 7HU. Tel 0394 283494

Deja Vu
7 Hollinbrook, Beech Hill, Wigan WN6 7SG. Tel 0942 495261

George Thompson Services
Cucumber Hall Farm, Cucumber Lane, Essendon, Herts AL9 6JB. Tel 0707 664654

NBS
1 Chain Lane, Newport, Isle of Wight PO30 5QA. Tel 0983 529594

PD Soft
1 Bryant Ave, Southend-on-Sea, Essex SS1 2YD. Tel 0702 466933

17 Bit Software
PO Box 97, Wakefield, West Yorks WF1 1XX. Tel 0924 366982

Software Expressions
Unit 4, 44 Beauley Road, Southville, Bristol BS3 1PY. Tel 0272 639593

Upgrading your Amiga

Sometimes the Amiga you bought isn't the one you ultimately want. Sometimes the more you explore the potential of your Amiga, the more hardware power you need. Extra floppy drives let your Amiga handle more data, more RAM lets it handle bigger jobs and an accelerator lets it do them quicker! Mark Smiddy shows you how to upgrade your Amiga…

Define an upgrade. Literally the word means to augment or enhance: but enhance what? Upgrading is a (often expensive) process whereby we improve the performance or usability of a micro by adding bits to it or changing elements of the design. Strictly speaking therefore, software utilities are upgrades too, but the type of upgrades the expression is usually applied to are hardware only.

You need more RAM!

RAM is the most precious commodity in any computer system, and the Amiga needs generous amounts of memory to gain full advantage of the machine's multi-tasking operating system.

Most Amigas come with at least 1-2Mb RAM (some older models with as little as 128K). The available memory is divided electronically into two sections known as CHIP and FAST. CHIP memory, depending on model, is allocated from the first 512K to 2Mb of RAM; FAST is taken from any memory above the CHIP boundary. The actual difference between CHIP and FAST RAM is quite complex and few users need worry about the particulars: they're regularly argued and explained in the technical Amiga press.

Extra RAM is a commodity you will need at some point – it is impossible to have too much. How much you should have is difficult to quantify, so here are a few guidelines based on the total you've got fitted now.

- 512K — (or less) upgrade now to at least 1Mb.
- 1Mb — consider upgrading to 2Mb at your earliest convenience.
- 2Mb — extra RAM (say another 1Mb) would be handy.

RAM
Stands for Random Access Memory – it's what your Amiga 'thinks with' as it goes along. The more it's got, the better.

MULTI-TASKING
The Amiga's ability to run more than one program at once.

Upgrading your Amiga

These guidelines assume you are using the machine for simple tasks such as playing games, simple Workbench tasks and (basic) serious applications such as simple music and art packages. If you intend using the machine for the more powerful (RAM hungry) applications such as desktop publishing, 3D rendering and advanced business use the recommended minimum limit should be doubled and preferably tripled – especially if you have a hard disk fitted.

The actual process of upgrading the machine varies considerably, depending on which model you have. Base machines have a slot located on the underside of the machine which can accept 512K-1Mb and this is usually the cheapest upgrade path – somewhat cheaper than the PCMCIA slot found on the later base models (A600 and A1200). This slot is also utilised by the KCS Power PC board – a remarkable design which allows the Amiga to run IBM PC compatible software. A500 machines have an expansion port located at the left of the keyboard often used for combined RAM/hard disk expansion units – a pricey but cost-effective solution.

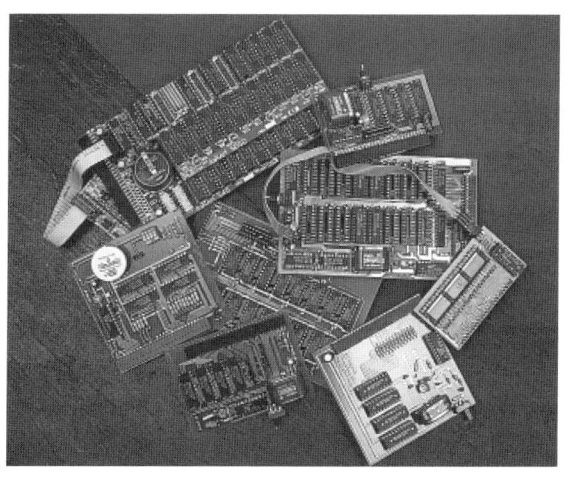

Whatever Amiga model you own, the chances are it could benefit from a RAM upgrade.

Two drives are better than one

RAM is an expensive commodity. Consider that 1Mb RAM costs £50 – the same amount of permanent (floppy disk) storage costs under one fiftieth of that! Moreover, Amigas are much simpler to use when more than one disk drive is fitted (you'll never find an experienced Amiga user with a single-drive machine). The single drive supplied is just enough to get the system going for serious use, although it is sufficient to play most games.

A second disk drive must be regarded as essential if you do anything else but play games. Some owners fit two or even three extra drives to the machine – although this is an unnecessary expense unless you use floppy disks to back up a hard disk. A third floppy drive may be useful if you regularly use a large business, DTP or programming application. In this case the third drive can be used for Workbench and the other two for program and data disks. The Amiga will automatically find the information it requires from the appropriate disks.

Generally speaking, though, the extra cost of a hard disk over extra floppy drives is outweighed by the extra convenience and storage

An extra floppy disk drive makes a huge difference to your Amiga's usefulness for 'serious' applications.

space. For the full story on hard disks, see the next chapter. But assuming you're interested in the floppy route, read on...

Choosing a floppy disk is very much a matter of personal preference. At the time of writing the market is flooded with a vast number of drives, all offering the same performance with a good variation in price. Some of the older designs are not suitable for use with the later Amigas because of power supply requirements. Check with your supplier.

Choosing the best floppy drive

During its life an external floppy drive will get a lot of abuse, no matter how careful you are with it. For this reason it is a good idea to choose a drive with a metal case over the more common (and often better-looking) plastic moulded ones. Plastic cases are more prone to attack from heat (cigarette burns) and dyes (ink or cellulose paint) than their metal counterparts. However, minor scratches are easier to remove using a proprietary cutting compound, albeit a last resort. Metal cases tend to be heavier, too, making them less likely to accidentally slip off a worktop.

If budget allows, a couple of manufacturers offer "double-decker" drives with their own power supply. This avoids the problem of connecting two external drives to base machines and possibly overloading the power supply "brick". Although some suppliers claim the low power drain from modern drives is sufficient to avoid this problem, such claims must be treated with scepticism. Certainly, misuse like this will invalidate the warranty in case of failure.

Standard Amiga drives have an unformatted capacity of 1Mb, reducing to 880K once the disk has been made usable. The extra 120K is used by the hardware for necessary timing information and not merely wasted. Recent developments have seen the introduction into everyday use of 2Mb unformatted drives. These have been slow to reach the Amiga but at least two developers are known to have succeeded in using this hardware with the machine and more will probably follow. The drives will work on any Amiga and give a usable 1.76Mb of storage.

> **STARTUP SEQUENCE**
> *A user-definable AmigaDOS program which is used to activate Workbench.*

How to stop your drive "clicking"

Before making any final decision, there are a couple of further points which you should think about. Amiga drives "click" incessantly while they are waiting for a disk. This is caused by the operating system continually "polling" the drives while it waits for a disk to be inserted.

The fault is not with the Amiga, but the way in which the disk drives operate. Nevertheless, drive click is a nuisance and can be cured in two ways. You can either add software patch called "NClick" to the startup-sequence or use a more permanent solution by getting a drive with hardware to cure the problem. Several manufacturers offer drives with this gadget and it should be available at no extra cost.

Another useful addition, fitted to many drives in recent years, is the disable switch. This allows you to permanently 'remove' the drive without physically unplugging it. Although this is less useful for owners of late machines it is generally considered worthwhile.

Something that cannot be adequately performed by software though, is the ability to protect track zero from the more common, and virulent strains of computer bootblock viruses. Such protection is built into a few of the high-performance floppies and although not infallible, goes some way to combat the menace of rogue programmers.

Get the most out of your Amiga 1993

THROUGH-PORT

If you have a disk drive with a throughport, you can plug another peripheral in the back of it.

Last, and by no means least, check out the length of the connection lead and the availability/compatibility of a throughport. Lead length might raise some eyebrows but if the lead is too short it might restrict choice when positioning the drive. Similarly, too long a lead may defeat the drive's throughport mechanism — this allows you to "chain" two or more drives in parallel.

Do you need an accelerator?

Before finishing off, a word about the stuff of legend; or at least the stuff of dreams: accelerators. While men dream of fast cars and faster women – computer users appreciate the finer things in life, like faster processors. Even the latest Amiga 1200 models are only based around a 14MHz 68020, and while this offers a great increase over previous models, it still finds the machine trailing a little in some (albeit biased) benchmarks.

BENCHMARK

A test to discover how fast a computer can perform a specified action or job (usually meaningless in the real world).

'Acceleration' is a process whereby a more powerful processor and faster RAM is shoehorned into existing hardware to make it run more rapidly than it did before. The sort of speed improvements we're talking about are the sort of things that, if applied to a Formula One car, could propel Ayrton Senna into the next race, never mind pole position. Hardware developers generally refer to these things as "Turbos".

If you're planning on fitting an accelerator, you need to follow several rules.

- Does it have 32-bit RAM or the option to support it? This is essential if you are accelerating beyond the menial 68010. Besides, such processors are behind the times and hardly worth the bother.

- Does it have hardware 68000 fallback mode? Even if you just play the odd, very occasional, once-in-a-blue-moon game, it probably won't work properly, if at all – bear that in mind.

- Is the speed higher than 14Mhz? If not, don't even bother. A standard 68000 or 68010 could run at 100Mhz and you still wouldn't see a great improvement in performance.

- Does it have an FPU? The floating point co-processor (68881 or 68882) does IEEE maths many times faster than any software ever could and more accurately too. This is going to be great if you use something that supports it – like VistaPro or Professional Calc; and as useful as a chocolate fireguard if it doesn't (and not even as tasty, either).

- Does it fit your machine? Sounds daft, but maybe you've already fitted too many extras to the machine and there isn't enough room left inside the case. This applies to "three-box" models just as much as it does to base machines.

- Do you need one? We're talking big bucks here! Spondoolicks; brass; dosh; loadsa money. An accelerator is going to set you back an arm and possibly a large part of your lower anatomical regions too. So think: will it really benefit your use of the computer? An accelerator is a nice gadget to have, but most people would be better off investing the money in a bigger, better machine or some more substantial hardware like a hard disk.

If you decide your Amiga really is underpowered, never fear! It's a highly expandable machine, and the above guide should give you an idea where to go next.

> **FPU**
> Stands for Floating Point Unit. It's a gadget that speeds up certain sorts of programs, thanks to the way they carry out complex mathemical calculations.

Get the most out of your Amiga 1993

Choosing and using a hard disk

What's the difference between a floppy disk and a hard disk? At least 19Mb, basically! As the Amiga and its software grow steadily more sophisticated, so the need for more and more storage space grows. A simple disk drive and a collection of floppy disks is no longer enough for serious Amiga users. For DeskTop Publishing, graphics work, business… for a whole host of Amiga activities, you need the bulk storage and rapid access time of a hard disk. Mark Smiddy is the man with the explanations…

In days gone by, the hard disk was considered a true luxury item, almost to the point of folly, and a preserve of the rich enthusiast. The development and widespread use of more powerful processors brought with it the need for increasingly larger mass-storage units. Demand creates production; production – development; development – lower costs; lower prices create more demand and so the cycle repeats.

A hard disk is no longer a luxury item and must be considered essential for any non-leisure computing use. Coupled up to a hard disk, the Amiga becomes a new machine – the relationship between the two is symbiotic.

The Anatomy of a Hard Disk

At grass roots, hard disks are similar to the floppy disks you use daily. Remove the shell (casing) from an old 3.5-inch floppy and you'll see a disk of Mylar film coated in a fine film of magnetic material. The disks (or platters) inside a hard drive are the same but made from a more rigid material such as ceramic or a non-ferrous metal like aluminium. Such materials are carefully chosen to avoid interfering with the magnetic dust.

There's now a wide range of plug-in hard drives to choose from. Prices are coming down too, making them attractive (and equally compact) alternatives to floppy drives.

Choosing and using a hard disk

CRASH

Any catastrophic failure, either of hardware or software. Usually, it's your program that crashes, but if it''s your hardware you'd better reach for (a) the aspirin bottle, (b) the cheque book.

The major difference between hard disk and floppy disks is the former is a complete, vacuum enclosed unit. Several platters are fixed to the same axle and a moveable carriage carries a set of heads over the surfaces.

In use, the discs revolve at great speeds – over 100mph at the circumference. It takes several seconds for the motors to accelerate the discs to this speed – the spin-up time – so they run constantly. Accordingly, if the platters were flexible the read/write heads could impact the surface with catastrophic results. (The sound of a head "crash" is quite unlike any other.)

A crash is much more likely when the disks are spinning (modern hard disks can withstand several "g's" worth of impact when switched off). For this reason they should never be moved when the disks are still revolving. Even a frustrated fist hammered on the table can totally wreck a drive.

Which is the best for you?

Choosing a hard drive can be a difficult decision – since there are a lot to select from: but never forget they cost a lot of money and you'll have to live with them for a long time. Hard drives come as external and internal fittings, depending on which Amiga you have – all the modern Amigas (A600, A1200, A4000) have an internal IDE drive, while older and larger models also have the option for a SCSI unit. There is little difference between the two, although IDE is typically cheaper and SCSI is more versatile and expandable for the rich enthusiast.

IDE

Stands for Integrated Drive Electronics. Amiga IDE drives are compact and designed for internal fitting.

One thing dominates the buying decision: size. No matter what you do, a hard disk's capacity is fixed. Clever compression techniques can cram more into available space – but the space is finite. Workbench needs at least 3Mb for comfort – more (say

Get the most out of your Amiga 1993

6Mb) if you use a lot of fonts. Subtract this value from the size of your hard disk and this gives an approximate 'available' size.

Using this rule, a 20Mb drive will have about 14Mb free – enough for three or four applications and maybe a game or two. That said, there is a temptation to leave a lot of redundant information on the drive and fill it up. Therefore, reckon up how much storage you think you'll need then double it and get the nearest capacity within your budget. Never buy less than 40Mb, though.

Speed should be a secondary consideration – although it's often quoted as the most important. The figures you'll see mooted are in thousandths of a second – and bigger drives tend to be faster because of the way they work (there is insufficient room to explain why here). Very fast drives are really only useful for massive databases which require a lot of searching, and therefore, a lot of heavy disk access.

The difference a few milliseconds makes here and there for merely loading applications and saving data does not warrant the extra

SCSI
Stands for Small Computer Systems Interface. It's an industry-standard connection and leads to much greater interchangeability between peripherals.

IDE drives fit inside the latest generation of Amigas, leaving you with a neat, 'invisible' upgrade.

HEAD PARKING
Moving the hard disk heads away from their working position, where they could damage the surface of the disk platters and thus destroy data. These days heads are usually parked automatically when not in use, so don't worry about it.

cost. This money would be better invested in some back-up software.

Living with a hard drive

If you get a hard drive fitted or buy a complete unit, most suppliers will set it up for you ready to go. Partitioning – the action of dividing up one hard drive into two or more distinct parts is best left to experienced users. Every partition uses valuable memory and, although useful, they are rarely necessary.

Modern hard drives are exceptionally reliable but that doesn't mean they will never fail. Most systems automatically "park" the heads when the drive is switched off, thus reducing possibility of a breakdown even further. (If a parking utility is supplied, use it immediately before switching off.) However, software and hardware faults can contribute to failure just as much as Sod's Law. The failure rate is difficult to quantify, but most users will suffer some data loss at least once every year.

The vast majority of errors are "soft" (in the magnetic material) and can be recovered by formatting the drive just as you would

SCSI drives plug in externally, via the Amiga's SCSI port.

format a floppy disk. More rarely, portions of the drive have to mapped out permanently – but this requires expert assistance and drive-dependent software. In either case, data will have to be restored from a backup set – usually floppy disks. Backups are time-consuming and a thoroughly hateful job – but you'll thank yourself when the crunch comes and the drive comes to a grinding halt.

Good software and the machine's multi-tasking nature will at least allow you to tinker quietly while the backup takes place. Most backup systems also allow you to only backup or restore specified items – and given the number of disks involved it makes sense to only copy your own work; applications can be installed from their master disks.

If you don't already have a hard drive (and some Amigas already come fitted with them), think very seriously indeed about getting one. They don't cost the earth, but do they make the sky the limit. (Groan)

BACK-UPS

The data you store on your hard drive may be irreplaceable. If so, you'd be well advised to 'back-up' its contents on to floppy disks regularly. It's a pain, but not as much of a pain as losing your entire and only just completed novel, or your entire year's business accounts...

Choosing a printer

If you're a writer or into DeskTop Publishing, you're not going to get far without a printer. Programmers, artists and business folk also need hard copies from time to time. But printers aren't always cheap, and they aren't always easy to set up. Just as well, then, that Mark Smiddy has trodden that path many, many times…

Choosing a printer

When computers first came into being, there were no monitors – only printers! And when monitors came along, this gave us the name VDU – visual display unit. Until then, every interaction between the terminal operator and the computer was echoed on a printer. Technology, by today's standards was crude, and these days a 'terminal printer' is a museum piece. Printers have been replaced by high-resolution monitors capable of representing text and graphics in a multitude of colours. The humble printer is a thing of the past.

However, the pundit's prediction of a paper-less office run entirely by computer has not arrived. Although computers do indeed do most of the work they still produce nothing as tangible as a piece of paper. You can hold it in your hand, feel the texture, judge its physical dimensions in finite space and so on: everything you can't do with a monitor (ever tried carrying one up a flight of stairs? – ed). Moreover, there's nothing quite as instantly portable as paper. The dream of a paper-less office has been transformed into an environmental nightmare: modern computers are efficient enough to gobble acres of rain forest faster than some people could say laser printer.

TERMINAL PRINTER
Back in the dark ages of computing, there was no such thing as a monitor. As you sat and typed away at your computer 'terminal', the results were printed out on a 'terminal printer'.

Dot-matrix printers work by 'firing' pins through an inked ribbon on to the paper. Each letter is made up of a series of 'dots' produced by these pins.

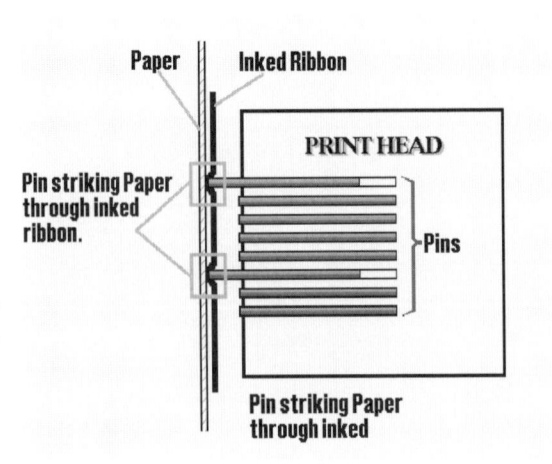

Choosing a printer

LASER PRINTER
A laser beam applies a charge to a roller, which then attracts toner particles. Expensive technology, but excellent results.

Printers are therefore often desireable, but also expensive items – so before proceeding any further, ask yourself: do I really, really need one? Before you part with your cash, read the reviews and consult an independent expert who isn't trying to sell you something.

Every printer has its pros and cons and in general you get exactly what you pay for in terms of price and performance. A good general purpose printer is going to cost in excess of £150. If that makes you flinch consider that less than ten years ago, the same performance would cost over £400 in unconverted currency or something in the region of £600-800 taking account of inflation! That sort of cash today will buy you a budget laser printer or a snazzy colour ink jet.

Be practical!

What do you (and the family) use your machine for? If everyone treats it as nothing more than a versatile games console then a printer is a waste of time and money and you can stop reading now. If, on the other hand, you use the machine for just about any

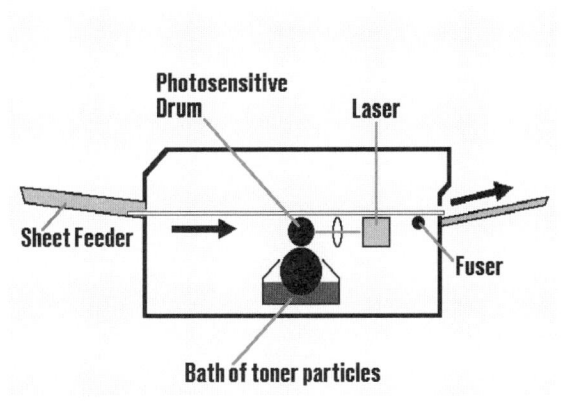

Laser printers work by attracting toner particles to an electrostatically-charged drum, which then 'rolls' the image out on to a moving sheet of paper.

Get the most out of your Amiga 1993

other application, then a printer could be a useful and productive addition.

The most obvious use is for word processing – after all what use is the ability to create a letter without having the ability to print it? Propeller-head enthusiasts could point out the "Cuckoo" principal – using the machine to generate the text then borrowing someone else's printer, possibly via a remote link over a telephone. This is not as daft as it sounds: many journalists do exactly that – their copy never gets onto paper until it physically reaches you in the form of a magazine, or this book for instance.

A more sober and practical approach is to figure out what you are going to want from your printer – because unless your budget is unlimited, some compromise will almost certainly be necessary.

Printers can be divided into many categories, but the most common are dot-matrix graphic types. These come in many forms, from simple impact to high quality laser diode types. The price you pay will determine how good the final output is and what other facilities are on offer. If your penchant is for pure word processing

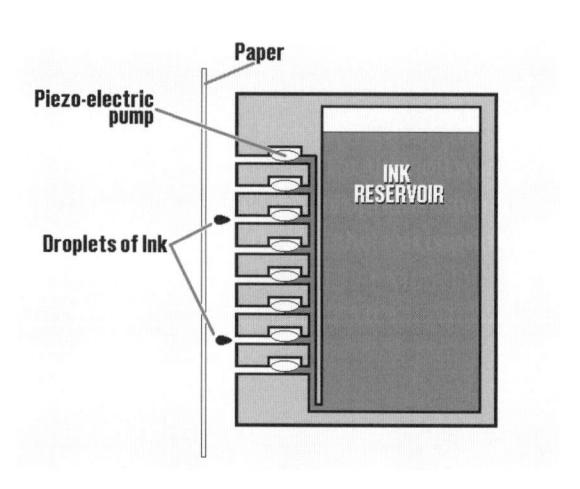

INKJET PRINTER

Ink is 'squirted' at the paper rather than being applied via an inked ribbon. More expensive than a dot-matrix printer, but better results.

One step up from dot-matrix printers, inkjet models spray the paper with tiny dotsof ink, rather than 'stamping' it. A good inkject printer can rival a laser printer for quality.

Get the most out of your Amiga 1993

Choosing a printer

GRAPHIC PRINTER
The best dot-matrix printers accept a 'graphical' input from the computer rather than coded instructions to print a specific character. The bottom line is much greater flexibility, including the ability to print a range of different typefaces and sizes, plus graphical images too.

only, and budget is limited, the other main group, letter-impact printers are the only choice. These machines are less common, incredibly noisy and often are better purchased as custom electric typewriters. That said, there is nothing stopping you connecting both a graphic printer and an electric typewriter to the same machine.

Plain graphic printers

General purpose graphic printers are often the best choice for the beginner or enthusiast since they are by far the most versatile. Manufacturers realised this a long time ago and such machines are available to suit almost any wallet. They are readily available from most stockists and the potential buyer is spoilt for choice.

Six manufacturers dominate today's market, these are (in no particular order): Star, Citizen, Epson, Canon, Hewlet-Packard (HP) and Oki. The latter three specialise in more up-market ink-jet and laser printers whereas the others produce a wider range to suit all tastes.

Now's the time to decide what you want from the machine. Colour capability is something a lot of beginners think they want until

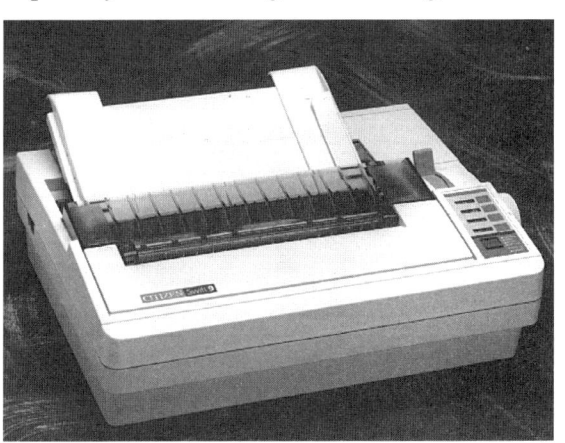

For simple word processing, a 9-pin dot-matrix printer like the Citizen Swift 9 may be all you need.

Get the most out of your Amiga 1993

they get the printer running and find the colour rendition is less of a practicality and more of a gimmick. Consider that the most expensive machines on the market (£10,000+) are geared to producing black and white output ONLY and you'll start to get the picture.

Think back to those salad days in the classroom where the art teacher wore a beard, sandals and a tie-dyed smock. Remember how you produced green from a mix of blue and yellow pigments? Add more blue to get a darker green and more yellow to get a lighter shade – it's simple enough. Now ask yourself, how does a printer do it? Take a simple impact dot-matrix machine: since the ribbon has three primary colours and black, it has to mix the colours on the page by overprinting dots and dithering colours. The plain (and sad) fact is, it doesn't work very well. It is impossible for a dot matrix printer to deliver exactly the right amount of pigment to represent the required shade. In fact, the average colour printer is only capable of printing red, yellow, blue, green, purple, orange and black. Every other shade must be created by dithering.

DITHERING

Displaying two colours close together to produce the appearance of a different shade. It's a bit of a bodge, and only works properly when you view the results from a certain minimum distance.

Laser printers don't come cheap, but offer the ultimate in print quality. If you're interested in DTP, look for 'PostScript-compatibility'.

Choosing a printer

EPSON-COMPATIBLE

In order for printers to be able to work with computers, they have to talke the same language. Printer-makers Epson invented one which has since become an industry-standard amongst dot-matrix printers.

PRINTER DRIVER

Different printers may talk different languages (see jargon box above). A 'printer driver' is a piece of software your computer uses in order to communicate with a printer.

What's this 'pin' business?

Modern dot-matrix printers come in two major forms defined by the number of "pins" in the print head: usually 9 or 24. Older printers and possibly the odd cheap one will only have 8. Such a machine can be easily identified by the lack of true descenders: the little curly bits on small letters like "g", "y", and "p". 9-pin printers were devised to overcome this shortfall and are the most common machines available.

Most of these models will have a standard carriage capable of accepting a sheet of A4 paper in "portrait" orientation. Such machines will print 80 standard sized letters across the full-width of the page. Wide-carriage machines can print up to 132 standard characters but this is only useful for spreadsheet users.

Better quality printers come with 24-pin print heads. The greater number of pins occupying the same area of the page means the dots are physically closer together, and therefore, the quality is improved. (Watch out for cheap 24-pin machines which may have a 16-pin fallback mode.) If quality is a major consideration, then a no-frills 24-pin such as the Citizen 124D is an excellent choice. Remember, a printer does a job – it does not have to look good, so don't be put off by Citizen's functional looks over Star's more aesthetic approach.

What you need to look for

Printers are always a source of confusion. A lot of folks blame the Amiga – but a lot of the blame lies with the almost complete lack of standardisation. You can connect just about any printer to the Amiga but your problems are just starting. There's enough jargon to fill a book, indeed at least one author has written an entire tome using printers on the Amiga. Overleaf is a checklist to help you get a good buy.

- Look for Epson compatibility – it's a simple way to get started.
- Ask if an Amiga-specific printer driver is available. Canon and Citizen have produced their own drivers which offer greatly improved performance over the standard ones supplied by Commodore.
- Ignore the specifications. It's easy to be foxed by an impressive-looking set of meaningless figures.
- Get a demonstration and take the final output away with you – don't get fooled by a simple self-test. Compare same thing printed on several machines before making a final choice. If you can, take something you have prepared yourself. This is especially important if you have a specific application in mind such as colour from Deluxe Paint or word processing. If one shop will not co-operate, find another that will.
- If you fancy an ink-jet machine, ask about the availability and price of consumables. Ink cartridges can work out very expensive (£15-20) and a special paper is required to get the best from the machine. A low-cost laser can work out cheaper in the long run, the output is better and they're faster too! Oki make an excellent range.
- Some printers are louder than others. Ink-jet machines are the quietest and golf-ball text printers are probably the loudest – think carefully about where the machine will live and whom it's going to disturb. Does anyone in your household work nights, for instance?
- Never buy a laser (or LED) printer second-hand. They are incredibly complex machines and very expensive to repair.
- Go home and think about it – don't just make a snap judgement and regret it later on.

The disks

Inside the back cover of this book are two disks crammed with the very best Amiga public domain/shareware software. Ian Wrigley explains what it does, and how to use it…

You should have received two disks with your copy of Get The Most Out Of Your Amiga 1993. On them are samples of some of the best PD and shareware around, including a fully-featured word processor and the industry-standard file compression package. Each program comes with full instructions in the form of a 'read me' file on the disk, written by the author, but on the next few pages we'll guide you through the basics to get you started quickly.

Using the disks

Before you start doing anything, make sure that your master disks are write-protected – that is, slide the plastic tab so that you can see through the hole at the top right-hand corner of the disk. If your disks are write-protected, you can't accidentally erase files from them, and no virus can infect them.

You should make backups of your master disks, and only use those backups – keep the masters somewhere safe. Backing up is easy; open a new shell window (double-click on the Shell or CLI icon which you'll find on your Workbench disk) and type in the following:

Diskcopy from df0: to df0:

(Note that '0' is a number, not the letter 'Oh'.)

Then press the Return key. Your Amiga will ask for the Source disk – that's the master disk that you want to copy. Place it in the disk drive and hit Return, as requested. The Amiga will read the information from the source and, eventually, ask for a destination disk. This should be a blank floppy that you want to copy the data to. Eject the master and insert the blank disk, then press Return – again, as requested. Your Amiga will tell you that it's writing data

> **MANUAL BOOTING**
> *To make sure that as much space as possible was kept for software, we haven't made these bootable disks – you will need to boot your Amiga from a standard Workbench disk before you insert either of the two Get The Most disks.*

Get the most out of your Amiga 1993

The disks

VIRUS KILLERS

Why haven't we included a virus killer on the disks? Well, they were created a couple of months before you'll have bought this book – so any anti-virus program would be out of date. And there's nothing worse than an outdated virus killer – it gives you a false sense of security, while not really protecting you properly at all. So you really should get hold of the latest version of a program like Virus Checker as soon as possible – any PD house will stock a range of options. And make sure that you keep updating your copy!

to the disk. You may have to insert the source disk again at some point, depending on how much memory your machine has – if that's the case, just follow the instructions that your Amiga gives you. Remember, you can't accidentally overwrite your master disks if you have write-protected them.

Using the software

Using the disks is easy. First boot your Amiga up from a standard Workbench floppy (or allow it to start up from your hard disk, if you own one). Then put either of the two Get The Most disks in the drive, double-click on the disk's icon using the left-hand mouse button and a window will appear showing the contents of the disk. It's that easy!

Some of the packages require files to be placed in special places on your boot disk in order to work properly. All these details are contained in the 'read me' documents that come with the programs. You can read these with a text viewer such as More, which comes as part of your Amiga's standard system software, or you can use TextPlus, the fully-featured word processor on disk 2.

We haven't compressed any of the files on the disk – often you'll find that when you get software from a PD house or via a bulletin board it's been 'shrunk' using a program like LhA (which is on disk 1, in fact). We decided that compressing the files would probably confuse matters – this way, you can use the programs straight off the disk.

So, on with the programs...

SysInfo checks your Amiga's specs and performance.

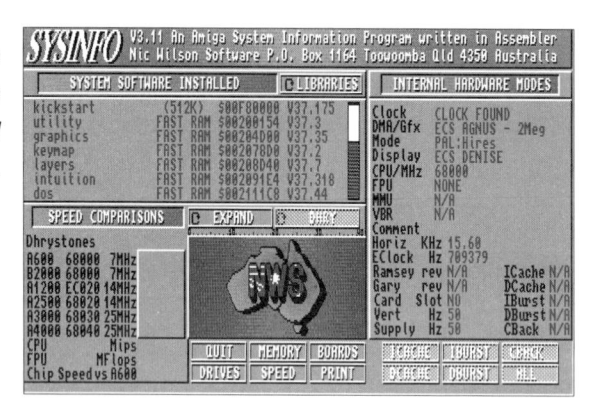

SysInfo   Disk 1

SysInfo is a program designed to tell you all about your Amiga. It was written by Nic Wilson, and is now the accepted benchmarking program. To run it, just double-click on its icon from the Workbench screen, and you'll be presented with a display similar to the one shown above.

You can quite easily access the speed checks and diagnostics, simply by clicking on one of the buttons marked Memory, Boards, Drives or Speed. Each runs tests and reports back the results – which you can print out if you want. The program also lists things like what versions of Libraries you have installed, what background tasks are running and, of course, your exact hardware configuration.

Play around with the options; for a full description of what everything means, check out Nic's documentation, which you'll find in the same drawer as the program.

FileMinder   Disk 1

FileMinder is a sophisticated piece of software which will help you to control the programs on your hard disk – or, indeed,

The disks

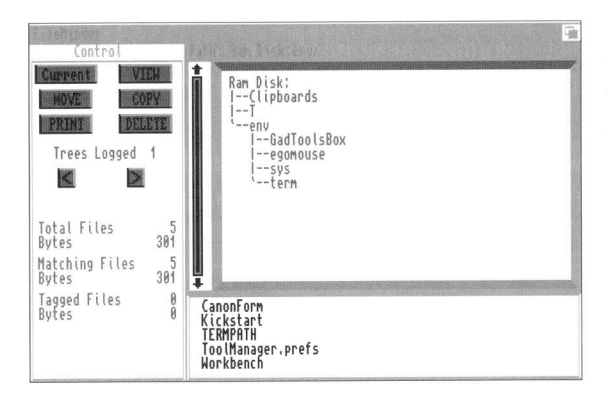

Fileminder is an excellent file-handling utility.

floppies. Double-click the icon from the Workbench to start things up, and you should be presented with a screen which displays the contents of your RAM: disk. As you'll see, the display takes the form of a 'tree' – and will be familiar to anyone who has used XTree, a PC-based directory utility.

Clicking on a directory name produces a list of files in that directory; this list appears under the tree diagram, and clicking on it opens a full window of the contents. Files can be 'tagged' by clicking on their names; you can then move or copy all tagged files to a different directory, which means that moving batches of documents or whatever around the disk is far easier than normal.

If you find that the initial colours are difficult to read, there is a Palette menu item in the Configuration menu, which gives you a choice of different colours. Or, by selecting ColorWindow (again from the Configuration menu) you can choose your own colours.

FileMinder is a complex, but relatively easy-to-use program. We suggest that you read the documentation before you play with it too much – things will make far more sense that way. After you've used the program for a few days, you won't know how you ever did without it!

AZspell   Disk 1

This program is a great addition to a word processor – it checks your documents to make sure that all the words are spelled correctly. To use it, you must either create a blank floppy disk called AZspell, on to which you should copy the files AZspell, AZdictionary and AZmerge, or you should run the AZassign program, by double-clicking on its icon, before you try to run the program proper.

Once you've done this, you can launch AZspell by double-clicking on it. Wait a few seconds – the program takes a while to load – and you will be asked for the file name of a document to be checked; you must specify the full path name, including drive name – for instance, 'DF0:AZspell/AZspell.DOC'. The file that you are checking must be in ASCII format, not a word processor's proprietary format.

You will see the text from the file being checked scrolling across the bottom of the screen. If AZspell doesn't recognise a word, the display will pause and you are given the option to add the word to the dictionary, ignore it, or correct it – either by typing in the right spelling or by selecting the correct word from the scrolling list on the right of the window.

Once you have corrected the entire document, you can add any new words to AZspell's permanent dictionary – the documentation tells you how to do this.

AZspell can check the spelling in any ASCII text file.

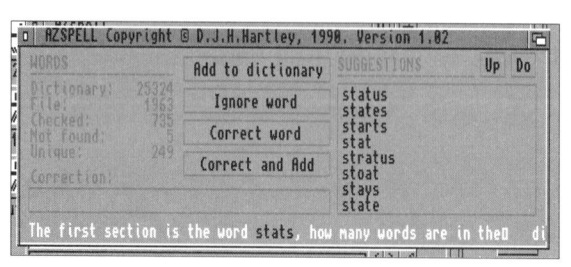

The dictionary supplied contains over 12,000 words; not a vast number, but you'll soon build it up as you check your own documents.

LhA   Disk 1

LhA is probably the best archiving utility available for the Amiga. Its purpose is to 'shrink' files so that they take up less space on the disk, or so that they are smaller when transferring them by modem. Because of its wide range of features, it's not easy to use – it can only be called from the Shell or CLI, and has an enormous number of options that can be invoked. For that reason, you should spend some time reading the file 'LhA.man', which is a complete manual. If you get stuck while you're using it, typing 'lha ?' at the Shell will produce a brief(ish) list of available commands.

If you're keen to get stuck in, you should copy the file itself to the C: directory of your Workbench boot disk – that way, it can be called just like any other Shell command.

TextPlus   Disk 2

TextPlus is a fully-featured word processor. It features such things as block copy, move and delete, a range of type styles, left, right, centre and full justification, multiple tab stops which can be set simply by clicking in the ruler, and much more. You may never need to buy a commercial word processor after you've registered this shareware program!

Two versions of the program are supplied by the author: one in English and one in German. They both feature what he calls the 'nerve wracking requester' – a requester which pops up from time to time, telling you that you haven't registered your copy. Register, and you'll get a version without this 'feature'.

WOT, NO ICON?
Because LhA can only be run from the Shell, it doesn't have an icon. Don't worry, though – it is in the drawer! If you're running Workbench 2.04 or above, you can choose Show All Files from the Window menu to see it. Otherwise, doing a DIR from the Shell will show that it's present and correct.

Get the most out of your Amiga 1993

To install, you need to copy some files to special places on your Workbench disk. Copy 'TxP.Config' and 'TxP.Printer' to your S: directory, and 'TextPlus-Handler' and 'null-handler' to your L: directory. You'll find these files in the L: and S: drawers within the 'English' drawer (itself inside the 'Text Plus' drawer) on disk number 2. Also, copy 'req.library' and 'powerpacker.library' to your LIBS: directory. These are in the LIBS: drawer, which is just inside the main 'Text Plus' drawer on the disk. Don't worry – it isn't as tricky as it sounds! There are some other files that you might want to copy to get maximum use from the program – these are all detailed in the documentation.

Now you're ready to start. Double-click on the TextPlus icon, and a blank window will appear. The first thing that you should do is read the program's documentation, so select Load from the Project menu and, from the subsequent requester, find 'TextPlus3.0E.doc'. It will take a few seconds to load; when it does, it will look like there's nothing in the file – the window will still be blank. Don't worry; the author has just included some blank lines at the beginning of the file. Scroll down using the arrows at the bottom right of the screen and you'll soon see text appearing.

TextPlus is a fully-featured and extremely powerful word processor.

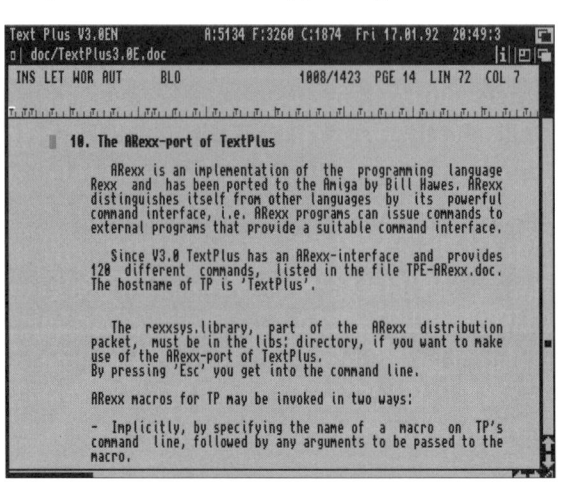

NickPrefs (needs WB 2.04)   Disk 2

We included NickPrefs on the disk because they are neat little utilities which prove that just about everything on your Amiga can be customised if you want it to be. They are Preferences-type files, and allow you to have a picture instead of a boring pattern as the backdrop to your Workbench; to animate the pointer when your Amiga is busy (for instance, to have an hourglass that fills up and then turns over), and to stop empty floppy disk drives from clicking.

To install, just copy the NickPrefs file (which doesn't have an icon, although it can be displayed by selecting Show All Files from the Window icon) to your C: directory, and edit the 'startup-sequence' file in your S: directory so that the word 'NickPrefs' comes on the line below 'IPrefs'. Then copy the three prefs files into your Prefs directory, reboot your Amiga and you're ready to start playing!

Disk doesn't work?

If either one of your disks is physically damaged or the contents are corrupted and unreadable, you should return it with an SAE to: **Discopy Labs, Unit 2+3, Amiga, Technology Centre, Drayton Fields, Drayton NN11 FR1** for a free replacement.

AmigaDOS reference

Workbench is the 'friendly' face of the Amiga, but if you want to control the machine at its most basic level, you need to master AmigaDOS. AmigaDOS works via the 'shell'. Instead of handling icons and menus, you work using a 'command line' where you type in commands manually. What follows is a list of those commands, the form they must take and what they do. This section covers the latest version, AmigaDOS 3 (A1200/A4000), but the commands are similar in most respects to those in AmigaDOS 2. Mark Smiddy is your guide...

AmigaDOS is the most complex and comprehensive operating system this side of UNIX and far more powerful than anything on any comparable microcomputer — for the home or office. This power comes a price: complexity. AmigaDOS is one of the most difficult operating system to get to grips with because of the sheer number of commands and the possibilities those commands provide.

Unlike UNIX and other DOS systems, AmigaDOS does have the advantage of built-in help as standard and most of the commands have quite meaningful names. It is fully programmable and affords quite low-level control of the many devices the Amiga is capable of controlling: including the printer and serial ports.

This reference section has been constructed to get you started with this amazing system. While not exhaustive, it is based on the most comprehensive and recent version, AmigaDOS 3. This is the system you will be using on Amiga A1200 or A4000 machines and similar in most aspects to that on a 2.04 or 2.1 system such as an A500+ or A3000. All the examples have been taken directly from the machine using a process known as output re-direction.

The examples follow two different patterns: commands which can be entered directly at the keyboard and scripts which must be entered and executed using a special AmigaDOS instruction. Commands are always preceded by a simulated screen prompt:

```
1>This_is_a_command
and this is the result!
```

which is in a different type style to the rest of the text. In cases where the AmigaDOS output has also been shown, this is shown in bold type. Script examples are introduced without a prompt and should be left well alone unless you are aware of how to enter them.

The AmigaDOS jargon is quite extensive and unavoidably complex — so when in doubt just try the examples: most are more explanatory than a ream of text. For more detailed descriptions and earlier versions see Mastering AmigaDOS 2 Vols 1 & 2. Pub. Bruce Smith Books.

Command Arguments

All AmigaDOS commands can be made to generate their command templates by entering the command followed by a question mark. For instance:

1>Dummy ?
FILE/A,BUF=BUFFER/A/N,UNIT/K/N,OFF/S:

For clarity these arguments are separated by an extra space here, but what is more important is the meaning of the argument types starting with /:

/A   Argument is required and must be supplied.

/F   Final. Must be last argument on the line.

/K   Keyword. Must be entered with the parameter.

/M   Multiple. One or more arguments may be supplied.

/N   Number. A numeric value is expected.

/S   Switch. Function is active if supplied.

Some of these can be mixed, depending on the command in question. In this case for instance, the argument is a numeric keyword:

MouseBlanker CX_PRIORITY/K/N

so a correct command line is:

```
1>MouseBlanker CX_PRIORITY=5
```

AmigaDOS reference

Command Reference

AddBuffers DRIVE/A, BUFFERS/N
Add or read the number of sector cache buffers assigned to a drive. **Examples:**

```
1>AddBuffers DF0: 22
1>AddBuffers DF0:
Df0: has 20 buffers
```

AddDataTypes FILES/M, QUIET/S, REFRESH/S
This is a private system command used by AmigaDOS to activate the translations for Multiview.

Alias NAME, STRING/F
Assigns a short name to an AmigaDOS command. Square brackets may be included in the string to add an optional argument. **Examples:**

```
1>Alias Destroy Format Drive DF[]: Name Empty
1>Alias NS NewShell
1>Alias TrashIt Rename[] :Trashcan
```

Alias can be used just like normal AmigaDOS commands and your favourite ones should be defined in S:Shell-Startup. Extra arguments can be added when the Alias is called. For instance, Destroy defined above works like this:

```
1>Destroy 0 NOICONS
Insert disk to be formatted in device DF0:
Press RETURN to begin formatting or CTRL-C to abort:
```

AmigaDOS reference

Ask PROMPT/A

Gets a "yes" or "no" response from a user in a script file. A "Y" answer sets the warn flag; anything else clears it. ASK can be used from the command line but this is a little pointless:

```
ASK "Do you wish to continue Y/n?"
IF WARN
  ECHO "OK, here we go..."
...
```

Assign NAME, TARGET/M, LIST/S, EXISTS/S, DISMOUNT/S, DEFER/S, PATH/S, ADD/S, REMOVE/S, VOLS/S, DIRS/S, DEVICES/S

Assigns logical device names to directory paths, reads the current settings or checks for the existence of a specified assignment.

Assign is a complex command which cannot be examined in detail here. However the following examples give the most common uses. Used without arguments the command generates a list of all the current devices and assignments. The VOL, DIRS, and DEVICES switches can be used to narrow the display list.

```
1>ASSIGN
Volumes:
Ram Disk [Mounted]
KCS
Apps [Mounted]
37MB [Mounted]
WB3.0 [Mounted]

Directories:
HELP <LOCALE:Help>
LOCALE WB3.0:Locale
```

Get the most out of your Amiga 1993

AmigaDOS reference

```
KEYMAPS  WB3.0:Devs/Keymaps
PRINTERS [DEVS:Printers]
REXX WB3.0:S
CLIPS Ram Disk:Clipboards
T Ram Disk:T
ENV Ram Disk:ENV
ENVARC WB3.0:Prefs/Env-Archive
SYS WB3.0:
C WB3.0:C
S WB3.0:S
LIBS WB3.0:Libs
  + WB3.0:Classes
DEVS WB3.0:Devs
FONTS WB3.0:Fonts
L WB3.0:L

Devices:
PIPE RAM CON RAW SER
SER PAR PRT WB_2.x DF0
DH0 DH1 KCS
```

Volumes:
These are the current disks fixed to the system. Disks listed as "[MOUNTED]" are available in some drives; others are locked but not physically available.

Directories:
These are the logical names for defined paths added by a line like this:

```
1>ASSIGN WORK: SYS:Wordworth/Text
```

You can access the assignment names just like any disk drive — the following are valid:

```
1>DIR WORK:
```

Get the most out of your Amiga 1993

```
1>LIST WORK:
1>MAKEDIR WORK:Letters
```

Several options control how this works: names listed in square brackets are "late-binding" assigns (DEFER/S); names listed in angle brackets are "non-binding" assigns (PATH/S); and finally names preceded by "+" are additional directory paths (ADD/S) — not all software can read these however.

Devices:
These are the current physical devices or device emulations. When a device has been mounted it will appear in this list.

You can check for the presence of an assignment in a script like this:

```
ASSIGN >NIL: FONTS: EXISTS
IF WARN
  ECHO "Fonts dir missing or inactive!"
  QUIT
ENDIF
```

AutoPoint CX_PRIORITY/N/K
Starts the AutoPoint commodity to activate any window as the pointer passes over it.

This command should either be directly executed from Workbench or RUN as a background process. The CX_PRIORITY is the utilities Exchange priority and will not normally be used. If this command is called in a Startup-sequence input and output MUST be directed to NIL: or the initial CLI window will not close. Examples:

```
RUN AutoPoint
RUN <NIL: >NIL: AutoPoint CX_Priority=3
```

Get the most out of your Amiga 1993

Avail CHIP/S, FAST/S, TOTAL/S, FLUSH/S

Reads the current memory usage and (optionally) clears out freed resources. The output from this command can be controlled to give the total amount of memory in any type or to break down in more detail. All values are returned in bytes like this:

```
1>AVAIL Chip
1890528

1>AVAIL
Type    Available   In-Use    Maximum    Largest
chip    1890528     205600    2096122    1837432
fast    1012336     1609104   2621440    518464
total   2902864     1814704   4717568    1837432
```

The Available count shows how much memory is free for use — this is tied to the largest count which shows the biggest contiguous block of free memory. Maximum (total) shows the amount of memory fitted and In- Use shows how much is physically in use at the time.

Note: this command can only provide an instant snapshot of the available memory at any time due to the machine's multi-tasking nature.

BindDrivers

Activates certain old hardware drivers. This command is retained for ancient compatibility and is used to mount certain types of software drivers located in the Expansion drawer: typically hard disks and RAM modules. BindDrivers is only called once during the startup sequence.

AmigaDOS reference

Blanker CX_PRIORITY/N/K, CX_POPKEY/K, CX_POPUP/K, SECONDS/N/K, CYCLECOLORS/K, ANIMATION/K

Activates the commodities screen banker. Typically this command will be executed at Startup (where it is most useful) although it can be activated at any time from the Workbench. Typical use in User-startup for a three minute blank period is as follows:

```
RUN <NIL: >NIL: Blanker CX_POPUP=NO SECONDS=180
```

Break PROCESS/A/N, ALL/S, C/S, D/S, E/S, F/S

Sends a break signal to a running process. Break is most often used in scripts to stop commands which have no interactive Shell window attached to them. Although it is possible to send a single break code, it is more common to send everything.

```
1>BREAK 5 ALL
```

Here's an example using STATUS to find a process number:

```
STATUS >T:PRO{$$} Command=WAIT
BREAK <T:PRO{$$} >NIL: ALL ?
```

CD DIR/A

Changes or reads the current directory. Change directory is used to navigate around the system paths. Used without arguments it returns the current path. With an argument containing using zero, one or more of the following delimiters it moves through the tree — patterns can also be used in AmigaDOS 2 or better:

:	-	**Root of this device**
/	-	**Next level up tree**

Examples:

```
1>CD
Workbench2.04:Utilities
```

Get the most out of your Amiga 1993

AmigaDOS reference

```
1>CD :
1>CD SYS:
1>CD DF0:
1>CD Utilities
1>CD /Tools
1>CD DEVS:Printers
1>CD :Devs/Printers
1>CD //
```

In AmigaDOS 2 and higher, CD can be omitted in these examples. However it must be used to obtain pattern matching:

```
1>CD T#?
```

If more than one entry matches the pattern the directory level remains the same and an error is generated.

ChangeTaskPri PRI=PRIORITY/A/N, PROCESS/K/N
Change the priority of the task attached to any running process or Shell. This command should be used with care. Allowable parameters for the priority range between -128 and +127 although a realistic range is -5 to +5. The process argument can be omitted to set the priority of the current Shell which is 0 by default. **Examples:**

```
1>ChangeTaskPri -1 ; this shell's priority
1>ChangeTaskPri 5 Process=6 ; process 6 (whatever that is)
```

ClickToFront CX_PRIORITY/N/K, QUALIFIER/K
Activates the commodities ClickToFront tool. ClickToFront brings a window to front of the display by holding down a key and clicking any part of it. This can be very useful if you have a lot of windows on the screen and the depth gadgets get hidden. The command is best used from a User-startup like this:

```
RUN <NIL: >NIL: ClickToFront
```

Get the most out of your Amiga 1993

Clock DIGITAL/S, LEFT/N, TOP/N, WIDTH/N, HEIGHT/N, 24HOUR/S, SECONDS/S, DATE/S, FORMAT/N, PUBSCREEN/K

Activate an Intuition-based clock. This utility has been with the Amiga since the early days. Although the latest incarnation has changed somewhat, it still looks like the original did. The clock can be started at any time, although it should be RUN to avoid clogging the CLI.

The Left and Top arguments set the position on screen, whereas the width and height set the size of the default analogue display. The Digital and 24Hour switches make the clock a digital type which is more convenient and less demanding on screen real-estate. The date switch enables the date display and the PUBSCREEN option allows the clock to be displayed on any public custom screen.

Examples:

```
1>RUN <NIL: >NIL: Clock
1>RUN <NIL: >NIL: Clock Top=5 Left=20
1>RUN <NIL: >NIL: Clock
1>RUN <NIL: >NIL: Clock Digital Date 24hour
```

ConClip UNIT/N, OFF/S

Activates the console clipboard device. When this command is running, text cut from the console can be pasted directly into any application which can read text from the Amiga clipboard device. Multiview can display the current clipboard contents. This command is called during startup and never really needs to be used by user-scripts.

Copy FROM/M, TO/A, ALL/S, QUIET/S, BUF=BUFFER/K/N, CLONE/S, DATES/S, NOPRO/S, COM/S, NOREQ/S

Copies data from a source device to destination device until end of file is reached. In its most basic form this command is used to copy (duplicate) a file. However, it is much more powerful than that. A "*" can be used in place of source or destination arguments to copy text to or from the current console window. If the source is a pattern and destination is a name, the destination directory will be created on the destination device.

AmigaDOS reference

Examples:

```
1>COPY C: RAM:
1>COPY DF0: DF1: ALL
1>COPY C:#? RAM:C QUIET
1>COPY S:SPAT TO *
1>COPY S:DPAT TO CON:0/0/320/200/MyWindow
1>COPY * TO T:NewFile
```

In the last example you must send an EOF (CTRL+\) to close the input stream. See NewShell for more details on the CON: device. The remaining options have the following effects:

ALL: Copies all files in the source directory and all sub- directories below it.

QUIET: When pattern-matching is being used, this suppresses non- interactive output.

BUFFER: Sets the buffer size – default 100K. A value of 0 sets the buffer to the size of the file up to the largest available memory block.

CLONE: Makes an exact duplicate of the file's datestamp, protection bits and comment (see FileNote, SetDate, Protect).

DATES: Copies the file's datestamp information.

NOPRO: Sets the default protection bits (RWED) only.

COM: Copies any comment attached to the file.

NOREQ: Suppresses any interactive (pop-up) requesters.

```
CPU CACHE/S, BURST/S, NOCACHE/S, NOBURST/S,
DATACACHE/S, DATABURST/S, NODATACACHE/S,
NODATABURST/S, INSTCACHE/S, INSTBURST/S,
NOINSTCACHE/S, NOINSTBURST/S, COPYBACK/S,
NOCOPYBACK/S, EXTERNALCACHE/S, NOEXTERNALCACHE/S,
FASTROM/S, NOFASTROM/S, TRAP/S, NOTRAP/S,
NOMMUTEST/S, CHECK/K
```
Change the CPU settings and check for hardware. This command is reserved for experts and is technically beyond the reach of this section. It is most useful on its own like this:

```
1>CPU
System: 68030 68882 FastROM (INST: Cache Burst) (DATA: Cache Burst)
```

CrossDOS CX_PRIORITY/N/K, CX_POPKEY/K, CX_POPUP/K
Activates or changes the settings of CrossDOS system. **Example:**

```
1>CrossDOS
```

Date DAY, DATE, TIME, TO=VER/K
Sets or reads the system time and date. The AmigaDOS version of Time preferences :

```
1>Date
Thursday 25-Feb-93 20:30:28
```

A time, date or both can be entered in the same format to change the settings there and then (note times are in 24 hour clock). For instance:

```
1>Date 19:00:30
1>Date 30-Jun-93
1>Date Date=12-Feb-96 Time=09:00
```

Day names can also be used like this:

AmigaDOS reference

```
1>Date Tomorrow
1>Date Wednesday
```

Note: the time will be reset when the machine is switched off unless the current settings are saved using SetClock.

Date's output can also be sent directly to a file like this:

```
1>Date TO T:Today
```

Delete FILE/M/A, ALL/S, QUIET/S, FORCE/S
Permanently delete one or more files. This command MUST be used with care since it removes files from disk beyond retrieval and a simple mistake on the command line will delete everything. Examples

```
1>Delete ABC
1>Delete (ABC|DEF)
1>Delete ABC#?
1>Delete T:#? ENV:#?
1>Delete RAM:#? ALL
1>Delete RAM:Protected FORCE
1>Delete #? QUIET
```

Delete will not remove a directory that contains one or more files or sub-directories unless the ALL switch is used. Output can be suppressed using the QUIET switch. Also, files can be protected from accidental deletion by clearing the "D" flag with the PROTECT command, although the FORCE switch will delete a file protected in that way. It is not possible to delete a device or a file that is "in use" by another application.

Dir DIR, OPT/K, ALL/S, DIRS/S, FILES/S, INTER/S
Display the sorted contents of a directory. This command is used to get a listing of any directory in the hierarchy — and one of the most used in AmigaDOS. Typically the command is used without arguments to get a listing of the current directory or with a

AmigaDOS reference

directory path. The ALL switch can be used to search the entire hierarchy moving down from the current level and listing every directory below. The search files can be limited using a pattern. Directories or files may be listed using the respective DIRS or FILES switch. The INTER switch is used to trigger "interactive" mode. Examples:

```
1>DIR
1>DIR S:St#?
1>DIR FONTS FILES
1>DIR DEVS: ALL
1>DIR FONTS: FILES ALL
1>DIR DIRS
1>DIR ~(#?.info)
```

DiskChange DEVICE/A

Inform the Amiga of a new disk. The Amiga normally reads a disk as soon as it is inserted in the drive, however under certain circumstances it is necessary to re-read a disk so the system is aware of changes. Typically this command is used to inform Workbench when a disk's volume label has been changed with ReLabel. For example:

```
1>DiskChange DF0:
```

DiskCopy FROM/A, TO/A, NAME/K, NOVERIFY/S, MULTI/S

Duplicate an entire disk. This command is very important if you want to save yourself from a lot of heartache and misery — disks go wrong: it's just life. DiskCopy performs a track-by-track copy between one or two disk drives and can format a disk in the process. Single drive copies can be very efficient on machines with more than 1.5Mb memory since the entire disk can be copied to RAM first. On machines with 3M+ and two drives, two disks can be copied at once.

The NOVERIFY switch turns write verification off and is reserved for use when copying to RAD:. It can be used to copy floppy disks by the very brave or just plain stupid; the feature speeds up the copying process by about 50 per cent. The MULTI switch is used to make more than one copy of the same disk.

Examples:

```
1>DISKCOPY DF0: DF0:
1>DISKCOPY DF1: TO DF0: NAME=Workbench
1>DISKCOPY DF0: TO RAD: NOVERIFY
1>DISKCOPY DF0: TO DF0: MULTI
```

Echo /M, NOLINE/S, FIRST/K/N, LEN/K/N, TO/K

Display text on an output device. Echo is like the PRINT command in BASIC. It sends a string of characters to the current output device — usually, but not always, the console. Output can be forced to a file using the TO parameter. By default, ECHO prints a line-feed but this can be suppressed using the NOLINE option. Extra line feeds can be included using "*n". The FIRST and LEN options are used to perform basic string slicing and may be used individually or combined. Other special strings starting "*e[" are used to include colours.

Examples:

```
1>Echo "Hello World!"
Hello World
1>Echo "Hello" "this is AmigaDOS" "speaking"
Hello this is AmigaDOS speaking
```

now some string slicing…

```
1>Echo "1234567890" First=5
567890
1>Echo "1234567890" Len=5
890
1>Echo "1234567890" First=2 Len=5
23456
1>Echo "1234567890" First=255 ; last character in string
0
```

AmigaDOS reference

...and some colours...

```
1>Echo "*e[32mwhite foreground"
1>Echo "*e[33mblue foreground"
1>Echo "*e[31mblack foreground"
1>Echo "*e[42mwhite background"
1>Echo "*e[43mblue background"
1>Echo "*e[41mblack background"
1>Echo "*e[44mgrey background"
```

Reversed apostrophes can be used to execute a command within the ECHOed string:

```
1>Echo "The day is `date`"
The day is Thursay 25-Feb-93 12:00:04
```

Ed FROM/A, SIZE/N, WITH/K, WINDOW/K, TABS/N, WIDTH=COLS/N, HEIGHT=ROWS/N

Edit a text file using the full-screen editor. Ed is the big AmigaDOS Editor and the easiest to use when you are just starting out. This is the one you should use to create and edit script files. Ed is started by supplying a filename to edit: if that file does not exist it will be created. The following examples show how this is done:

```
1>Ed S:Startup-sequence
1>Ed S:NewScriptFile
```

In release 2 and higher, ED features menus which make it very easy to use. However, there is not enough room to list the extended commands here and knowledge of these is necessary to use the WITH argument. Also, ED is not suitable for working on very large files but the maximum memory usage can be set using the SIZE argument, for instance:

```
1>Ed S:BigScript 60000
```

By default, ED opens its own window, however you can open it on the current console window (to save memory) like this:

```
1>Ed S:Startup-sequence Window=*
```

When used in this way, ED will take the width and height of the current console to be the editing area. However, you can restrict this to a portion of the screen using the ROWS and/or COLS arguments.

```
1>Ed S:Spat Window=* ROWS=5
1>Ed S:Dpat Window=* COLS=40
1>Ed S:Spat Window=* ROWS=8 COLS=60
```

Note: When you use the ROWS argument the last row is reserved for use by ED. Therefore, if you specify five rows, only four will be used by the actual file.

Edit FROM/A, TO, WITH/K, VER/K, OPT/K, WIDTH/N, PREVIOUS/N

Edit a file using a line editor. EDIT primarily finds use in scripts where it is used to perform all manner of automatic text editing sequences which cannot be achieved any other way. It operates using commands typed directly from the keyboard and is far to advanced to warrant further descrption here.

Else

Mark an alternative path after an IF test. The ELSE command can only be used in a script file as part of a structured test. It marks the alternative route if the IF test fails. See IF for more information.

Endif

Terminate an IF construct. This command can only be used in a script file and is used to mark the end of a structured test. See "If" for more information.

EndSkip
Terminate a Skip branch. This command can only be used within a script and immediately stops the progress of a "Skip" jump. The WARN flag is set in this case and the command is only useful in the debugging stages.

Eval VALUE1/A, OP, VALUE2/M, TO/K, LFORMAT/K
Expression evaluator and calculator. This command can be used from the Shell to perform simple arithmetic or within scripts to make loop counters and so on. Expressions are evaluated from left to right although brackets can be used to fix the calculation order. The basic format is seen in the following examples:

```
1>Eval 2 + 2
4
1>Eval 2+2*4*8
128
1>Eval 2+(2*4*8)
66
```

Numbers can be specified in hexadecimal by adding "0x" in front, octal by supplying "0" or from characters using a "'", for instance:

```
1>Eval 077
63
1>Eval 0x77
119
1>Eval 'A
65
```

Similarly, you can convert to these formats using the LFORMAT operator like this:

```
1>Eval 'A lformat "It is: %n *n"
It is 65
1>Eval 255 lformat "It is: %x4 *n"
```

```
It is: 00FF
```

Note: You MUST supply the "*n" at the end of the string to get the line feed — this is exactly opposite to the way in which Echo works, but is necessary when writing to global environmental variables:

```
Eval $count + 1 to env:count
Eval $count + 1 to env:char lformat "%c"
```

Exchange CX_PRIORITY/N/K, CX_POPKEY/K, CX_POPUP/K

Activate the commodities master process. This command is best not used from AmigaDOS unless you want to start the master process and hide it away in the background for later use. In such a case it might be called from the user-startup file like this:

```
RUN <NIL: >NIL: Exchange CX_POPUP=No
```

Execute FILE/A

Execute a script. This command is used to execute any AmigaDOS script file — a text file of AmigaDOS instructions constructed as a program. Many commands only work in scripts or work better from them. This command can be implied automatically by setting a script's "S" protection flag. (SPAT, DPAT and PCD supplied by Commodore are scripts.) If a query operator is specified the script will display its own template.

The following special operators may be used as the first few lines of a script:

.	is an optional comment line.
.key	Optionally defines a simple argument template. Only /A, /K, and /S arguments are corréctly interpreted.
.bra C	changes the default opening bracket "<" to the character "C"

AmigaDOS reference

.ket C   changes the default closing bracket ">" to the character "C"

.dol C   changes the default dollar character "$" to the character "C".

.def Arg "Contents"   Sets the default contents of any argument if nothing is supplied by the caller.

Command-line arguments can be inserted at any position in the script by enclosing them in special "braket" characters (< and >). Here's a small example script:

```
.key Name
.bra {
.ket }
.def Name "Lazy bones"
Echo "Hello {Name} this is AmigaDOS!"
```

More examples:

```
1>Execute PCD
1>Execute AddPestEvent ?
Message, Time/K, Day/K, Wait/K
```

FailAt RCLIM/N

Change or read the failure limit for scripts. This command sets the lower limit for the return code necessary to stop a script in its tracks. Correctly written AmigaDOS commands only generate one of four return values:

0 OK
5 Warn
10 Error
20 Fail

Get the most out of your Amiga 1993

AmigaDOS reference

If the error is 10 or 20 the script will be stopped. The failure level may be raised to stop this occurring but extra error checking MUST be included using IF ERROR or IF FAIL. This, in fact, is the only way to read these results. The actual value is returned in the system local variable "RC" read by Set. **Examples:**

```
1>FailAt
Fail limit: 10
1>Failat 21 ; don't let anything stop me now!
```

Fault /N/N

Translate a fault code(s) into error message(s). This command is called by WHY to given an extended reason as to why a command failed. It reads the internal system variable, "Result2" which can be read directly by Set. The command can be executed with more than one argument to read several fault codes at once. Examples:

```
1>Fault 221
Fault 221: disk is full
1>Fault 10 120 121
Fault 10: Error 10
Fault 120: argument line invalid or too long
Fault 121: file is not executable
```

FileNote FILE/A, COMMENT, ALL/S, QUIET/S

Add or change a file's comment. This command can be used to attach a comment to one or many files since patterns can also be used. If the comment string is omitted, any note attached to the file is removed. The ALL switch moves progressively down through the hierarchy and the QUIET switch makes the command work without producing normal output when the ALL switch and/or a pattern is active. Comment strings should be no longer than 79 characters but it may contain non-printing characters such as ANSI colour codes. Comments are only shown when the file is LISTed and not when DIR is used.

Examples:

```
1>FileNote DIR "A very important command..."
1>FileNote C:LIST "*e[32mMajor command this one!*e[31m"
1>FileNote C:DIR ; remove the comment.
1>FileNote Diary:Text/#? "Don't read me!" QUIET
```

FixFonts

Update the dot-font files. This command may be called at any time but it only makes any sense when you have been adjusting the contents of the FONTS: drawer. Specifically, it checks to see what sizes are available in any particular font and updates the contents of its associated .font file to suit. If this is not done the system will think fonts are available when in fact they are not.

FKey CX_PRIORITY/N/K, CX_POPKEY/K, CX_POPUP/K

Activate the commodities function key tool. Use this to activate the function key helper — a utility to automatically insert a string of text into the input stream when a function key is pressed. This command will usually be started from the User-startup like this:

```
RUN <NIL: >NIL: Fkey CX_POPUP=No
```

Format DEVICE=DRIVE/K/A, NAME/K/A, OFS/S, FFS/S, INTL=INTERNATIONAL/S, NOINTL=NOINTERNATIONAL/S, DIRCACHE/S, NODIRCACHE/S, NOICONS/S, QUICK/S

Initialise a new floppy disk. This command is used to prepare a new floppy disk for use with the Amiga. Generally speaking from Workbench 2 it is better to call this command directly from the Workbench's icon menu or double-click its icon. The FFS option is best not used for floppy disk although the DIRCACHE (directory caching) is OK. Little information exists as to the function of the INTL and NOINTL switches. NOICONS tells Format not to copy the Trashcan drawer and its icon from the Workbench disk. If you want to use Format from Shell, here are a few examples:

```
1>Format DRIVE DF0: NAME Empty FFS
```

AmigaDOS reference

```
1>Format DRIVE DF0: Name "New Disk" OFS NOICONS QUICK
```

Important: OFS and FFS formats don't mix!

Get NAME/A
Read a local environmental variable. This command directly displays the contents of a named environmental variable local to the process. See Set for more information.

```
1>Get RE
object not found
1>Get RC
5
```

GetEnv NAME/A
Read a global environmental variable. This command directly reads the contents of a global environmental variable stored in the ENV: assignment. See SetEnv for more information.

```
1>SetEnv counter 1
1>Eval $counter +1 to env:counter lformat "%n"
1>GetEnv counter
2
```

IconX
Run a script from Workbench. This command is held in the C directory but is never called from AmigaDOS. It is only used as the "default tool" attached to a project icon. When the icon is double-clicked, IconX runs the script as if it had been executed from AmigaDOS and opens a default interactive window for it to work in.

AmigaDOS reference

```
If NOT/S, WARN/S, ERROR/S, FAIL/S, ,EQ/K, GT/K,
GE/K, VAL/S, EXISTS/K
```
Test for a condition in a script. This command can only be used in a script file to test for a single condition or event. The WARN, ERROR and FAIL switches test for command returns sent via RC — any one can be used. **Examples:**

1: Test for a string in a file.

```
Search S:Spat "Nothing"
If WARN
 Echo "Didn't find that string"
Endif
```

2: Ask a simple question and respond.

```
Ask "Are you over 21?"
If WARN
 Echo "Getting a bit old for this, don't you think?"
Else
 Echo "So , you're not over the hill yet"
Endif
```

The keywords EQ (is equal to) GT (is greater than) and GE (is greater than or equal to) are typically used in conjunction with the VAL switch where IF assumes the input condition is a number. NOT can be used to invert the test therefore:

NOT GE = Less than.
NOT GT = Less than or equal to.
NOT EQ = Not equal to.

Get the most out of your Amiga 1993

AmigaDOS reference

Example — a simple count up loop:

```
SetEnv count 0
Lab start
Echo "Count=$count"
Eval $count +1 lformat "%n" to env:count
If val $count NOT GE 10
 Skip start back
Endif
```

The "EXISTS" keyword is used to test for the presence of a file or directory, for example:

```
If NOT Exists "DEVS:Keymaps/gb"
 echo "Can't do this: UK keymap is missing"
 quit 10
endif
```

Info DEVICE

Get information about a device. This command is used to retrieve information on all available filing system devices. Used without arguments it generates something like this:

```
1>Info
Mounted disks:
Unit    Size Used Free Full Errs Status     Name
RAM:    68K  68   0    100% 0    Read/WriteRam Disk
DF0:    No disk present
DH0:    37M  28534473163 8% 0    Read/Write37MB

Volumes available:
Ram Disk [Mounted]
37MB [Mounted]
Workbench
```

Get the most out of your Amiga 1993

AmigaDOS reference

The column headings translate like this:

Unit physical device name.
Size storage capacity available in Kbytes or Mbytes.
Used capacity used in blocks.
Free amount of free store in blocks.
Full ratio of free/used store as a percentage.
Errs number of hard errors found by the validator.
Status Read only or Read/Write or Validating.
Name The volume name attached to the device.

The "Volumes available" list is the same as that returned by Assign. You can get specific information about a single disk or filing system device like this:

```
1>Info RAM:
Mounted disks:
Unit    Size  Used  Free  Full  Errs  Status       Name
RAM:    68K   68    0     100%  0     Read/Write   Ram Disk

Volumes available:
Ram Disk [Mounted]
```

Install DRIVE/A, NOBOOT/S, CHECK/S, FFS/S

Install, test or remove a boot block on a floppy drive. In order to boot the machine from disk, the disk must contain a valid boot block and this command is used to generate the correct code. The basic format is like this:

```
1>Install DF0:
1>Install DF0: FFS ; for Fast Filing System disks
```

You can remove the bootblock to disable booting like this:

```
1>Install DF0: NOBOOT
```

Get the most out of your Amiga 1993

AmigaDOS reference

The bootblocks can be checked in command mode or in script like this:

```
Install >NIL: DF0: CHECK
If WARN
  Echo "Caution: May not be a standard boot disk!"
Endif
```

IntelliFont VALIDATE/S
Start the Intellifont utility. This command is not normally executed from Shell. It starts the Intellifont, CG fonts utility, previously known as Fountain.

IPrefs
Start the IPrefs daemon. This is a private system function which is only called once in the AmigaDOS 2/3 Startup-sequence. It reads the current environmental preference settings and configures the machine accordingly. IPrefs must be started before the machine has any windows open because it can change the Workbench's screen mode.

Join FILE/M/A, AS=TO/K/A
Join several files together. Use this command to join several text files together. The destination (TO) file must not be one of the source files. **Example:**

```
1>Join File1 File2 File3 AS Files123
```

Lab LABEL
Mark a label position in a script. This command is not really a command in truth — it is used to mark the position in a script for the Skip command to jump to. See "If" for an example of use.

AmigaDOS reference

```
List DIR/M, P=PAT/K, KEYS/S, DATES/S, NODATES/S,
TO/K, SUB/K, SINCE/K, UPTO/K, QUICK/S, BLOCK/S,
NOHEAD/S, FILES/S, DIRS/S, LFORMAT/K, ALL/S
```

List a directory with file information. This command is one of the most powerful in AmigaDOS and due to space limitations cannot be given the coverage it deserves here (Mastering AmigaDOS 2 has almost eight pages devoted to it). Basically it lists complete file information in an unsorted list like this:

```
1>LIST SYS:Ex#?
Expansion              Dir    ----rwed  02-Sep-92 11:51:33
: Expansion directory
Expansion.info   632          ----rw-d  Yesterday 09:08:41
: Expansion dot-info icon file
1 file - 1 directory 5 blocks used
```

Very briefly the options work as follows:

PAT:	specifies an extra search pattern.
KEYS:	lists the positions of files on the disk.
DATES:	dates are listed for every file (no day names).
NODATES:	dates and times are omitted from the list.
TO:	send output to a named file (like Eval and Echo).
SUB:	find a sub-string.
SINCE:	List files since a defined date.
UPTO:	List files up to a specified date.
QUICK:	List filenames only (something like DIR).
NOHEAD:	Suppress the heading information.
FILES:	List files only (no directories).
DIRS:	List directories only (no files).
LFORMAT:	Use a format string.
ALL:	List all files and directories (see DIR).

AmigaDOS reference

LoadWB -DEBUG/S, DELAY/S, CLEANUP/S, NEWPATH/S
Activate the Workbench. This command is used to start the Workbench interface and is typically only called once during startup. The DELAY option waits for three seconds before the Workbench reads the mounted disks to allow disk activity to stop and CLEANUP cleans up the default icons (over-riding the snapshot settings).

NEWPATH can be used at any time to take a snapshot of the current path settings if these have been changed since the Workbench tool was first started. The "-DEBUG" option is provided for developers to test code and should not be used for any other purpose.

Lock DRIVE/A, ON/S, OFF/S, PASSKEY
Write protect an FFS hard disk. Use this to set write protection on any hard disk or hard partition. A four-letter password may also be supplied. **Examples:**

```
1>Lock DH1: ON
DH1: locked
1>Lock DH1:
DH1: unlocked
```

-now use a password-

```
1>Lock DH1: ON ABCD
DH1: locked
1>Lock DH1:
Attempt to lock drive DH1: failed
1>Lock DH1: OFF Passkey=ABCD
DH1: unlocked
```

Magtape DEVICE/K, UNIT/N/K, RET=RETENSION/S, REW=REWIND/S, SKIP/N/K
Operate a magnetic tape streamer. This command is a private system function and should not be used.

Get the most out of your Amiga 1993

AmigaDOS reference

MakeDir NAME/M
Create a new sub-directory. This command is the AmigaDOS level version of New Drawer (although it does not create an icon). It is possible to create several new directories in one go including sub-directories of the first. **Examples:**

```
1>MakeDir RAM:A
1>MakeDir RAM:A/B
1>MakeDir RAM:A/B/C
```

This can be shortened to:

```
1>MakeDir RAM:A RAM:A/B RAM:A/B/C
```

MakeLink FROM/A, TO/A, HARD/S, FORCE/S
Create a logical link. The uses of this command are somewhat limited. It creates a link between two files — so the file can be accessed by either name. Technically speaking, it creates another file header block which points to the start of the specified file's data block list. A link can be created to a user sub-directory anywhere in the hierarchy by using the FORCE switch. Soft links (links between volumes) are not supported in release 2 or 3 so although the HARD switch has no effect, it should be specified. Examples:

```
1>MakeLink T C:TYPE HARD
1>MakeLink D SYS:Devs FORCE HARD
```

More
View a text file. This command is an old file viewer which is still supplied with the system because it's actually still quite useful. You can use it to read any plain ASCII file such as a script or some instructions supplied with a program. (Press "H" for help when More's window is active.) For instance:

```
1>More S:Startup-sequence
```

AmigaDOS reference

By default, More opens on the current console window. If this is not desirable it can be RUN to make it open its own window:

```
1>Run More S:Startup-sequence
```

More is very effective when used with pipes between two (or more) separate Shells. Here the prompt number shows the different Shell windows — this technique should always be used with pipes to stop the sending process "freezing" when the pipe is full.

```
1>Type >pipe:a S:#?
2>More <pipe:a
```

Alternatively this method can be combined with Run to execute the command in parallel from the same Shell:

```
1>Run Type >pipe:a S:#?
[CLI 2]
1>More <pipe:a
```

Mount DEVICE/M, FROM/K

Add a new device to the device list. Mount is a special command used to add new "device drivers" to the system. The driver must be defined in a special driver description or, for older devices, a mountlist. The driver description just tells Mount what software to use and how to configure it: these are supplied by Commodore and by third-party hardware manufacturers so you need not worry how they work. With Workbench 3, devices (located in the DEVS:DOSDrivers drawer) are mounted automatically during startup so this command is not usually required. You may mount a device manually like this:

```
1>Mount SPEAK:
1>Mount BigRAD: FROM DEVS:BigRAD
```

AmigaDOS reference

A device driver is simply a piece of software which provides a simple interface between AmigaDOS and the hardware. Some devices (RAD:, PIPE: and RAM:) are emulated entirely in software whereas others (such as PRT:, DFx: SER:) and are connected to some hardware. As far as AmigaDOS is concerned the device must support one or more of the following commands:

Read   -   Read some data from the device.
Write -   Write some data to the device.
Seek   -   Locate a position on the device.

It is this ability that makes AmigaDOS so clever and easy to use (once you get the hang of it). Here is a list of the available devices and what they support:

	Read	Write	Seek		Notes
AUX:	-	X	-		Unbuffered serial
CON:	X	X	-		Console windows
DFx:	X	X	X		Floppy disks
DHx:	X	X	X		Hard disks
PAR:	-	X	-		Parallel untranslated
PRT:	-	X	-		Printer (parallel or serial)
PIPE:	X	X	-		Buffered process channel
RAD:	X	X	X		Reset proof RAM disk
RAM:	X	X	X		Basic RAM disk
RAW:	X	X	X		Unfiltered console device
SPEAK:	-	X	-		Speech device

The RAD DOSDriver is very important because it configures the size of the reset-proof RAM disk. Assuming you have moved the device into the correct drawer the device description can be edited like this:

```
1>ED DEVS:DOSDrivers/RAD
```

Get the most out of your Amiga 1993

AmigaDOS reference

The screen display will look like this:

Device	= ramdrive.device
Unit	= 0
Flags	= 0
Surfaces	= 2
BlocksPerTrack	= 11
Reserved	= 2
Interleave	= 0
LowCyl	= 0
HighCyl	= 79
Buffers	= 5
BufMemType	= 1

You can adjust the size of RAD by changing the value of HighCyl (called HiCyl in early releases) using the following formula:

HighCyl = (Size in Kbytes/11)-1

Changes will not take effect until the machine has been switched off and re-started.

MouseBlanker CX_PRIORITY/N/K

Activate the commodities mouse blanking utility. The commodities MouseBlanker utility is provided for people who use a lot of text based programs and find the mouse pointer gets in the way. Typically it can be called in the User-startup like this:

```
Run <NIL: >NIL: MouseBlanker
```

AmigaDOS reference

```
MultiView FILE, CLIPBOARD/S, CLIPUNIT/K/N, SCREEN/S,
PUBSCREEN/K, REQUESTER/S, BOOKMARK/S, FONTNAME/K,
FONTSIZE/K/N, BACKDROP/S, WINDOW/S
```
View a text, graphics or AmigaGuide file. MultiView is a powerful, general purpose file viewer along the lines of, but infinitely more powerful than, More. There is nothing like enough room to do it justice here other than supply some general guidance. For instance, if MultiView is started without arguments it presents a standard Amiga file requester. Examples:

```
1>Multiview
1>MultiView RAM:Picture.IFF
1>MultiView S:Spat
```

Briefly, the major switches have the following effects:

CLIPBOARD:	show the contents of the clipboard.
CLIPUNIT:	read the specified clipboard number.
SCREEN:	open MultiView on a custom screen — use this to display graphics in all available colours.
PUBSCREEN:	open MultiView on a public custom screen.
REQUESTER:	present a standard file requester on opening.
BOOKMARK:	go to a bookmark.
FONTNAME:	use the specified font instead of the system font.
FONTSIZE:	specify a font size (must be available).
BACKDROP:	place the window behind all other windows.
WINDOW:	open a window on a custom screen.

```
NewCLI WINDOW, FROM
```
Open a new CLI window. This command is retained for ancient compatibility with the original AmigaDOS system and is directly equivalent to entering NewShell.

Get the most out of your Amiga 1993

AmigaDOS reference

NewShell WINDOW, FROM
Open a new Shell window. This command is used to open a new interactive Shell process — a command interpreter in other words: call it what you will. The new Shell is completely free and independent of the calling Shell although it will inherit its local environmental variables. The Shell can start its own interactive Shell processes or background processes without affecting the calling CLI in any way. Typically, NewShell is called without arguments like this:

```
1>NewShell
```

However, it is possible to change the format of the window generated by the new Shell process by adding the window option which takes the following format:

Window=CON:X/Y/Width/Height/Name/Option1/Option2...

Options can be any mixture of the following:

Auto: The window will only open when some output is sent to it. (This option has no effect when used with NewShell since that command generates output instantly. It is provided for use when sending output via other commands such as Copy and More.)

Backdrop: The Window is opened as a backdrop behind all other windows on the screen. The title bar and close gadgets are not available in spite of any other active settings.

NoBorder: The window is opened without left and bottom borders. This option is most usefully combined with the Backdrop option.

NoDrag: The window's title bar is available but it cannot be moved around the display.

Simple: Activates simple refresh — the window's contents will not be refreshed automatically when the window is re-sized.

Smart: This option is default and the reverse of the Simple option.

Wait: The window will remain open until the close gadget is clicked or the EOF (CTRL+\) code is sent. It will not close when the process finishes.

AmigaDOS reference

Examples:

```
1>NewShell Window=con:0/0/200/200/Testing
1>NewShell Window=con:0/0/100/200/Testing/BackDrop/NoBorder
1>NewShell Window=con:50/50/200/100/Testing/Nodrag/Wait
```

By default, as the new Shell opens a special script file "Shell- Startup" is executed. This is used to define certain startup parameters such as resident commands, aliases and the prompt string. The FROM argument can be used to override this and read a different script. Example:

```
1>NewShell From MyStartup
```

This option may be combined with the Window argument to get some really flashy effects. For instance, to start a NewShell on a remote (serial) console with a special message and configuration you could use:

```
1>NewShell Window=AUX: From=S:Serial-Startup
```

(The script is not supplied — you must create your own.)

NoCapsLock CX_PRIORITY/N/K

Activate the commodities Caps lock disabling utility. This commodities utility is very handy when using a word processor or even for (cack-handed typists like me) using the Shell. It disables the effect of the "Caps Lock" key but allows use of the Shift keys to access upper case letters. Like most commodities this command is most used in the User-startup like this:

```
RUN <NIL: >NIL: NoCapsLock
```

Get the most out of your Amiga 1993

AmigaDOS reference

NoFastMem
   Stop further allocations of Fast memory. This command is used to disable automatic allocations of FastMemory (memory above the 2Mb Chip boundary limit in current Amigas). It is retained for compatibility with earlier systems software which tended to crash — quite spectacularly — when Fast memory was available. This is something of a falsehood when you consider some applications crash when Fast memory is not available. NoFastMem MUST be Run as a process or it will freeze the process. The effect may be switched off by Running the command again, viz.:

```
1>RUN NoFastMem
[CLI 2]
1>Avail Fast
0
1>RUN NoFastMem
[CLI 2]
1>Avail Fast
808168
```

Path PATH/M, ADD/S, SHOW/S, RESET/S, REMOVE/S, QUIET/S
   Add, read or alter the current path settings. This command can be used to check the current paths or add new ones. The paths are a list of directories which will be searched when you enter a command from the Shell. The command is located by name and the first occurrence found in the list will be executed. If no matching name is located an error (XXX: not found) will be generated. Used without arguments Path lists the current path settings, like this:

```
1>Path
Current_directory
Ram Disk:
WB3.0:C
WB3.0:Utilities
WB3.0:Rexxc
```

Get the most out of your Amiga 1993

```
WB3.0:System
WB3.0:S
WB3.0:Prefs
WB3.0:WBStartup
WB3.0:Tools
WB3.0:Tools/Commodities
C:
```

The most basic Path settings can be gained using the Reset switch like this:

```
1>Path Reset
1>Path
Current_directory
C:
```

Prompt   PROMPT

Change the default prompt string. This command is used to alter the default prompt and is best added to the Shell-startup file. You can make the prompt anything you want although it can be reset back to its default value by entering the command without an argument. The following codes have a special meaning:

%R Insert the last return code (RC).
%S Insert the current path read by CD.
%N Insert the current CLI number.

The default prompt is constructed thus:

Prompt %N.%S>

AmigaDOS reference

Examples:

```
1>Prompt "Your wish is my command>"
Your wish is my command>Prompt %R.%N.%S>
0.1.Ram Disk>Prompt >
>Prompt
1.Ram Disk>
```

Protect FILE/A, FLAGS, ADD/S, SUB/S, ALL/S, QUIET/S
Change the protection flags on any file. A file's protection flags determine how AmigaDOS responds to it. The available flags have the following actions when set:

- **R**   can be read from.
- **W**   can be written to.
- **E**   can be executed (is a command).
- **D**   can be deleted.
- **P**   is pure code — can be made resident.
- **S**   is a script (Execute will be called automatically).
- **A**   is archived (not used by AmigaDOS).
- **H**   is hidden (reserved flag).

It is important to note however, not all these flags are interpreted correctly by all software. For instance, all files are marked as "Executable" when they are created — even text. This does not mean the file can be executed, merely that AmigaDOS will attempt to execute it and generate an error "file is not an object module".

Typically protect is used to set or clear one or more flags in one go. The "+" and "-" characters can be used in place of the ADD and SUB switches. Patterns may be used and the ALL switch can be used to act on every file in the directory and sub-directories; the QUIET switch can be used to suppress confirmation output in this case.

Examples:

```
1>Protect S:MyScript +S ; make a script executable
1>Protect C:MyCommand P ADD ; set the pure bit.
1>Protect S:#? S ADD ; set the script bit on all files
1>Protect C:#? -D  QUIET ; protect all commands from deletion
```

Quit RC/N

Stop a script. This command may be used to terminate any script and return AmigaDOS back to the calling Shell. This applies even if Quit is executed from within a script which has been called by another script. To terminate a script naturally, Skip should be used to Skip to the end instead. Quit may be followed by an optional return code which will be sent via the RC variable to the calling Shell as the following fragment demonstrates:

```
If WARN
  Echo "Sorry, can't do that - exiting..."
  Quit 20 ; generate a fatal error
Endif
```

ReLabel DRIVE/A, NAME/A

Change the volume label on any disk. This command may be used to change any disk's volume name from AmigaDOS. Generally speaking this command should only be used in scripts, since it is usually faster and more convenient to perform the operation from Workbench. If the command is called from AmigaDOS, it should be followed by DiskChange to inform Workbench of the change: this example shows use in a script:

```
.key drive/a,name
.def name Empty
ReLabel <drive> <name>
DiskChange <drive>
```

AmigaDOS reference

RequestChoice TITLE/A, BODY/A, GADGETS/M, PUBSCREEN/K

Ask the user for input using a requester. This command was introduced for AmigaDOS 3 and is one of the most useful additions to the system. It presents an interactive system file requester and returns a number indicating which gadget has been pressed. The command finds all sorts of uses in scripts where Ask is far too limiting. The following script shows this:

```
RequestChoice >ENV:RT "Attention" "About to format your hard
disk*nAre you sure?" "Go ahead" "No way!"
If val $RT EQ 1
  echo "Your hard disk is being formatted...."
else
  echo "Chickened out then?"
endif
```

There is no limit to the number of gadgets that can be used: they're numbered from left to right starting at 1. The exception to this is the extreme right-hand gadget which always returns zero. On multi- gadget requests therefore, this should ALWAYS be the get out (cancel) gadget.

RemRAD DEVICE, FORCE/S

Disable the RAD device. This command is used to disable the reset-proof ram disk and remove it from memory. When this is executed RAD reliquishes all the memory it had reserved for data storage although the handler (which is quite small) remains in place until the machine is reset. The FORCE switch can be used to disable RAD: even if the drive is in use — this switch MUST be used with care. Examples:

```
1>RemRAD RAD:
1>RemRAD BigRAD: FORCE
```

AmigaDOS reference

```
RequestFile DRAWER, FILE/K, PATTERN/K, TITLE/K,
POSITIVE/K, NEGATIVE/K, ACCEPTPATTERN/K,
REJECTPATTERN/K, SAVEMODE/S, MULTISELECT/S,
DRAWERSONLY/S, NOICONS/S, PUBSCREEN/K
```

Get a filename using a standard selector gadget. This is another extremely powerful command added to release 3 and allows the user to select one or more filenames from a script. The selection is returned back via the console although this is normally re-directed to a variable. Here is a simple script example:

```
Lab start
RequestFile >ENV:File
Echo "You picked $File"
if "$File" NOT EQ ""
  Skip Start Back
Endif
```

Very briefly, the options have the following effects:

DRAWER:	Specify a drawer (directory) to display.
FILE:	Display this file in the selection box.
PATTERN:	Use pattern as a filter — #? is default.
TITLE:	Set the window's title.
POSITIVE:	Optionally defines the contents of the "OK" gadget.
NEGATIVE:	As POSITIVE for the "CANCEL" gadget.
ACCEPTPATTERN:	Defines the file pattern(s) to show. Disables the Pattern gadget.
REJECTPATTERN:	As ACCEPTPATTERN but sets the pattern(s) to hide away.
SAVEMODE:	Changes the requester's colour scheme to indicate Save (or some alternative action).
MULTISELECT:	The user can select multiple files by "shift-clicking" them.
DRAWERSONLY:	Only drawers will be displayed. The file and pattern gadgets are not available!
NOICONS:	Use this option to automatically suppress dot-info file.
PUBSCREEN:	Open the requester on a named public screen.

Get the most out of your Amiga 1993

AmigaDOS reference

```
Rename FROM/A/M, TO=AS/A, QUIET/S
```
Rename or move a file around a volume. Use this command to change a file's name or shift it from one place to another in the hierarchy. It is not possible to rename a file across volumes because that does not make sense. Patterns and multiple source arguments can be used provided the destination is a directory ON THE SAME DISK. The QUIET switch suppresses confirmations when multiple files are being worked on. **Examples:**

```
1>Rename TempFile AS Completed
1>Rename RAM:File1 RAM:File2 RAM:Text#? TO S: QUIET
1>Rename Rubbish TO :Trashcan ; move something to the trash
```

```
Resident NAME, FILE, REMOVE/S, ADD/S, REPLACE/S,
PURE=FORCE/S, SYSTEM/S
```
Make a command resident in memory or list resident commands. This command should be used to store commonly used commands in the C, System, Preference or Tools directories to the resident list and make them instantly available. Many AmigaDOS commands are already resident in ROM from release 2 and these can be shown using Resident without arguments. **Examples:**

```
1>Resident
1>Resident C:Dir
1>Resident SYS:System/Format
```

Other options have the following effects:

FILE: Add a command to the resident list with an alias
REMOVE: Remove a command from the resident list (complement to the ADD switch). Can also be used to disable an internal command.
ADD: Add a command to the resident list. Use this switch to avoid multi-tasking clashes in scripts but don't forget to remove the command afterwards!
REPLACE: This switch is default. The command is replaced on the resident list — but a conflict will occur if some other process is already executing the command.

PURE: Force load non-pure code on the resident list.
SYSTEM: Show the system's resident code segments or add code to the system resident list. Leave well alone!

Run COMMAND/F

Start a background AmigaDOS process. This command is used to execute AmigaDOS code from the current Shell without opening a new Shell window. All interactive I/O is performed on the current console window so this command should be used with care. Typically it is used to start "Quiet" commands, that is, commands which do not require input and do not generate any console output. Run usually echo's the new process number in square brackets but this can be suppressed using redirection to NIL:.

Examples:

```
1>Run More S:Startup-sequence
[CLI 2]
1>Run >NIL: More S:Spat
```

As a final example, let's see how Run starts a new process which must be completed before the file is available.

```
1>Run >NIL: DIR >T:T SYS: ALL
1>More T:T
Can't open file
```

To avoid such a conflict, the "+" parameter may be added like this:

```
1>Run >NIL: DIR >T:T SYS: ALL +
More T:T
1>
```

Note: the Run does not start until after you enter the second command.

Get the most out of your Amiga 1993

Search FROM/M, SEARCH/A, ALL/S, NONUM/S, QUIET/S, QUICK/S, FILE/S, PATTERN/S

Search a file for some text -or- search for a file. This command is a complex and comprehensive search utility that can find almost anything, almost anywhere. The following two examples illustrate this:

Example 1: Search for text in a file:

```
1>Search S:PCD "Assign"
    7 Assign ofrom<$$>:  ""
    9 Assign from<$$>:  ofrom<$$>:
   10 Assign ofrom<$$>:
   12 Assign from<$$>:  ""
```

Example 2: Search for a file:

```
1>Search SYS: "Startup-sequence" file all
WB3.0:S/Startup-sequence
```

The other options have the following effects.

ALL: Primarily used with the FILE switch, this forces search to search all sub-directories below the start level of the search.
NONUM: Line numbers are not displayed when searching a file for some text.
QUIET: The command does not generate any output, instead it sets the WARN condition if the search item was NOT found.
QUICK: Output listing is reduced in size — not very useful.
FILE: Tells search to look for a file, rather than text within file.
PATTERN: Tells Search that the search string includes a pattern; any valid pattern may be used to search files or search for them.

Set NAME, STRING/F

Set a local variable -or- list variables. This command is used to initialise a local environmental variable. That is: a variable which can only be accessed by the process which creates it or any processes launched by that process. Local variables are static and cannot be changed unless they are reset to a new value. More importantly, local variables have priority over global variables of the same name. All environmental variables can be inserted at any point in a command line by preceding their name with a "dollar" symbol, for instance:

```
1>SET MyName Smiddy
1>Echo "Hello $MyName"
Hello Smiddy
```

It is important to note also, when used without arguments, Set lists some current process information (plus any user-defined variables) like this:

```
1>Set
process 1
RC 0
Result2 0
```

RC is the result code tested by IF (WARN|ERROR|FAIL) and Result2 is the error code read by Fault when a command fails.

SetClock LOAD/S, SAVE/S, RESET/S

Set, read or initialise the battery-backed clock. Simple one this — use this to save the current date and time to the battery-backed clock or load it back again. The Reset option is provided in case some rogue program crashes the clock hardware. Example:

```
1>Date 12:00 ; set a new time
1>SetClock Save
```

AmigaDOS reference

`SetDate FILE/A, WEEKDAY, DATE, TIME, ALL/S`
Change the datestamp on a file. Every time you create or modify a file or directory, AmigaDOS changes its datestamp (shown by List). This command may be used to change the stamp on any file or user-directory. See Date for the time and date formats. The ALL switch affects every file in the selection and sub- directories and patterns may be used. Example:

```
1>SetDate S:Spat Today
1>SetDate DEVS: Saturday 12:00
```

`SetEnv NAME, STRING/F`
Set a global environmental variable. This command is similar in use to Set the only difference being it initialises a global environmental variable. Global variables can be altered directly by writing to them directly in the ENV: assignment. If this command is executed without parameters it lists the names of the current variables — unlike Set however, the current contents are NOT shown. See Eval and If for complete examples.

`SetFont NAME/A, SIZE/N/A, SCALE/S, PROP/S, ITALIC/S, BOLD/S, UNDERLINE/S`
Change the console font. This command is of limited use because it overrides the current setting for the current console font. Generally speaking only fixed- width fonts like Courier and Topaz should be used unless the font is being used for output ONLY. Examples:

```
1>SetFont Topaz 8
1>SetFont Courier 15 BOLD
```

The options have the following effects:

SCALE: This switch can be used to scale a font to a desired size if the requested size is not already available.
PROP: This switch must be supplied if a proportional font (like times) is requested otherwise an error (object not of required type) will be generated.

AmigaDOS reference

ITALIC: Algorithmically adjusts the font to have a slight slant.
BOLD: Gives the font a dark (heavy) appearance on screen.
UNDERLINE: Underlines the font.

`SetKeyboard KEYMAP/A`
Changes the current keyboard type. This command is not generally used by user script and used to be called SetMap. **Example:**

SetKeyboard UK

`SetPatch QUIET/S, NOCACHE/S, REVERSE/S`
Patch system functions. This command is only called once at the beginning of the Startup- sequence and is used to fix certain bugs in the system ROMS. The QUIET switch prevents it from generating output and the NOCACHE option switches the processor caches off for compatibility with smaller processors such as the 68000.

`ShowConfig DEBUG/K`
Display the machine's configuration. This command is used to list the current custom chips, processor information and other hardware options. The debug keyword can be used as a switch to gain extra information about ZorroII/III cards in higher end machines.

Example:

```
1>ShowConfig
PROCESSOR:   CPU 68030/68882fpu/68030mmu
CUSTOM CHIPS:    ECS PAL Agnus (id=$0020), ECS Denise
(id=$00FC)
VERS: Kickstart version 39.106, Exec version 39.47,
      Disk version 39.29
RAM:  Node type $A, Attributes $505 (FAST), at
                   $7F00000-$7F7FFFF (0.5 meg)
      Node type $A, Attributes $605 (FAST), at
                   $200000-$3FFFFF (2.0 meg)
```

Get the most out of your Amiga 1993

```
            Node type $A, Attributes $703 (CHIP), at
                      $400-$1FFFFF (~2.0 meg)
     BOARDS: RAM (unidentified): Prod=2102/4($836/$4)
                         (@$200000 2meg Mem)
```

Skip LABEL, BACK/S

Alter flow control in a script. This command only has any meaning in a script file and is akin to the GOTO instruction in BASIC. The BACK switch must be supplied if the label to be jumped to is above the position of the Skip instruction. See "If" for an example.

Status PROCESS/N, FULL/S, TCB/S, CLI=ALL/S, COM=COMMAND/K

Read the status of running processes. This command can be used to discover what AmigaDOS is up to at any particular point in time. The command generates its most meaningful output when used without arguments (the ALL switch is implied) viz:

```
1>Status
Process 1: Loaded as command: Status
Process 2: Loaded as command: C:ConClip
Process 3: Loaded as command: sys:commodities/blanker
Process 4: Loaded as command:
           sys:commodities/nocapslock
Process 5: No command loaded
Process 6: Loaded as command: Workbench
```

Similarly, the command can be used to list a single process like this:

```
1>Status 2
Process 2: Loaded as command: C:ConClip
```

AmigaDOS reference

The remaining arguments have the following effects:

FULL: Lists the TCB and general information.
TCB: Shows the task control block only — information about the process priority, stack and global vector table.
COMMAND: This takes a command name as an argument and returns the process(es) running that command. See Break for an example.

Type FROM/A/M, TO/K, OPT/K, HEX/S, NUMBER/S

Display the contents of a text or binary file. This is a very useful command that can display the contents of any readable file. It's faster and often more convenient than using More and its ability to show binary files makes the examination of IFF structures (like the Preferences for example) possible for experts. Type can optionally provided line numbering in cases where this is necessary — listing a script for instance. The OPT keyword is retained for compatibility with older versions.

Examples:

```
1>Type S:Spat
.key com/a,pat/a,opt1,opt2,opt3,opt4
.bra {
.ket }

; $VER: spat 38.1 (11.10.91)
; Do wildcards for single arg commands
(etc.)
```

Get the most out of your Amiga 1993

```
1>Type S:Spat NUMBER
1   .key com/a,pat/a,opt1,opt2,opt3,opt4
2   .bra {
3   .ket }
4
5   ; $VER: spat 38.1 (11.10.91)
6   ; Do wildcards for single arg commands
7
(etc.)

1>Type ENV:Sys/input.prefs HEX
0000: 464F524D 00000046 50524546 50524844
      FORM...FPREFPRHD
0010: 00000006 00000000 0000494E 50540000
      ..........INPT..
0020: 002C6762 00007464 69720000 00000000
      .,gb..tdir......
0030: 00000002 00000001 00004E20 00000000 ..........N
      ....
0040: 000927C0 00000000 0000C350 0080 ..   '¿......JP..
```

UnSet NAME

Clear a local variable. This command is used to remove a variable from the process completely and should be used when variables are finished with. Used without arguments it behaves like Set. (System variables: Process, RC and Result2 cannot be UnSet.) Example

```
1>UnSet MyName
```

AmigaDOS reference

UnSetEnv NAME
Clear a global variable. This command is used to remove a variable from the environment and free up any memory it used. If called without arguments it behaves like SetEnv. Any system-wide variable can be unset (deleted) provided it is not in use. Careful: once removed, the variable cannot be restored.

    UnSetEnv Kickstart

UnAlias NAME
Clear an alias. This command is used to completely remove an Alias from the process list. This may be necessary if you have inadvertently (or deliberately) defined an alias which clashes with an existing command name. Example:

    1>UnAlias Format

Version NAME, VERSION/N, REVISION/N, FILE/S, FULL/S, UNIT/N, INTERNAL/S, RES/S
Get version number of a command, script or library. This command is a very versatile way of checking what version any particular piece of system software is: either from the Shell or in a script. By default the command returns the current version numbers of Workbench and Kickstart. By providing the full path and filename, any command or library can also be checked. **Examples:**

    1>Version
    Kickstart 39.106, Workbench 39.29

Pattern matching is not supplied with Version, but this can be achieved with Spat. For instance:

    1>Spat Version c:#?

Version numbers are usually split into two parts: a version and revision numbers. Therefore 39.106 is version 39, revision 106. These can be tested in a script like this — if

Get the most out of your Amiga 1993

the version or revision number is not higher than specified the WARN flag is set, for example.

```
Version Kickstart Version=39 Revision=106
If WARN
  Echo "Sorry. This requires Kickstart 3.0"
Endif
```

The remainder of the options work like this:

FILE: Read the version number from a file — even if the command/library is already loaded. The file and pathname is also displayed.
FULL: Include any extra version information: usually the creation date.
UNIT: For multi-unit devices, this allows you to specify a unit number. Not much use.
INTERNAL: Read the version number of an internal command.
RES: Read the version string from a command which has been made resident with Resident. If a path is supplied, it is removed before making the test.

Wait /N, SEC=SECS/S, MIN=MINS/S, UNTIL/K

Wait for a time or until time. Although this command might sound useless, it is actually very handy. It is used to wait a specified period in seconds or minutes or until a specified time in the future. If the time has already passed, Wait will automatically wait until the next day. Generally speaking, this command should be used from its own Shell or Run as a separate process. Examples:

```
1>Wait 3 SECS
1>Wait 60 MINS ; wait for an hour
1>Wait UNTIL 12:20 ; wait until 20 past 12.
```

AmigaDOS reference

Which FILE/A, NORES/S, RES/S, ALL/S

Show the path of a file. This command can be used to ascertain the exact position of any file in the hierarchy: provided that it is somewhere in the current path — see Path. If a wider search is required, Search must be used instead. The RES and NORES switches determine whether the resident list is to be searched. The ALL switch determines if every occurrence, or just the first one, should be displayed. The resident list is searched FIRST, viz:.

```
1>Resident C:Wait ; just for this example
1>Which Wait
RES Wait
1>Which Wait NORES
WB3.0:C/Wait
1>Which Wait ALL    ; spot the bug!!!
RES Wait
WB3.0:C/Wait
WB3.0:C/Wait
```

Why

Ask why something went wrong. This command can be used to find out what you did wrong when a command returns its own internal error. It must be used before any other commands have executed and is only valid when the RC return (see Set) is 10 or 20. This command can also be used if a script command fails quietly for example:

```
1>Blurb
Blurb: Unknown command
1>Why
Last command failed because : object not found
1>Echo >NIL: " ; simulate silent failure in a script
1>Why
Last command failed because : argument line invalid or
                              too long
```

Get the most out of your Amiga 1993

Wildcards and pattern matching

AmigaDOS commands make extensive use of pattern matching. This is a technique whereby zero or more text strings (usually a filename) can be matched to a special sequence of letters. Wildcards are the special characters used to a build a pattern. Here are the current wildcards:

#	-	Any number of the following character.
?	-	One character.
%	-	Nothing (a null string).
|	-	Delimits an alternative pattern. (OR)
~	-	Negates a grouped pattern. (NOT)
()	-	Group patterns together.
'	-	Insert wildcard as a literal.

The most common pattern in use and the one you need to remember is "#?" this matches any sequence of anything. Positionally, the pattern can be used on its own or one or more places in a string. For instance:

```
1>DIR #?        ; get everything
1>DIR S:Start#?     ; get anything beginning with "Start".
1>DIR S:#?sequence  ; get anything ending with "sequence".
```

Negative filters can be introduced to eliminate, for instance, dot- info files from listings like this:

```
1>DIR ~(#?.info)
```

Similarly, the group can be extended with the "|" pattern to include other pattern strings.

```
1>DIR (#?.info|.backrop|.fastdir) ; get just these.
1>DIR ~(#?.info|.backrop|.fastdir) ; everything except these.
```

314

Get the most out of your Amiga 1993

Index

This book is packed with information, tips, reviews, diagrams, screen shots and jargon-busting explanations. To make it easier to find out exactly what you want to know, look it up in this index first! (Product names are picked out in bold type.)

Index

A

A300 8
A500 .... 2, 5, 6, 17
A500+ 2, 6, 17
A600 .... 2, 8, 9, 17
A1000 .... 2, 4, 5, 17
A1200 .... 2, 10, 17
A1500 .... 2, 8, 17
A2000 17
A2000+ 2
A3000 .... 2, 9, 18
A4000 .... 2, 12, 18
A-Train 138
AA chip set 44
About… command 30
Accelerators .... 47 (tip), 231
Advantage 89
AGA chip set .... 2, 3 (jargon), 119
Alfa Hand Scanner .... 122 (tip)
Amiga Assembly Language .... 205 (review)
Amiga Vision 61
AmigaDOS .... 20 (jargon), 258
AMOS .... 203 (review)
Animations 47
Another World .... 164 (game tip)
ANSI graphics 129
Anti-aliasing .... 57, 69, 70 (jargon)
AntiA .... 69 (review)
Apidya .... 148 (review)
Archer MacLean's Pool .... 143 (review)
Archive .... 130 (jargon), 215
Art Department Professional 67, 114
Art Department Professional 2 .... 68 (review)
ASCII .... 103 (jargon)
Assembler 199
Assembly language 199, 204
Asteroids .... 152 (review)

B

Audio Engineer Plus .... 77 (review)
Audiomaster IV 77
Auto-booting .... 6 (jargon)
Automix 83
AUX: device 27

B2000 .... 2, 7, 17
BABT approval 126
Backdrop command 29
Backing-up .... 95 (tip), 215, 238
BASIC .... 203 (jargon)
Batman – The Movie .... 164 (game tip)
BBS .... 126 (jargon)
BCPL 201
Benchmark .... 231 (jargon)
Binary .... 198 (jargon)
BMAP file format 108
Boot .... 21 (jargon)
Boot block .... 216 (jargon)
Boot options 21
Boot screen 22
Border .... 27 (jargon)
Broadcast Titler 2 .... 57 (review)
Brush .... 49 (jargon)
Bug Bomber 146
Bulletin board .... 124, 208, 211 (jargon)
Bureau .... 118 (jargon), 122

C

C .... 201 (jargon)
C compiler 201
C Programming Language .... 205 (review)
Cache .... 22 (jargon)
Caligari 51
Capture feature 128

Get the most out of your Amiga 1993

Index

Carrier Command .... 164 (game tip)
Cash Book Combo .... 94 (review)
Cash-flow .... 88 (jargon)
Cashbook Controller .... 95 (review)
Cell .... 89 (jargon)
Chaining drives 231
Chase HQ 150
Chip RAM 226
Cinemorph .... 59 (review)
Cix 124
Clean Up command 32
Clicking drives 230
Close command 31
Closing windows .... 35 (tip)
Colour displays .... 9 (jargon)
Colour printing 243
Colour separations 122
Colour splitter 63
Columns 151
Combat Air Patrol 142
Command arguments 259
Compiler .... 200 (jargon)
Composite video .... 66 (jargon)
Compositing .... 66, 68 (jargon)
Compression .... 214 (jargon)
Compugraphic fonts 118
Compulink Information eXchange (Cix) 124
Copy command 35
Copyright 208
Crash .... 235 (jargon)
Crazy Cars 3 .... 150 (review)
Cursor .... 14 (jargon)

D

D/Generation .... 161 (review)
Data bus .... 10 (jargon)
Database 90
Database language (jargon) .... 93 (jargon)
De-interlacer 11
Debugging .... 202 (jargon)
Defender of the Crown .... 165 (game tip)
Delete command 38
Deluxe Paint 47, 113, 114
Deluxe Paint IV .... 48 (review)
Demo .... 210, 213 (jargon)
DeskTop Publishing 109
DeskTop Video 6, 55
DevPac 3 .... 204 (review)
DEVS/Printers drawer 27
Dice C .... 202 (review)
DIF file format 88
Digitising 63
Direct mail .... 91 (jargon)
Disable switch 230
Disk navigation 219
Display options 21, 22
Dithering .... 244 (jargon)
Dot-matrix printer 240, 242
Double-clicking .... 35 (jargon)
Double-decker drives 229
Dr T's KCS 3.5 Level 1 .... 83 (review)
DR2D file format 109
Dragging .... 24 (jargon)
Drawer 39
DTV 6
Dyna Blaster .... 146 (review), 165 (game tip)

E

E-Motion .... 165 (game tip)
Early Startup screen 20, 21
ECS chip set .... 2, 3 (jargon)
Eight-channel sound 80
Empty Trash command 38
Emulator .... 114 (jargon)

Epic .... 166 (game tip)
EPSF file format .... 108, 111 (jargon), 114
Epson-compatible (jargon) .... 245 (jargon)
Eric and the Floaters 146
Execute Command… command 29
Exile .... 139 (review)
Expansion port .... 7 (jargon)

F

F-29 Retaliator .... 166 (game tip)
Falcon .... 166 (game tip)
Fantasy World Dizzy .... 167 (game tip)
Fast RAM 226
Fast scan digitising 63
Field (as in database) 90
File compression 215
FileMinder .... 220 (review)
Final Accounts 95
Fire and Ice .... 167 (game tip)
First Samurai 148
Flat-file database .... 92 (jargon)
Floating Point Unit 11
Flood .... 169 (game tip)
Floppy disk drive 228
Font (jargon) .... 105 (jargon), 107
Font preferences 26
Format Disk command 38
Formula One Grand Prix .... 134 (review)
FPU .... 232 (jargon)
Fred Fish 211
Freely distributable software .... 208 (jargon)
Freeware 208
Future Wars .... 135, 168 (game tip)

G

Gadgets 23
Gem'X .... 151 (review), 167 (game tip)
Genlock .... 60 (jargon)
GIF file format .... 71, 72 (jargon)
Gobliiins .... 168 (game tip)
Graphic printer .... 243 (jargon)
Graphics formats .... 66 (jargon)

H

HAM mode .... 9, 44 (jargon)
Hard disks .... 46 (tip), 114, 234
Harlequin .... 147 (review)
Head parking .... 237 (jargon)
Hexadecimal .... 198 (jargon)
Hi-Res Interlace Overscan screen mode 45
Hi-res Interlace screen 44
Hi-Res Interlace screen mode 45
Hi-Res Overscan screen mode 45
Hi-Res screen mode 45
Hi-Torro 3
Hook .... 169 (game tip)
Hotlink .... 117 (jargon)
Humans .... 170 (game tip)
Hunter .... 158 (review), 172 (game tip)
Hypertext 202

I

Icons 24
IControl preferences 26
IDE .... 16 (jargon), 235
IFF file format .... 47 (jargon), 70, 71
IFF24 file format 72
Image Master .... 67 (review)
Image processing 49, 66

Get the most out of your Amiga 1993

Index

Imagine 2 ....51 (review)
Indiana Jones and the Fate of Atlantis 135
Information window...39
Information... command....................................30, 36
Inkjet printer...242 (jargon)
Input preferences...26
Integrated office system ....86 (jargon)
Interceptor ....174 (game tip)
International Karate + ...153 (review)
Interpreter ....200 (jargon)
Intuition ....26 (jargon)

J

Jaggies..57, 69
Jimmy White's Whirlwind Snooker ..143 (review)
John Madden Football...137
JPEG file format................................50 (jargon), 71
Justification 107, 111

K

K-Spread 2 ....88 (review)
K-Spread 4 ....88 (tip)
KCS Power PC board...227
Kick Off 2 ....172 (game tip)
Kickstart..21 (jargon), 205
Kindwords 3...106 (tip)
Klax 151

L

Last Message command 30
Last Ninja 3 ....175 (game tip)
Leading 113
Leave Out command 38
Left Out icons..37 (tip)
Lemmings ....144 (review), 175 (game tip)
Letter-impact printer 243

LhA ....129 (review), 215
LhA-Win..129 (review)
LhArc 215
License fee 208
Licenseware 209
Lightwave 3D...51
Lisa 4
List command..34
Llamatron 153
Lo-Res Interlace Overscan screen mode................45
Lo-Res Interlace screen mode.................................45
Lo-Res Overscan screen mode................................45
Lo-res screen mode 44, 45
Locale preferences 26
Looping samples ....78 (jargon)
Loraine 3
Lotus 1-2-3..89
Lotus Esprit Turbo Challenge..........176 (game tip)
Lotus Esprit Turbo Challenge II ....178 (game tip)
Lotus Esprit Turbo Challenge III ...179 (game tip)
Low level language 199
LZ 215

M

Machine code ....198, 204 (jargon)
Macintosh..4
Macro 89
Mail merging.....................................92 (jargon), 107
Mail Shot Plus ....91 (review)
Maxiplan 89
MED v3.21...79 (review)
Mega Lo Mania...............................180 (game tip)
MHz ....8 (jargon)
MIDI...76 (jargon)
MIDI sequencing 81
Midnight Resistance ....179 (game tip)
Modem 16, 125
Modulator..15

Get the most out of your Amiga 1993

Monkey Island .... 135 (review), 189 (game tip)
Monkey Island 2 .... 135 (review)
Morph Plus .... 58 (review), 114
Morphing .... 55 (jargon)
Motorola 4
Motorola 68000 5
Motorola 68020 10
Mouse .... 14 (jargon)
Mouse mat 14
Moving morph .... 58 (jargon)
Moving warp 58
Multi-tasking .... 20 (jargon), 201, 226
Multimedia 60
Multisync monitor .... 115 (tip)
Multitrack recorder 81
Music-X .... 82 (review)
Music-X 2 82
Muting 80

N

NClick 230
NComm .... 128 (review)
New Drawer command 31
New Zealand Story .... 181 (game tip)

O

Object code .... 199 (jargon)
OctaMED Pro .... 79, 80 (review)
Oh No! More Lemmings! .... 144 (review), 181 (tip)
Oktalyser 79
Open command 35
Open Parent command 31
Operating system .... 5 (jargon)
Outline .... 90 (jargon)
Outline fonts 108
Overscan preferences 26

P

Pageliner 112
Pagesetter 3.0 110
PageStream 2.2 .... 117 (review)
PAL .... 44 (jargon)
PAL/NTSC option 22
Palette preferences 26
Parking heads .... 237 (jargon)
Partitioning 237
PCMCIA expansion 8, 227
PCX file format 108
PD house 211
Peritel connector 16
Personal Paint .... 49 (review)
Pinball Dreams .... 154 (review)
Pinball Fantasies .... 154 (review), 183 (game tip)
Pitch bending 80
Pixel .... 44 (jargon)
Pixel 3D 2 .... 54 (review)
Pointer 27
Pointer preferences 27
Populous 140
Populous .... 185 (game tip)
Populous II .... 140 (review), 186 (game tip)
Post 1.7 121
PostScript .... 27 (jargon), 110
PostScript interpreter .... 120 (jargon)
PostScript output 116
PostScript printer 27
Preferences 25
Premiere .... 181 (game tip)
Printer driver .... 27, 112 (jargon), 120, 245
Printer preferences 27
PrinterGfx preferences 27
PrinterPS preferences 27
Printers 121
Pro Clip file format 109

Procalc 89
ProData 1.2 .... 92 (review)
Professional Calc .... 89 (review), 232
Professional Page 4.0 .... 110, 119 (review)
Program 198
Project 40
Protext 92
Protext 5.5 .... 104 (review)
Pseudo icon 35
Public domain .... 124, 203 (jargon)
Put Away command 37
Putty .... 156 (review)
PVG 83

Q

Qualifier .... 26 (jargon)
Quantizing .... 82 (jargon)
QuarkXPress 110
Quick Formatted 38
Quickscore 83
Quit… command 30

R

R-Type II 149
Rainbow Islands .... 133 (review), 187 (game tip)
RAM .... 226 (jargon)
Real 3D Classic .... 53 (review)
Record (as in database) 90
Redraw All command 29
Registration fee 208
Relational database 92, 93
Rename command 31, 36
Rend24 .... 71 (review)
Rendale 8802 FMC Genlock .... 60 (review)
Reporting feature 95
Reset WB command 39
Resolution 44

Reverser .... 70 (review)
RGB 63
RGB port .... 60 (jargon)
RKM (Rom Kernel Manual) 205
Road Rash 150
Robocod .... 133, 148, 188 (game tip)
Robocop 3 .... 182 (game tip)
Rodland 133
Rotoscoping .... 63 (jargon)
RS232 port 27

S

S-VHS video .... 65 (jargon)
Sampling .... 76, 77 (jargon)
SAS C 6.2 .... 202 (review)
SBase 4 .... 93 (review)
Scala 47, 61
Scala HT .... 61 (review)
Scala MM .... 62 (review)
Scala VS .... 62 (review)
SCART connector 16
Score writer .... 80 (jargon)
Screen mode 44
Screen resolution .... 44 (jargon)
Screen saver 214
ScreenMode preferences 27
Scribble! 103
Script handling 129
Script language 127
Scroller 2 .... 56 (review)
SCSI interface .... 16, 17 (jargon), 235, 236
Sculpt 3D 51
Search & replace 107
Second disk drive 228
Select Contents command 32
Sensible Soccer/v1.1 .... 132 (review)
Separations 122
Serial preferences 27

Get the most out of your Amiga 1993

Serif .... 107 (jargon), 112
Shadow of the Beast II .... 185 (game tip)
Shareware .... 124, 204 (jargon)
Show… command 33
SID .... 218 (review)
Sideways expansion 7
Silkworm .... 184 (game tip)
Sim City .... 137 (review), 191 (game tip)
Simpsons .... 187 (game tip)
Slow scan digitising 63
Snapshot command 32, 33, 36
Sound preferences 28
Source code .... 199 (jargon)
Spaces, in names .... 36 (tip)
Speakers 16
Speedball 2 .... 136 (review)
Spellchecking 106
Spindizzy Worlds .... 186 (game tip)
Spreadsheet .... 87 (jargon)
Stack 40
Starglider 2 .... 189 (game tip)
Startup sequence 230
Stereo sound 16
Still morph 58
Still warp 58
Street Fighter II .... 154, 192 (game tip)
Structured graphic .... 109 (jargon)
Studio 113
Super Denise chip 57
Super Hang On .... 190 (game tip)
Super Hi-Res .... 57 (jargon)
SuperBase Personal 2 93
SuperBase Professional .... 93 (review)
SupraFaxModem V32bis .... 125 (review)
SupraFaxPlus .... 125 (review)
Surface mapping .... 54 (jargon)
Switchblade II .... 188 (game tip)
SWIV .... 192 (game tip)
Synth control .... 83 (tip)

Sys-Ex .... 83 (jargon)
System 3 .... 96 (review)

T

Tags 113
Technosound Turbo 2 .... 78 (review)
Term .... 127 (review)
Terminal printer .... 240 (jargon)
Terminal program 125
Terminator 2 .... 191 (game tip)
Text Plus .... 221 (review)
Text runaround 107
The Works, Platinum .... 98 (review)
Thesaurus 103
Throughport .... 77, 231 (jargon)
Tiger 83
Time preferences 28
Time-stretch 77
Titus the Fox .... 192 (game tip)
Tool .... 25 (jargon), 40
Tooltypes 40
Trackball .... 14 (jargon)
Tracking 79
Tracks .... 79 (jargon)
Transwrite 106
Trashcan 39
Treasure Island Dizzy .... 193 (game tip)
Troddlers .... 193 (game tip)
True Print 113
Truecolour mode 45
Turbo Print 113
Twilight Zone .... 213 (review)
Type style 117
Type weight 117
Typeface .... 56 (jargon), 117

Get the most out of your Amiga 1993

Index

U

Unsnapshot command 32, 38
Update command 30, 32
Upgrading 226
User group 208, 211

V

V32bis .... 127 (jargon)
Vaxine .... 194 (game tip)
VDU 240
Video Toaster 51
Vidi-Amiga 12 .... 64 (review)
View 3.0 .... 72 (review)
View By... command 32, 34
Viewtek .... 72 (review)
Virtual Reality .... 51 (jargon)
VirusZ .... 216 (review)
VistaPro 51, 232
VLab .... 65 (review)
VLab Par .... 65 (review)
Vroom .... 159 (review)

W

Warp .... 59 (jargon)
WBPattern preferences 28
WIMP interface .... 6 (jargon)
Window .... 23, 29 (jargon)
Wizkid .... 157 (review), 195 (game tip)

Word count 107
Word processor .... 102 (jargon)
Word publisher 105
Wordworth 2 .... 106, 108 (review)
Workbench 2 20
Workbench 3 20
WWF 154
WYSIWYG .... 105 (jargon)

X

Xenon II .... 195 (game tip)

Z

Zak McKracken 136
ZModem protocol 128
Zoo 215
Zool .... 160 (review), 196 (game tip)
Zorro 2 bus 7
Zorro 3 bus 11
Zorro bus .... 7, 11 (jargon)

8-bit/16-bit/32-bit .... 4 (jargon)
9-pin printer 245
24-bit card 47
24-bit colour 45
24-bit files 71
24-pin printer 245
32-bit architecture 10
68000 .... 205 (jargon)

Get the most out of your Amiga 1993